SEX AND THE INTELLIGENCE OF THE HEART

SEX <small>AND THE</small> INTELLIGENCE <small>OF THE</small> HEART

NATURE, INTIMACY, AND SEXUAL ENERGY

JULIE MCINTYRE

Destiny Books

Rochester, Vermont • Toronto, Canada

Destiny Books
One Park Street
Rochester, Vermont 05767
www.DestinyBooks.com

Text stock is SFI certified

Destiny Books is a division of Inner Traditions International

Library of Congress Cataloging-in-Publication Data
McIntyre, Julie.
 Sex and the intelligence of the heart : nature, intimacy, and sexual energy / Julie McIntyre.
   p. cm.
 Includes bibliographical references and index.
 ISBN 978-1-59477-397-6 (pbk.) — ISBN 978-1-59477-698-4 (e-book)
 1. Sex. 2. Nature. 3. Mind and body. I. Title.
 HQ21.M4634 2012
 306.7—dc23

                                                                    2012002238

Printed and bound in the United States by Lake Book Manufacturing, Inc. The text stock is SFI certified. The Sustainable Forestry Initiative® program promotes sustainable forest management.

10 9 8 7 6 5 4 3 2 1

Text design by Virginia Scott Bowman
Text layout by Jack Nichols
This book was typeset in Garamond Premier Pro with Bodoni and ITC Legacy Sans used as display typefaces

For permissions information please see page vi.

To send correspondence to the author of this book, mail a first-class letter to the author c/o Inner Traditions • Bear & Company, One Park Street, Rochester, VT 05767, and we will forward the communication, or visit the author's websites at **www.sexandtheintelligenceoftheheart.com** or **www.gaianstudies.org**.

This book is, in essence, a love story. It is a falling in love with self, with another, and with Earth story. The journey of being in love—of letting love in to shape you, grow you, change you—takes you through many landscapes, territories unknown and unfamiliar to you, to the windy, rocky precipice of deep change. The journey is punctuated with surprises, brilliant insights, deep joy, and a discovery of rich, dynamic, internal strengths, and genius. Travel well.

Dedicated to
Hailey Elizabeth Kennington
and
Araina Marie Kennington.
And for Darian Sahara Marie Ronan—to the day we meet on this extraordinary journey.
Also, to the young girl inside each of us.

May your spirits stay wild, unbroken, and joined to Earth.
May your bodies be strong and your hearts beat passionately.
May your minds always be hungry.
May you know deep love and ecstatic joy.
May wonder and awe be your constant companions.
And may your souls be whole and thrum from the adventure.

Thanks are extended to the following authors, translators, and publishers for granting permission to reprint:

"Who Makes These Changes?" by Rumi, which appears on page 67, is from *The Essential Rumi*, translated by Coleman Barks, and is used by permission of the translator. *The Essential Rumi* was originally published by HarperSan Franciso.

"A Third Body" and "One Source of Bad Information," which appear on pages 198–99 and 213–14, are from *Loving a Woman in Two Worlds* and *Morning Poems* by Robert Bly, and are used by permission of the author. *Loving a Woman in Two Worlds* was originally published by Dial/Doubleday. *Morning Poems* was originally published by HarperCollins.

"Flowers" and "The Movement of Great Things," which appear on pages 98–99 and 169–70, are from *The Taste of Wild Water: Poems and Stories Found While Walking in Woods* by Stephen Harrod Buhner, and are used by permission of the author and the publisher, Raven Press, Silver City, New Mexico.

"Fearing for My Life," "Do You Recognize Me Now," and "A Third Body," which appear on pages 33, 187–89, and 202–3, are from *Dancing with the Beloved* by Paul Ferrini, and are used by permission of the author and the publisher, Heartways Press, Inc.

The text from *The Sexual Teachings of the White Tigress: Secrets of the Female Taoist Masters* by Hsi Lai, which appears on page 118, is used by permission of the author. *The Sexual Teachings of the White Tigress* was published by Destiny Books, Rochester, Vermont.

The poem by Rumi beginning "If you want to know god," which appears on page 166, is from *The Spiritual Practices of Rumi* by Will Johnson, and is used by permission of the author. This version of the poem is Johnson's rewording of the Coleman Barks translation published in *The Essential Rumi*. *The Spiritual Practices of Rumi* was published by Inner Traditions, Rochester, Vermont.

Contents

❧

PART THREE

Challenges You May Meet on the Road

Acknowledgments

For all those who've awakened my heart, which beats stronger because of you.

This being my first book, there are many people—friends, companions, associates, partners-in-crime, pioneers, and believers—for whom I am deeply grateful and who I would like to acknowledge. To all of you, who in no small way encouraged me to lift the bushel basket and reveal what has been tenderly hidden.

To Stephen Buhner, more than you know, I am eternally, deeply grateful to you, for believing in me, for your love, companionship, deep friendship, and for claiming my soul from the lost and found. Thanks to Trishuwa for your love, for transformation, and for friendship; and to Margaret Rhode for your friendship, love, and all the treats you left at my door. I thank M. John Fayhee for encouraging me to hold nothing back; Jaxon Burgess for your enduring and caring friendship; and Mark Heffernan for your original songs, stories, and friendship. Thanks to Julie and Tanya for giving me a column in *Tapestry* magazine month after month in which to practice. And thanks to Phil for being a great pen pal.

I thank the men in my life: my lovers, husbands, and partners; James P. Ronan for marriage and friendship and Jon (Hawk) Stravers Sr.; for the Driftless adventures; and Jon Stravers Jr., whose spirit kept showing up in moments of deep grief—may you be whole in spirit on the other side, you are missed dearly. And I thank my son, Garrett Ronan who helped me along the way.

I thank the gang at Isaac's Bar, the Buffalo Bar, and Diane's Parlor in Silver City, New Mexico; the Buckhorn Saloon in Pinos Altos, New Mexico;

and the Main Entrance in Prairie du Chien, Wisconsin. I thank you for your companionship and laughter, support and friendship. I thank you all for being part of my life and encouraging me to be who I am: Allan, Shawn, Fred, Farhad, Luan, Jean, Gay, Erika, Hans, Aleisha, Colette, Benjamin, Challa, Calixte, Kevin, Sahuara, Stephanie, Lisa, Jay, Rebecca, Merla, my Irish family—Lucy, Joseph, Michael, and especially Nikki, for your friendship and support and for reading the manuscript.

I thank Flick, who with aging arthritic joints and loss of hearing traveled countless miles up and down the stairs to my loft and napped on the floor near me while I wrote, fretted, and, at times, excavated this book.

I gratefully acknowledge John Seed, Arne Naes, Johanna Macy, Dolores La Chapelle, and the early Deep Ecologists whose fearless devotion has been a well of inspiration and influence. I thank Rosemary Gladstar for giving me a place to start teaching this work, and the women at the Women's Herbal Conferences, my apprentices and students, who sat in my classes and said to me afterward: "You have to write this book." I am grateful to the life-drawing classes at Western New Mexico University, where I was paid to pose nude while I spent time in interior work.

I thank Jon Graham whose initial letter of acceptance of the manuscript I referred to countless times to keep me going; and Laura and Kate, editors from heaven, who corrected my grammatical inadequacies, made suggestions, and who work to make authors' dreams come true.

And thanks to my birth family—for provoking my destiny.

To the invisibles: I am deeply indebted to the spirits of the Driftless Region of the Upper Mississippi River Valley, the Land of Enchantment, those of Southwest New Mexico who have heard and seen all of me and my internal world and who have walked through the writing of this book side by side with me; Venus, the goddess of love, beauty, and sexuality who rules my Libra sun and Taurus moon; Eros, the god of sexual love (and the chaos that ensues) and beauty, and from whom the energy and word *erotic* originates; Psyche, the soul, for drawing forth character; the Muses whose names inspire art, science, and wonder; Dionysus, god of the vine, half-mortal son of Zeus, born of fire and nursed by rain; Artemis, lover of woods and the wild chase over the mountain; and Pan, whose home is all the wild places— thickets and forests and mountains.

I pray I have not disappointed any of you.

INTRODUCTION

It Stops with Me

The basic problem is that everybody has sexual thoughts.

JUNE JORDAN, "A COUPLE OF WORDS
ON BEHALF OF SEX (ITSELF),"
IN *SOME OF US DID NOT DIE*

*Everything that people do is connected with "sex": politics,
religion, art, the theater, music, is all "sex."*

G. I. GURDJIEFF, *PARABOLA*

I placed my feet on the trailhead, half hidden under leaf litter. Ideas, thoughts, and images of where this trail might lead, written on disjointed notes, were scattered about the forest floor. Some were stuck on branches set there by winds, still others continued dancing about, flitting here then there. Once the start of this journey called "writing my first book" began, there was no turning back, no u-turns allowed, no way of knowing where it would lead, who would appear, or what news they would bear from distant lands. And though I could feel the presence of invisibles—those of myth, of Earth, early travelers of old, writers of the territory and my own destiny—falling in stride behind and alongside me, not knowing where this trail was going was as important as the trail itself.

Writing this book was an exercise in personal psychological restructuring. The experience was the best, and most difficult, therapy I've had,

1

ever. At times I was torn up inside, and at other times, the experience brought me unbounded joy and confidence. There were days when the only reason I wrote was because I had given my word. I have always wanted to be a writer; to not write would be an abomination to my soul. To say it was a love-hate relationship is trite; however, true it is. This book, and the process of it, became my therapist, my lover, my companion. We loved and hated each other. I thought about it all the time; I talked to it, dreamed of it, woke with predawn thoughts of it, with whole chapters lingering in the interworld between sleep and wakefulness.

Eros and Psyche spiraled through this journey with me. Eros, the god of love and passion, irresistible and clever, seduces the psyche with temptations of pleasure and occasions for suffering. Love always leads to the interior world of reflection and contemplation.

Eros always leads to Psyche.[1] Touching fingers to keyboard, each stroke took me deeper into the meaning of this book, the spirit of which came to sit in my room day by day, taking me around this bend and that, exposing unusual connections and insights, showing things I hadn't, wouldn't have, thought of on my own. Often, it would stand over my shoulder and whisper sweet inspirations and musings in my ear. We walked, trotted, strolled, ran down back alleys and side streets and down the stairwell into the cavern (or abyss as it felt on some days) of my psyche to rattle her awake, to shake the foundation of my beliefs, hang-ups, fears, dreams, history, to emerge fresh and ragged, awake, and drunk from the long, strange trip.

All serious daring starts from within.

EUDORA WELTY

Until I gave myself over to the writing and the magic and the struggle, I did not know, could not know, where this book would lead and what it would ultimately become. When you first discover that you are pregnant, you nurture the fetus, the baby, as it grows, and you pray that the baby is healthy, has all its functions and parts, but until the baby is born, you have no idea what she'll look like, how healthy she'll be, what sort of person she'll mature into, and, especially, what'll she do in the world. Such has been my relationship with this book. What it will do in the world I do not know. And like children, it does not belong to me; it never did. I have been merely the messenger.

Saying out loud my personal and family secrets sent me into a three-year spin before I got clear enough that I could be devoted to writing this book. As I wrote the chapter on sacred sex, a wee voice inside me insisted "You can't say that," "No, don't say that either," "What are you doing describing that intimate thing?" That part of me and I were able to reach an agreement so I could continue. Conversations with myself continued throughout as I also found myself writing things that confront social, cultural, religious, and political values around sex, sexuality, and our relationship with Earth.

I'm making two assumptions at the beginning of this book. The first one is that if you're reading this, you feel something is missing from your relationships, your love life, and maybe even your life. We have all felt such a sense of something missing—of emptiness—at least once in our lives. Many feel it most poignantly in those quiet moments just after sex, or sometimes after a conversation with a friend: a bit of emptiness like something is absent. There is a knowing in our deep selves that there is the possibility of something more, and perhaps, from time to time, you strive to name it and sometimes even strive to find it. This book is about that missing thing. It explores the nature of deep intimacy, the juice of life, the food that feeds the soul of love and relationships. It also (and necessarily) challenges deeply held beliefs about sex, intimacy, and relationships that are often carried from a young age. It challenges the way we see, think, and feel about sex personally and as a culture, for all these things are involved in the generation of that emptiness that we sometimes feel. And it explores the ecological function of sexuality and our relationship with Earth and the world of the invisibles.

So, I think it's safe to say we all carry baggage, some lack of clarity, and (to greater or lesser extents) shame about sex and intimacy and about our sexuality, our bodies, our relationships, and our feelings. It is nearly impossible to grow up without some of that detritus, particularly in the United States. We also carry an ecological dysfunction, a disharmony within our personal ecology and with our relationship with the deep ecology of Earth. Thus, the second assumption I am making is that you are looking for some resolution, some healing around all of this.

Most of our parents had issues around sex. They didn't talk to us about sex or bodies or relationships. Many of us grew up thinking, if we ever even heard the word, that intimacy only meant the act of sex or making love. Intimacy often involves sex, but it does not mean sex. Nor is sex the only arena for intimacy. Real intimacy takes place between real people, or rather, people being real—unguarded, undefended, unconcealed, and vulnerable. To be real, without a façade, requires a willingness to be naïve, to see what's in front of you as if for the first time.

Even if we did get some sex education in school or from our parents, it was almost never from a place of deep caring and genuine sharing. Often, it was guarded, haphazard, or superficial. It almost never included talk about intimacy, emotional openness, masturbation, pleasure, or consciousness. A lot was missing from those teachings, and in the West, it still is.

All of us grew up being lied to, blatantly or by omission. Shame grew around our sexual longings, sexual interest, and our bodies. Shame grew because it was all a secret and because those who told us about it carried shame in themselves. The baggage and misinformation around sex has not changed in any meaningful way. And since the sexual revolution of the '60s, it has not gotten better. It's gotten worse.

The use of sex toys—dildos, vibrators—was all hidden. We found out about them from friends and magazines and through our own curiosity driving our need to know. We covertly sought them out where information and access to them hid—in shadows. In seven states (Alabama, Georgia, Texas, Indiana, Mississippi, Louisiana, and Virginia), it is illegal to sell sex toys. Information is systematically withheld from our children. Government, schools, and church programs deliberately lie to children and withhold health services and health products in order to promote abstinence-only propaganda.[2]

The most powerful thing you can do for yourself, the most healing thing you can do for your children, nieces and nephews, grandchildren, and students is to become a subversive activist. Someone, who by means of thinking for yourself, will cause the system of lies and regulations to disintegrate from within bit by bit. But thinking for yourself is only one part of the dynamic; you must think behaviorally and act differently from new choices. Sexual patterns *are* social constructions; as Carol Hanisch is credited with saying, "the personal is political."[3]

The way to begin is to inventory and take an honest, penetrating look at your beliefs and values around sex, sexuality, intimacy, eroticism, shame, masturbation, and your body and your relationship with Earth and all her inhabitants. Begin to clear out all the old impediments and deformities around being a sexual, sensual, erotic, fully alive human being. Where did your beliefs and ideas come from? Why do you still hold them, or why do they still hold you? What do they serve? Is there another way of seeing things? What is true for you and why is it true for you? What beliefs and behaviors support you being a fully alive, fully sexual, empowered human being? What are your fears and how do they dictate your beliefs and behaviors?

When we stop contaminating sex, love, and intimacy with lies and misinformation, we start shaping our own ecstatic sexual experiences and we begin to decolonize the ideas we carry around sex and intimacy. Until we have thoughts and ideas that are our own, that we have come to through feeling them, through analysis, experimentation, and contemplation, only then can we be free to travel in the realm of the sacred, a realm that our sexuality opens up to us, the realm of the gods. The veil between their realm and this world is thin; sacred sex is one of the ways we can pass through the veil. And traveling in that realm is our birthright. Let no one tell you different.

> *To tell the truth is to become beautiful, to begin to love yourself, value yourself. And that's political, in its most profound way.*
>
> JUNE JORDAN

Sometimes you just have to say: Fuck it, it stops with me. Owning our sexual nature is a subversive act. Giving our children permission and encouragement to think for themselves, to own their sexuality, to be curious is an act of political, emotional, spiritual, and cultural restoration. It is an act of relationship fostering and trust building. And it is a reclamation of the sacred. Giving our children honest information is empowering to them and to our relationship with them. They have a right to know. We have an obligation and a responsibility to tell them and to be present for them when they have questions. It is a loving thing to do. We cannot begin to tell the truth, to step up to the plate of honest information, if the beliefs and information we carry are contaminated. Thus the need for unearthing and sifting through what is true for us and discarding what is not, of separating the wheat from the chaff.

It means healing the splits between our sexuality, our sexual behaviors, the sexualized Earth, and how sex is pretended to be in our culture. At the time of this writing, Christine O'Donnell, Republican candidate for the Delaware senate (thankfully, she lost), has been on an antisex campaign for ten years. She is antisex, antimasturbation: "It is not enough to be abstinent with other people, you also have to abstain alone. The Bible says that lust in your heart is committing adultery, so you can't masturbate without lust."[4] Tiger Woods, the world's best golfer, finalized his divorce and announced that he was taking a break from golf to work on his "infidelities." As a result, he has entered sex addiction therapy. AT&T, one of his largest corporate sponsors, withdrew sponsorship without stating why. The "public" is outraged at his "immoral" behavior; yet, we are secretly fascinated with the juicy details. This is part of the hidden world of sex—our secret fascinations.

Magazines use sex, eroticism, and sexiness to sell their products; yet, we refuse to admit we are sexual beings, that we have sexual longings and fantasies, except in those magazines and pornographic Internet sites openly devoted to doing so.

Imagine this (fantastic) scenario: People take responsibility for their needs and talk with each other honestly about them. What if we (those of us who feel this way) said to each other that one person is not enough to satisfy all our needs, that we need multiple sex partners, and that those who wish to be monogamous should do so without putting fears and moral codes onto other people? What if we gave up that disintegrating toxin, shame, and lived a life of empowerment rather than one of victimhood?

How can we ever expect to change anything if we are unable to shape our own sexual and core experiences? If we continue to feel oppressed, repressed, and victimized by something that happened chapters ago in our life, by the rules of behavior fed to us by the religious right, neoconservatives, our parents, our culture, and the media, how can we imagine ever changing or having an influence on anything? When will we get our priorities in order and start saying no to political and religious meddling that is mucking up the sanctity of relationships, pleasure, and our spiritual destinies?

> *You've got to have something to eat and a little love in your life before you can hold still for any damn body's sermon on how to behave.*
>
> BILLIE HOLIDAY

Any energy or inspiration we may have to influence our own lives, communities, schools, and government is diminished while we insist on feeling shame, guilt, and unworthiness about ourselves and while we keep ourselves repressed in the bedroom. As long as we persist in letting others think for us and tell us what appropriate behavior is and acquiesce to scare tactics that threaten to withhold love or money if we don't behave, we will remain utterly powerless in the face of any real or imagined power outside ourselves. If we don't own and take charge of our sexuality, someone else will. (Oh, wait, they already have.) It's time to bring it all back to its rightful owners, to each of us as autonomous individuals. For you must understand, Nature, Gaia, is sexual, sensual, and highly erotic. Nature is having sex all the time; that's one of the reasons why it feels so alive, and it's one of the reasons why, when we are immersed in Nature, we feel alive. Birds and bees are pollinating flowers every day. And flowers? They are the reproductive organs of plants.

Trees, heavy and dripping pollen, rub their branches against each other in sexual friction. Plants have gone through countless metamorphoses in their sexual organs since before the beginning of time, developing ingenious and innovative ways to spread their pollen and propagate their species. Every flower we put on our dining table is the sex organ of a plant. Each time we eat corn on the cob, wrapped in pubic corn silk, we are ingesting corn ovules, which hold the ovary that becomes a seed when fertilized by corn pollen. Flowers exude a seductive odor when ready for mating, causing birds, bees, and butterflies to join in ritual dances of reproduction. Some male plants exude an odor that remarkably resembles the seminal emissions of men and animals. The ailanthus species (tree of heaven) will produce flower clusters that are either female, male, or both. Only the male and male/female flowers produce the odor that fills the air with the unmistakable scent of a man's ejaculate.

Human sexuality and our reproductive organs have evolved from plants. Plant reproductive systems were the template or prototype that Gaia innovated on as animals and humans evolved. The semen of animals and men performs the same function in almost precisely the same manner as does the pollen of plants. Pollen enters the sticky folds of the flower's stigma, much like a human vulva, and traverses the whole length of the style, which is analogous to a vagina, until it enters the ovary and comes in contact with the ovule.

Slugs, hermaphroditic (possess both sex organs) and slow moving, make love for hours. Each slug inserts a penis into the other and are then simultaneously impregnated. Bonobos, or pygmy chimpanzees, are one of the most peaceful groups of mammals on the planet. They have evolved a unique system of peacekeeping and bartering: exchanging sex for food. Bonobos engage in tongue kissing, mutual masturbation, face-to-face sex, homosexuality, anal sex, and oral sex. And instead of fighting, they have sex, lots of sex.

We are inspired and transfixed by mating songs and the tandem flights of birds during courtship. How can we deny our curiosity upon seeing animals being tender and affectionate with each other and even having sex? None of us is unmoved upon seeing spectacular sunrises or the way a full moon enlightens and casts shadows in a dark forest. Nor are we unmoved while sitting on the porch and smelling the rain as a storm thunders toward us across the horizon. Sometimes we are so moved we take the feelings that have been stirred up into the bedroom or to a bed of leaves in the forest.

If you have ever let your hands caress the slow, smooth curves of water-worn boulders, you have been touched by the erotic, sensual, elemental power of Gaia. However much we try to deny or control Nature, we cannot separate ourselves from her; we are part of Nature. Nature is our nature.

Gaia is in a constant state of heat: expanding, reproducing, and expressing herself. Volcanoes and earthquakes—Earth orgasms—shudder and quiver in ecstatic rhythms. The moon pulls on the waters of Earth, causing the ebb and flow of tides. Women's wombs respond to the moon's influence on their bodies and psyches as they circle through menstrual cycles. Semen of the gods rides the ocean waves as foam. Sex is a basic drive in all living organisms. Without sacred sex, how can we imagine the sacredness in land and ecosystems? Indigenous peoples around the world have an ongoing concept of sacred sex that is incorporated into their seasonal and yearly ceremonies to increase abundance.[5] West African tribes have elaborate sex ceremonies that may last for weeks at a time.

> *Oh, what a catastrophe, what a maiming of love when it was made a personal, merely personal feeling, taken away from the rising and the setting of the sun, and cut off from the magic connection of the solstice and equinox! This is what is the matter with us, we are bleeding at the roots, because we are cut off from the earth and sun and stars, and love is a grinning mockery, because, poor blossom, we plucked it from its stem on the tree of Life, and expected it to keep blooming in our civilized vase on the table.*
>
> D. H. LAWRENCE,
> *LADY CHATTERLEY'S LOVER*

Perhaps our deepest fear is not that we would be uncivilized and out of control but that we would be free to rediscover the sacredness of being alive. The enchantment of Gaia and the split between wild Earth and our wild natures would be healed. Do we fear the power that is there in the deep Earth, in our deep sexual selves, would be too great? It would seem that we are more afraid of sex, of our sexuality, than we are of drugs, prescription medicines, corporations, or governments.

There is a tremendous amount of rhetoric coming from the pulpits and benches of religious and political edifices admonishing us on "right" or "moral" behavior and what is customarily acceptable sexual behavior in and out of the bedroom. Jeffrey Escoffier writes that "[t]housands of case histories have been researched and published to illustrate the dangers, penalties and pitfalls of any deviation from the prevailing sexual morality."[6]

There are equally similar admonitions regarding our behaviors and relationships to the environment, though those who would have us behave accordingly are incapable, at least not demonstrably capable, of following their own precepts. We need not look any further than current politics, policies, and legislation regarding logging, mining, oil drilling, water-use rights, and so on to find a fairly comprehensive picture of our relationship to the natural world and finite resources. There are just too many rules, rules that never have been and never will be the solution to the problem. If they were, we would all be sexually and ecologically healthier and happier and more secure in the future survivability of the human species. No, rules are not the solution, and moreover, the rules are creating more problems. If they serve anything, it is in forcing us to examine what works, what needs re-working and what needs abolishing.

I assert in the pages that follow that there is a direct relationship between our beliefs, values, and behaviors about sex, sexuality, and intimacy and our beliefs, values, and behaviors toward and about the environment and Earth. I also assert that healing one relationship will heal the other, that the two are intimately, inherently intertwined; how we treat our bodies and ourselves is how we treat Earth. If our sex isn't sacred, we won't treat Earth as sacred.

Sex has been around since the first single-celled bacteria duplicated through mitosis in the primordial ooze 3.85 billion years ago. Gaia took that single-celled organism, split it into two, and inserted a drive to reconnect, to be one again. It is that drive to reconnect that urges us toward a more intimate sexual experience. It is that same drive that pulls us out of our four walls and into the wild. In *Dazzle Gradually,* Lynn Margulis and Dorion Sagan explore the origins of sex—that drive to reconnect.

Sex has many origins: evolutionary, sociolinguistic, and perhaps even unconconsious or metaphysical origins that are not really origins at all, since they stand, at least psychologically, outside of time. Metaphysically, the conjunction of two individuals in an act of mating recalls the original split of each individual in his or her essential solitude from the universe of which he or she is a part. Thus, biology aside, the union of opposites resembles a sort of awkward "healing" of the primordial condition in which each of us finds ourselves: separate and alone.[7]

Honoring that innate drive is to acknowledge the gift of life, and it calls us to do deeper healing of the damage caused from secularizing and marginalizing sex.

What we would see around us in the natural world, if we choose to take in the view with wonder and awe as if for the first time, is what is inside us, what has always been inside us: our true nature. We would see, as Thoreau said, "The earth which is like a map spread out around me is but my inmost soul revealed."[8]

> *This leads us to the concept of most primitives, that "the sacred" is power. The "power" flows through animals, plants, waterfalls, mountains, humans, etc. in endless abundance.*
>
> GREGORY BATESON,
> QUOTED BY DOLORES LaCHAPELLE
> IN *SACRED LAND, SACRED SEX*

Many are the attempts to heal that separation, to restore the sacredness and spirit of sex, often through a resurgence of Eastern tantric practices and pagan Earth fertility rites. However, even in these practices there is a tendency to reduce them to techniques and mechanical uses. Western practices of tantric sex are more a hybridization of new age techniques, including yoga, aromatherapy, massage techniques—"a single invented tradition," says David Gordon White in *Kiss of the Yogini*. "What passes for Tantric sexuality in the West has almost no connection with its original inspiration in medieval India."[9] And in *Shamans, Mystics and Doctors*, Dr. Sudhir Kakar says, "New Age Tantra is to medieval Tantra what finger painting is to fine art . . . a remarkably unimaginative series of yogic exercises applied to the sexual act . . . a *coitus reservatus par excellence* . . . a sad attempt to mechanize the mysteries of sexual love."[10]

Our separation from our sexuality is equivalent to damaged ecosystems, so eloquently described by Aldo Leopold, John Muir, and so many Deep Ecologists. And like damaged ecosystems, our damaged human ecosystem, separated from sex, is in need of repair. As Deep Ecology principles are applied to heal ecosystems, healing the damaged human ecosystem requires that we be sensitive to our spiritual, physical, and psychological needs and evolution. It is important to seriously consider and explore what role a sense of place, a sense of our place, plays within the circle of all life.

The healing begins when we shift our perspective from seeing sex as some *thing* (the character of being either male or female) or a *thing* (technique) that happens between two beings and move sex into the realm of relationship. Seeing and experiencing sex from a place of communication and relationship takes us into the realm of the sacred and a state of sacredness. Sex as technique will always maintain a level of one-dimensional superficiality, the flat and parched landscape of human secularized experience. Dropping below the surface level of sex brings us to the source of all healing, in the deep waters of relationship and intimacy. Holding sex, our bodies, our relationships, and our place in the great scheme of biological diversity and evolution will return us to the ancient and archaeological roots of our species origins, to the primordial ooze where the first single-celled bacteria split. It returns us to the realm of the invisibles, the gods and goddesses of myth and legend who are more than storybook characters.

Sacred sex heals the split that has occurred between spirit and matter, between male and female, between physical and the numinous. It heals the dichotomy between humans and the sexuality of Earth. Sacred sex transmutes the sex act into the rejoining of the original split into male and female and the secularized split of body and soul.

Most of us today are hungering for intimacy in our lives, to feel a deep connection that was lost when extended families broke up and when we fell away from the wild sexuality of Earth that expresses itself through every life-form. First, we must feel connected to and be intimate with ourselves and get to know all the voices inside. Georg Feuerstein writes, "Intimacy is conditional on our acceptance of embodiment. We must be intimate with ourselves before we can be intimate with another person."[11] Once we are intimate with ourselves, we can be present with another human being, and then we can sense the sacred, the numinous, the spirit that enlivens all of life.

Sex is a union of the energy of two bodies, two lives, two spirits, two souls. Sex is explosive. It's the process for creating life and for rewriting a life. Sacred sex transforms a physical act into a prayer, a devotion. And in sacred sex, a life, a relationship, a story is transformed. Old wounds are healed. Stories become narratives and not predetermined fatalism for the way our life unfolds. Each becomes something new, something different, something other than what he or she was before. Each being becomes whole, and as a result of that wholeness, Earth moves closer to a state of wholeness.

In the pages that follow, we'll go beyond and below superficiality, traveling into the territory of the sacred as we repossess and restore the lost connections of intimate relationships with another human being, with Nature, with Gaia, with wildness. In the territory of the sacred, we will once again return to our lives and our world the sacredness of sex and the healing that comes from knowing our true nature and Nature outside us, as well as how the two natures are inextricably interwoven. We will learn to navigate the world with a sense of wonder and awe as we once did as children. Do not let time and familiarity destroy the mystery.

As I wrote this book, I was primarily telling all this to four people: my three granddaughters Araina and Hailey Kennington and Darian, and the fourth person is the young girl I was that so desperately needed to hear these words so long ago.

This book is meant for anyone wanting to have a life ensouled with sexual vitality, intimate human and nonhuman relationships, and for those wanting to heal the separation between humans and Earth. It is written from one woman to women in heterosexual relationships, though the work is meant to be used for anyone in any form of relationship: It is transferrable. In the interest of full disclosure, I want to say that this book does not affirm the limited reality you may currently live in. But, it does affirm a reality that you could live in if you give up limitations.

PART I

The Fall from Earth

1

Intimacy

Food That Feeds the Soul of Love

Love, I know, is essential if death is to be put in its place, and it has a place, but love is essential even if I do not know the words that give it flesh and scent. That is why we find it so difficult to write about sex. Not because we are so inhibited and prudish but because when we write about sex, we get acts and organs, a breast, a vagina, a cock, juices and tongues and thrusts—and wind up with recipes but no food. Orgasm is just a word. We have a hunger and love fills it, however briefly, and our accounts of having sex do not catch what drives us into the night seeking light.

CHARLES BOWDEN,

BLUES FOR CANNIBALS

Why isn't love enough? For over fifteen years I have been asking the Universe this question. I had the naive notion that if you love someone enough, have enough integrity and keep your agreements, everything else will take care of itself. I have loved much, deeply, and passionately. But something has always been missing. I hungered for more depth in my relationships, for talks deep into the night about the meaning of life, talks of the personal struggles we all go through. I hungered for soul-to-soul bonding and to be seen at the deepest parts of myself. As much as I ached and fought for more, the missing feeling was always present, pushing on my psyche like a bone spur in the bottom of my foot.

What was this hunger, this consuming passion and desire? I wanted to name it, to know its shape and texture. I wanted to know its taste and smell. But it was elusive, some invisible thing I chased in the dream corners of my heart. The reality that was present in my family and relationships never satisfied my heart and soul. I wanted, needed to know the truth, what was real.

This yearning, this appetite scared me at times for it seemed insatiable. I felt its powerful force pushing on me from the pit of my stomach; a soul hunger always wanting the next meal. Nevertheless, I was driven by an inborn, deep-seated belief that the depth I sensed was possible; it really could be.

When many people think of intimacy, it's often oriented around thoughts of making love or having sex, but this was not enough for me. It was emotional and spiritual intimacy that I longed for. Ideally, I wanted to marry it with physical sharing. I wanted a depth of intimacy, a bonding of spirit with another person. Through this bond, in the act of sexual union, my partner and I would travel together in the world of Spirit. That is what I wanted. And eventually, that is what I found.

The journey of learning the steps to the dance of intimacy was long and well worth the work of transforming myself, of unlearning and dropping defenses that kept intimacy out of my reach.

THE YEARNING FOR CONNECTION

I was born with a belief that love was supposed to be this way, not the way I saw it in the faces and distant behaviors of my parents, lovers, husbands, and friends, people who said they loved me. I felt love from them. Still, I was unsatisfied. Something was missing, and there was too much space, too much drama, too many games, too much unspoken, between people who said they loved each other.

When I was six years old, each night at bedtime my younger sister and I kissed my parents good night. It was an organic movement on my part, an impulse that arose naturally from within, for I had not witnessed that behavior in any of my older siblings. At six years old, I didn't understand why my father wouldn't show his love. Why, when I kissed him on the cheek, didn't he return the kiss, or look me in the eye, or hold me? I needed him to return the affection. I needed to feel his love for me. But he couldn't bring himself to do it. He never allowed himself to drop the façade of strength that he had spent a lifetime building. I felt that he didn't love me. But to my child's mind, it didn't make any sense. How could a father not love his children? So I believed that something was wrong with me, that I was somehow damaged and unlovable.

As a child, I spent a great deal of time and energy trying to show my father how much I loved him, trying to get below the surface, hoping my love would be returned. As a young adult and well into adulthood, I would bake his favorite desserts and take them to him on Sundays. My parents came to depend on me visiting them with fresh-from-the-oven home-baked cakes and cookies in hand. My mother was often gracious. On a few occasions, my father thanked me. I knew he enjoyed the treats but what I needed was to hear him say something genuine and sincere. At that time I didn't have the skills or permission to ask directly.

When I was thirty-eight years old, I moved two hours away from my parents. After years of being a devoted daughter, going through two marriages and two divorces, and raising a son, who was then seventeen, I was finally starting my own life (I'm a late bloomer, but bloom I did). I stopped baking for them, and my visits became irregular. My mother made it clear to me how disappointed my father was. I felt like the bad daughter, which is how I was supposed to feel. Families do that; they have an ingenious way of trying to get you to keep up the old, familiar behavior and family script, to maintain the status quo.

For forty-seven years, my father and I walked in each other's life, but we never got to know each other. We didn't know how. For seventeen years we were strangers to each other, living under the same roof, eating the same food, working side by side in pained silence. I ask myself if I knew him. Did I know what made him happy, what fed his soul? What drove him to rise each morning? Did intimacy terrify him so much that he'd do about anything to avoid it? Or was it simply that he didn't know how to go there? How did he deal with the pain of his own family,

I mean, deeply, inside himself? Outwardly, he didn't hide the rage and betrayal he felt. How did he feel watching his wife of fifty-five years suffering a slow death, helpless to make her well? How could I have made better our time together here on Earth?

IN THE LUMINOUS WORLD OF INTIMACY

Without intimacy to feed love, relationships are lonely and desperate. In the deepest sense, even among friends, there should be an invisible, yet palpable, flow of trust and love between people. Though rare, I did sometimes experience it, like the time a friend shared a part of himself he had long kept secret.

The two of us had made a conscious, out-loud agreement to have a deep and intimate relationship where we would actively work to reveal hidden parts of ourselves. In the beginning of our friendship, he found the courage to ask me to sit with him so he could tell me this thing he had carried inside him, hidden. We sat under the grape arbor partly shaded from the afternoon midsummer sun. Sitting across from him, looking into his eyes, I could see how afraid he was, how difficult it was for him to tell me his innermost secrets. His body tensed up as it responded to the inner voices telling him that saying secrets out loud was too risky, that something bad would happen if he did. He sat, uncomfortably at first, on the edge of his chair, facing me with the sun at his back.

Seeing him in distress, I felt the invisible fingers of my heart go out to touch him. My entire being swelled with love and compassion for this man. Gently, I wrapped my heart field around him and held him in it as he began to speak. His body slowly began to relax. It seemed as if with each word he uttered, some resistance flowed out of his body with it. The stress left his face, and then his shoulders relaxed. We held each other's gaze. As the sounds and meanings of each word came up to meet me, I greeted every one, breathed it in, and let it find a place to rest inside me.

As he talked, I silently acknowledged him with frequent nods of my head. I leaned forward, resting my elbows on my knees or my chin in my hand. Only a few moments had passed when I realized that he and I had moved from the mundane world into some extraordinary, other, and sacred territory. The sounds of the world around us began to fade from our awareness.

Water flowing in the nearby stream, an occasional car passing on the road, even the slight breeze in the trees, all these sounds retreated from the world we had entered. My senses were heightened, the warmth of the sun moved from the surface of my skin into the marrow of my bones. Colors took on an iridescent glow. My gaze softened, and the hard edges of the physical world became soft and out of focus, like the edges of a ball of cotton.

Without diverging from the telling of his own story, my friend and I shared an aware, unspoken understanding that we had slid through an opening between worlds. As we held taut the unseen realm we found ourselves engaged in, a small wild bee flew over to us and then stopped. She hovered at the edge of us, seeming to touch, to taste the bond that was being birthed between the two of us. She hovered, and then moved along the edge, the arc, of an invisible force field from me, to my friend, and back again. As if drinking in nectar from a beautiful, invisible flower, the bee would stop and taste this wonderful food. She never altered her course as she traveled in a curved sweep back and forth from my friend to me. She would stop for a moment, near each of us, in midair, the way a kite pauses momentarily in the air held by the tension of the string and air currents before some imperceptible force gently alters its position.

In that moment, the three of us were immersed in an ecstatic, luminous world. We had found the key to a door that, until this moment, had been locked. We had entered the world I had hungered for. And in that moment I realized that that world exists side by side with ours. Intimate, deep sharing and a communion of souls collapses the separation of the two worlds. I sensed that all of creation responds to such intimacy as we did. And I wanted that closeness, that experience of the luminous world as a way of life, every day of my life. It took me a long time to get to that place where the two worlds overlap.

FOOD FOR THE SOUL OF LOVE

After enough relationships had gone awry, with me going away feeling empty and disappointed, I realized I had taken on the smell of resentment. The need I carried stirred some aspect of my soul, or some need in my soul stirred up the question. It's difficult to know which happened first and doesn't, in this case, really matter. What matters is that I followed it.

I revisited the question.

Sitting in a coffeehouse with pen to journal, I held the question in my heart and awareness. "What is this depth I hunger for?" "Why isn't love enough?" As I wrote, authentic knowledge from the Universe entered my conscious mind, traveled down through my fingertips, out my pen, and appeared on the page:

"Intimacy is food that feeds the soul of love."

I looked at the words I had written. I kept writing to fill out my understanding and to anchor it inside me. Love has a soul that needs tending, feeding, and nurturing. Like a newborn infant that needs to suckle milk from her mother's breast, the food of intimacy is a vital food, a life essence that is chosen daily and given freely. When the infant leaves the womb, she enters a new world of unknown terrain. If we choose the path of intimacy, we must leave the womb of familiar old habits that prevent us from having the love we deserve. Intimacy is our birthright.

Intimacy requires taking risks, going beyond your comfort level. To have a life of intimacy, you must do that which you are most afraid of. The intimate, sacred life asks you to be vulnerable and exposed. It requires sensitizing yourself to the full range of feelings and emotions; from gross to subtle in increasing elegance. Being present with what you are feeling is the ground from which intimacy grows.

You must be willing to be seen in the deepest part of you and to give up hiding and lying. It requires rigorous self-examination (or as Data from *Star Trek* says, self-diagnostics) to see yourself clearly so that all of who you are can be present. And it asks that you see and marvel at the world and all that is part of it through the eyes of wonder.

Harriet Goldhor Lerner in *The Dance of Intimacy* says: "An intimate relationship is one in which neither party silences, sacrifices, or betrays the self and each party expresses strength and vulnerability, weakness and competence in a balanced way."[1]

I had learned not to let love in too far or too deep. I adopted this from early childhood based on my belief (at that time) that there was not enough love to go around anyhow, so someone was going to get shortchanged and be brokenhearted. And I was afraid that if love got in all the way, or if I allowed myself to open to it, someone would see that something truly was wrong with me, that I wasn't loveable. The risk of someone finding that out was, for too long, far too great. When love started to come into the hidden places inside, like water finding its way through sand, rock, and crevices, I created dams that prevented it from going too far or too deep.

To have the level of intimacy I longed for, I had to break deeply held beliefs and patterns of behavior. I began to give up ideas of who I thought I was. I gave up the romance of being alone, of marginalizing and privatizing my feelings. I gave up the façade of strength that I had crafted over the years, the strong, tough part of me that people first met. I crafted that skill from watching my father. It seemed to work for him, and the world is, after all, a dangerous place. I created that strong part to hide how terrified I was underneath. But my strength shielded the secret, tender heart inside me. I kept my natural childlike self in a closet. And as I gave these things up, I found that not many people wanted to look past the illusions or the pain to see the truth of who lay beneath. Eventually, I had to give up wanting to keep others comfortable to have the life I knew I wanted and was meant to live.

I gave up these things because, like razor wire, they hindered the path to what I wanted most: intimacy and the freedom to be intimate. Primarily, I wanted to be free, truly free, the kind of freedom that comes only from being awake, aware, and in charge of my own life; the freedom that is birthed when I am present inside my own body and thoughts and feelings; and the freedom that comes from strength of character, flexibility of options, and not feeling like a victim of anything that is happening around me so that I can choose how I feel, what I think, and how I am in each moment. I gave up hiding, gave up creating fights to make distance because being close was too scary. I chose over and over to do the things that frightened me the most. I could measure the level of intimacy each thing hid by the degree of fear I had around it. If there was tremendous energy running inside me, if I was shaking or felt pressure building, it was a clue that saying something out loud was important, for in my birth family, I had learned at a young age to not make noise and to become invisible. How many of us do that? Learn to remain silent as our deep needs and right to be alive are sacrificed to maintain the status quo?

I don't want the cheese, I just want to get out of the trap.
SPANISH PROVERB

LEARNING TO HIDE

When my father's farming partner, an old man who had been a state champion wrestling coach, grabbed my newly blossomed breasts while we were on the hay wagon together, I said nothing.

When I was molested and sodomized at age eleven by the hired hand, an all-star eighteen-year-old high-school wrestler, I said nothing.

When my first husband beat me and created a bone spur in my hip, I lied and said I had slipped down the stairs. I believed I had to make up something to tell the physician and my family to explain why I couldn't walk or move without pain for days.

I didn't know what to say, how to say it, or whom to say it to. As a survival mechanism, I learned to freeze up and shut down emotionally. Anything else was far too frightening. Though my body was still present, I was somewhere else deep inside my mind, unreachable.

Never did my mother or my older sisters ever talk about a woman's body and the changes it goes through, about sexuality or being sexual. We didn't talk about moon-time cycles. When my first menstrual cycle began at age twelve, I didn't know what was happening. I was visiting a friend when it happened, and she knew. Her stepmother took care of me. She talked to me about what was happening and how to take care of myself. It was the shorthand version about how long the bleeding might last, how I might feel, and what to do about it. What she left out was all the mystery and potential power inherent in the bleeding time. I didn't know it was a rite-of-passage time and that in indigenous cultures a young girl's first moon time is met with great celebration and the young girl is honored and welcomed into the circle of womanhood. What I knew was that I felt alone, confused, and ashamed. I wanted to hide. I spent time wishing I was a boy and doing as many boy things as I could. Not until I was much older did I come to love and work with my female body and the sacredness of her cycles.

I knew my friend's mother had called to tell my mom that I had started to bleed. But when I returned home, not a word was said. After a few hours, I finally asked, "Did Sharon call you?" My mother said yes. That was the end of the talk about menstrual cycles. When I was thirteen and wanted to use tampons, my mother accused me of being sexually active. She didn't know that you didn't need to have had sex to be able to use them. Thankfully, my sister, ten years older than me, informed her that it was possible to use tampons without first having had sex. Where my sister got that information I'll never know, but thankfully, she had it and offered it in my defense.

A year into my first marriage my mother took me into her bedroom, fished around in her underwear drawer, and pulled out of one of her size 36 C bras. She handed it to me and suggested I wear it for something that sounded like a cliché: to show off what God had given me. It worked. If you like the torpedo look. I got the point.

I have to thank my mother here, for despite our problems and dysfunction, she had a sexiness that she carried and a classic, movie-star attractiveness to her. She was a strong woman with a sense of justice. She loved wearing barely enough clothes to keep herself covered, and in the protestant Midwest, she stood out. Only now, after years of working on myself, can I see the impact her behavior had on me, which outweighed the difficult and ill-equipped verbal communication between us. On an unconscious level, she was giving me permission to have my own sense of inner strength and sexuality in the world.

When I reached puberty and came into my sexuality, my father pulled away from me completely. I was emotionally cast away from him. An unconscious part of me was learning the power of sex, and without elders or mentors to guide me through it, I was in free fall. For some reason, unknown and unbelievable to me for a long time, older men were attracted to me. I learned quickly, and painfully, that sexuality is a form of power. For me, it became a sideways attempt to get love from men that I couldn't get from my father. But because I thought I was unlovable, I put myself in more than a few dangerous situations proving to myself that I was what I believed I was: damaged goods. The damaged part of me acted out fiercely and desperately.

I watched my family. No one seemed happy. None of us would show genuine love and caring daily as a way of life. We were too afraid, too ignorant, too much asleep and shut down. I lived in an atmosphere of emotional and spiritual poverty, starved of love and affection. We would have fun now and then; but even in the croquet, volleyball, and softball games we played, there was an air of seriousness to them. And we all held

back some part of us, as if it were illegal to abandon ourselves to spontaneous, childlike fun and let unrestrained joy be a part of it all. It's taken
years for me to be able to play cards again. There was always a deck of
cards on the dining table alongside the condiments, and if we weren't
working or watching television, which was on all the time, there was a
card game going on. It was not fun to me. It was serious, cutthroat, with
fists of cards slamming the table. It was passionate, as if the card game
were the only place for passion to have expression. Playing cards was how
we dissociated from ourselves and each other. We could pretend we were
close. My mother dealt with the pain of it by disappearing into the world
of crossword puzzles. She would be bent over them at the kitchen table
early in the morning, at the end of each meal, and into the late hours of
night.

Something was deeply wrong. I could taste the acridness that hung
in the air with each inhalation of breath. I actively began to find something different, unconsciously and clumsily at first. Without a guide or
elder, I created my own tattered map from scraps of existential poems,
glue sniffing, self-tattooing, my mother's stash of prescription diet pills,
Jack Daniels, and advice from the older friends I gravitated toward. They
at least had a few more years of time in the territory than I had and they
taught me how to swear.

In my sixteenth year, I began to fight for my own life. I began to
make noise and demand to be noticed and I caused outward disturbances.
It felt good. No, it felt great. Sixteen years of repressed rage began to leak
out the edges as I rebelled against the silence, family lies, and games. I
rebelled against being put to sleep, dulled by unspoken codes of behavior
and family scripts. The waking up was slow for some years as I fumbled
my way along. Incrementally, I began to have some sense of myself, to
feel my own boundaries, and to take charge of my life, though from the
outside I'm sure it resembled nothing like taking control of my life. From
my parents' and counselor's perspectives, I was definitely not in control.
I started the habit of running away from home, which dominoed into
a ridiculous cycle that no one seemed to know how to break. No one
seemed to care enough to find out short of grounding me.

I quit going home after school on Fridays. As soon I was absent
without leave for twenty-four hours, my parents reported me missing.

Eventually, the police caught up with me, and I was deposited at the police station to wait for my parents to pick me up. The next weekend, it happened all over again. They assigned a probation officer to my case for a year. It was a valuable experience, I must say. I learned things during my brief stint in "the system" that showed me the template for how our society operates. I learned how to be crafty, how to play their superficial games and still get what I wanted: older boys in butch cars, sex in backseats, rock and roll, and drugs.

At the end of that year, I was beginning to feel desperate for a way out of the bottomless, directionless, meaningless existence I had carved out. It was exceedingly uncomfortable and becoming increasingly dangerous. A few of my friends had begun to seek drug and alcohol counseling and attend meetings. Well, I thought, I could surely use someone to talk to, so I went weekly to a counseling session. I also went to that AA meeting place where you say, "Hi, my name is Julie and I'm an alcoholic." During that time, I was not so politely asked to leave school and not come back. Twice. At seventeen I moved out of my parents' house, rented a room, and took a shit job at a capon factory. Was fired twice. I managed to get fired from a capon factory. Twice. That is fucked up.

I thought about one of those twelve steps where you say: "I am powerless (over alcohol)." It left a bad taste in my mouth. I didn't like feeling powerless (and I still don't), so I set out on a journey to feel powerful (and I still am).

I admitted myself to alcohol and drug rehab. More than once. I was in and out of detox, the psyche ward, and half-way houses for two years. During one of my tours in the detox ward, a remark my counselor made had a lasting impression on me. "You have to learn how to talk." Maybe yes, maybe no, I thought. There is power in silence. But I respected her, so I ruminated on that and concluded that it would be nice to know how to interact, to be socially adept and expressive. It became a personal project and a life goal. I watched people all the time. I watched how people changed when given the opportunity to talk about themselves, to say what they felt out loud. I learned how to engage them and keep the conversation going in directions we were mutually interested in. I began to understand the importance of talking from a simple place about how I felt and what I needed. The daily practice of refining my expression and language choices and calibrating the impact was tiring at first, and frustrating. It's a choice I made again and again even when it made others uncomfortable.

I had to learn discretion and how to do "readings" on people and circumstances. I would go into a tailspin, terrified afterward that I had said too much, made someone uncomfortable to the point of him not returning, had revealed too much of myself, and as a result, as sure as hell never freezes, something really bad was going to happen to me.

BIRTHING THE AUTHENTIC SELF

Looking in the rearview mirror at my life, I can see now just how brave, how determined I was. I didn't know I was those things at the time, but that's why a rearview mirror is helpful—it gives you a perspective of the distance and the terrain that you've covered. It may be that you have friends who are able to see the calluses on your feet from walking the path and are willing to remind you.

To make changes takes courage and fortitude: those qualities of soul that enable you to go head on into the darkness, into uncertainty and difficulty. You must have *spiritus* and *coeur*, inspiration and heart. Being intimate takes you into uncharted and uncultivated territory. There is no place there for survival mechanisms of defensiveness, paranoia, or making up what other people are thinking or saying. To be in the presence of true intimacy, one must lay down the sword that maintains distance, separation, and game dynamics. In tilling the soil of intimacy, you prepare the ground by doing your own internal work, faithfully, devotedly, as if your life depends on it.

In the process, you meet your *intimus;* your inmost nature. Over time you become your own best friend advocating for your needs, wants, and happiness. You learn to craft a life of joy so that all you do, how you make your home and life, brings you a sense of wholeness. The child parts of you begin to relax and trust you to take care of them. You speak on their behalf so their needs and wants get tended to in the open. The old and familiar habits of behavior begin to break down as you choose to do something different.

This new way is frightening. And liberating. Simple and most difficult. There is a very young part of each one of us who knows that life can be more full, enriching, and deeply rewarding. Begin by discerning wants from deep needs. Needs can be felt in the body somewhat like a slight pressure. The more fear you feel about speaking out loud on your behalf, the more energy there is around the need. And the greater the freedom there is in voicing it. For example: "I need a hug." Adding the phrase *will you* empowers you and activates the other person. "Will you give me a hug? I really need one." There is natural childlike energy and naïveté in those two words. Say them out loud. Or practice saying them inside yourself to get the feel of them. You can feel how the energy of the words comes from a younger part inside you. Notice how you hold your body when you say it. How is your breathing? What expression does your face take on? With practice you can call up this part of you at will. Allow that part of you to look through your eyes, to speak through your voice. The self of you, who is at the center of all you have been and will ever be, becomes a witness to this small person you once were being born into the world once again.

It's not unusual to feel a bit shaky inside after speaking so vulnerably. The shakiness is normal for a while until you flex those muscles often enough that the new behavior patterns find their own groove. You literally shake up your internal structure to allow something new to replace the old. Like bushwhacking a new trail in a deep forest, the first swath is difficult. Subsequent trips get easier as the path becomes clearer, well marked. You are essentially creating new neurological pathways. Think of it as adding a new software program to the mainframe of your consciousness. You are breaking the rules about intimacy, about sharing secrets and trusting another human being with your heart and the truth of you. It's important that you understand that you are breaking covert agreements about being a certain way with those close to you, for there may be repercussions. Those close to you may not be happy with the new you. Keep going. Others have gone this way before you and have left maps of the territory. But they are just maps, not the territory itself.

You are birthing your authentic self. The birthing of self is frightening, uncomfortable, and awkward. It really is like going through the birth canal when you were first born into the world. The journey was fraught with distress, pressure, and uncertainty; an unknown world lay before you. Even so, you made it through (even caesarian babies find a way through and out). And that is exhilarating, to express yourself through the birth canal and continue to be authentic in each moment thereafter.

It's important to say what you're feeling out loud. "I feel shaky and kind of scared." Ask from the little and undefended parts of you all the questions you need to ask so there is nothing unsaid. Simple and direct questions as a child would ask: "Do you still love me?" "Will you hold me?" "Do you still want to be with me?" "Do you like being with me?" "Do you think I'm pretty?" "Will you tell me what you like about me?" "I feel funny. Will you sit and talk with me?" This is a scary experience for many of us, finding a new way to be often is. But, there is life on the other side.

Very few of us were raised in families where talking honestly about how we feel was encouraged. Most of us grew up feeling scared of saying how we feel, and we learned to lie or hide to keep ourselves safe, to not disrupt the unspoken agreements we'd made with those we lived with.

NO SUCH THING AS SAFE

Security is mostly superstition. It does not exist in nature, nor do children of men as a whole experience it. Avoiding danger is no safer in the long run than outright exposure. Life is either a daring adventure, or nothing.

HELEN KELLER

I want to say something about the word *safe*. We like to think we can create an environment in which we feel safe, where our life and well-being are not threatened. Safe does not exist. At most, we can take a calculated risk, which means we consider all the possible variables and potential outcomes and, based on an analysis of the circumstances and risk factors, we decide on a particular action. Take learning to skydive for example. We may decide to skydive after we've taken into account each factor and its potential for danger. When we consider an instructor, we look at his years of training and experience, number of accidents, attitude, awareness, and attention to detail. We inquire about the integrity of the parachute equipment, the condition of the airplane and the pilot's experience, and the wind and terrain. We balance our need for this particular adventure against our fears of it and disappointment if we decide not to do it. When we finally decide, it's a result of weighing all the possible outcomes and agreeing to the risk involved. We take responsibility for the choice.

In intimate situations, we may want to ask, "Is it safe to say something?" First of all, it's a trick question. It's a setup: No matter how the person responds—yes, no, or maybe—the outcome will always be their fault. Responsibility for your well-being is unfairly put in the other person's hands, letting you off the hook of any personal responsibility. Whether or not you feel a situation is safe for you to proceed is ultimately your decision and responsibility. Deciding to take personal responsibility is the first step toward ultimate freedom.

> *There's no safety in numbers . . . or anything else.*
>
> JAMES THURBER

When we were young and chose to hide or not say something, we felt it was the safest thing to do to keep from being beaten or to help us fit in. Making those decisions as children was a smart way to survive; it got us through painful and frightening situations. And it was survival. As grown-ups, we get to do things differently, and the price we pay for not saying or doing something is often our self-respect and dignity and a postponement of freedom as we continue to keep parts of us shut down, hidden, and compromised.

Eric Berne said, "Parents, deliberately or unaware, teach their children from birth how to behave, think, feel and perceive. Liberation from these influences is no easy matter, since they are deeply ingrained and are necessary during the first two or three decades of life for biological and social survival. Indeed, such liberation is only possible at all because the individual starts off in an autonomous state, that is, capable of awareness, spontaneity and intimacy, and he has some discretion as to which parts of his parents' teachings he will accept. At certain specific moments early in life he decides how he is going to adapt to them. It is because his adaptation is in the nature of a series of decisions that it can be undone, since decisions are reversible under favorable circumstances."[2]

The significance of being intimate is that in being close, you are thrown back to a time when you decided that being close was too scary, so you folded in on yourself. When you go back to that time, you give yourself the opportunity to be a child again, but this time with the power of an adult. You learn that you no longer have to hide your feelings to survive. You learn that it's ok to have feelings, needs, wants and desires and to say them out loud to another person who will receive all of you without judgment or fear. You learn that you no longer have to hide your feelings to survive but that you can feel alive. You learn to take your place in the relationship rather than adapting to what is there. In so doing, you reclaim the precious parts of yourself-your trust, your faith, your honesty, your integrity, your child like joy and enthusiasm for life. All the things that you locked away in a place where they would not be touched by the devastation in your family.

GENEEN ROTH, *WHEN FOOD IS LOVE*

When you choose a life of intimacy and all that it requires and affords, a door opens to some new adventure, to awareness and intuitive development. Light is able to penetrate the shadowed places in your interior house. There comes a point on each journey when you know, without doubt, without hesitation, that you cannot go back to your old life; you cannot be who you once were and also have a new life with new riches. If it were possible, I would have found how to do it. I tried to keep one foot in each life, the old and the new. It's a recipe for crazy making and relationship messes. You have to choose one or the other, and the old life is like the line from *The Matrix*: "You've been down that road before, Neo."

Sexuality is not a thing, an act, or a behavior, but rather a state of being who you are, what your nature is. And it is bound tightly to creativity. Sexuality is used to create, not just life but art, poetry, food, a home. It is given from Eros—the God of sexual passion, that longing for the divine, and it is the instinctive drive to connect to the larger world—and when Eros is made part of all that we do, all that we do becomes alive, enhanced, animated. Food tastes juicier, colors are brighter, and life takes on a luminous sexiness.

Hans Hofmann, in *Sex Incorporated,* writes about the broader meaning of sex.

> Sex is the action through which we accomplish what sexuality prompts us to do. The term *sex* should be rescued from its promiscuous meanings in common usage. Restored to its precise significance, sex connotes the interaction by which persons express their most intimate union. *Expression* is here the most crucial term. The intimacy and mutuality of two people's relationship with each other is not limited to or by sex. But sex expresses most intensely the character of such a union, for better or for worse. That is why sexual intercourse represents the quintessence of sex. From this center, sex radiates in a descending line of significance into all other forms of human interaction and intercourse.[3]

If you choose a life of awareness and attention to detail, a life dripping with sensuality and intimacy will belong to your true self as you emerge into the light of day. That life asks you to pay attention to the details, to awaken your senses, to relinquish limiting behaviors and beliefs, to be present with what is right in front of you, with what's real from moment to moment.

2

Autonomous Personhood

Fearing for My Life

Meeting you,
I shuddered,
fearing for my life.
Now I understand why.

Death has come
in the guise of the beloved.
The one I used to be
is gone forever!

Paul Ferrini,
Dancing with the Beloved

All my life I've wanted nothing but to bring sex and
friendship together—and I seem to be farther away from
it than ever.

Erica Jong,
Any Woman's Blues

The Self is not a known territory, but a wilderness. Too often we forget that. Too often we reach the boundaries of what we know about ourselves and turn back.

PAUL FERRINI,

THE WISDOM OF THE SELF

The privilege of a lifetime is being who you are.

JOSEPH CAMPBELL,

REFLECTIONS ON THE ART OF LIVING

The gods cannot give you anything that you cannot imagine for yourself.

JULIE MCINTYRE

So you want intimacy and meaning in your life. The want, the desire to have something, is the beginning, the acorn from which all else will grow. In the wanting, inside that acorn, is an intimation of what it might look like when the want is made manifest, comes to fruition, like the great oak that is inside the acorn. Some part of you has suggestions about how to have that thing in your life, what it will look like, and having the desire sets the creating of it in motion. There becomes a movement in the direction of that thing, in this instance, a relationship. Not just any relationship but one that has a particular feeling and quality to it, and when you imagine it, you get a warm and fuzzy feeling inside and parts of you relax just imagining it, and you say, "Yes, that's it, that's what I want." Anything that is created begins in the imagination with images.

Creating the life you want begins with desire and imagination. Imagining the love and intimacy you desire and the life you want, a rich life, ecstatic life, creative life, interesting life, romantic life, passionate life, ensouled life. To be in a life other than the life you have been living, imagination and desire to be a person other than the person you have been must be the initiator. Imagination and desire can be the key that turns the ignition of change. You know the definition of insanity—doing the same thing over and over and expecting different results. To get different results, you must do something different. You have an image of what you desire, but you haven't been able to have that in your life. Something has to change at a fundamental level. We keep looking for Mister Right to come along; but even if he did, we're still the same person, doing the same things, with the same unhappiness, the same feelings of unworthiness, the same psychoses, and we're still reading from the old scripts our family gave us.

Intimacy comes from the Latin *intimus,* meaning "innermost." To be intimate with another, we first must become intimate with ourselves, our primary relationship, which is the foundation of intimately relating to others, to Earth, to anyone and anything. There is a problem with being intimate with ourselves when we are more concerned with what others are feeling than what we are feeling. Lacking intimacy with ourselves creates or at least maintains a fragmentation within our self, an incompleteness, an unfinished business of the soul to make itself whole. The soul has its own desires and purposes. It is here to make itself, to remake itself, to be educated in the journey of becoming a human being.

Intimate moments assert themselves into our lives when we least expect it. Consider how uncomfortable it is to see a friend or acquaintance in the grocery store. It's an intimate thing to have someone see what we are buying and taking into our homes. Some of the things in the cart are . . . intimate. Remember the experience of visiting a friend's home for the first time? There is almost always the requisite tour of the house. As you move more deeply into the heart of the home, a little unease begins to push on you for you see intimately how people live and what is important to them. Those feelings of unease build as you approach the bedroom, since we know what goes on in there, in that bed, under those blankets, and suddenly we turn to leave the room, quickly. These are two examples of how uncomfortable we can get simply with superficial intimacy.

> *To be what we are, and to become what we are capable of becoming, is the only end in life.*
> ROBERT LOUIS STEVENSON

A primary focus of this book is to go beyond and below casual superficiality and assumptions to the place where real and lasting transformation happens. My goal is to get to the source of those uncomfortable feelings and eventually, ultimately, not let them unhinge you.

WHAT IS THE SOUL?

Before I go further, I feel it's necessary to come to a working understanding and definition of the word *soul* for the duration of this book.

We know what love is, and we know it has different meanings with respect to the relationship. "I love my granddaughter" has a particular kind of meaning, and you know it when you read it or hear the words. "I love steamed artichokes" has another kind of meaning, different from "I love my granddaughter." "I love my horse" has still another meaning in it, particular to my relationship with my horse.

But soul is something that, after more than 3 million years of human habitation on Earth, we cannot seem to agree on. There are other invisibles that we can agree not only exist, we can agree on the meaning of them as well. Wind, for example, and heat and cold are invisible, but we know them through feeling and how our bodies experience them. We know love through feeling it and experiencing it, just as we have the experience of heat and cold.

Soul, like love, is an invisible thing; you can't see it, but you can feel it. The soul of a song that stirs you to the core, the soul of a great poem or story or painting. When we are touched by a great work of art, it is a soul-to-soul touching. A person who is a good soul walks into the room, and you feel the soul of that person walking in. But feeling, knowing our own soul, is even more elusive to us than the soul of a song that moves us deeply. Most of us can agree that the thing that is present in a living body that is not present in a dead body is soul. Soul is not a flat, two-dimensional phenomenon.

The concept of soul is ubiquitous around the globe and has been since antiquity. Socrates made the appeal that it is the soul that animates the body of a living thing. If a person is clinically brain dead from an accident is the soul still present? Does the soul need a fully functioning body to be present? I have met paraplegics and people with missing limbs and have sat with my dying father-in-law while he was unconscious. I have experienced their souls to be intact, present, and available. We've heard from scientists and from people who have come out of a coma that comatose people are not only able to hear conversations around them but remember them and the feelings in the room.

Who is remembering? Contrarily, I have met people who are healthy in body and sick in soul. Soul is the bearer of moral qualities and moves toward ideals of justice, courage, and truth.

The idea that the soul animates the body doesn't fit when we consider stones, mountains, or trees or even in the way we think of humans and animals as being animated and moving about. Have you met a stone outcropping or stood gazing out from a mountaintop that moved you to stillness and awe? What was it that struck you, caused you to stop in your tracks and stand still, to inhale deeply in those moments? The energy coming off the stone face or rising up from the valley below, from the breathtaking view—is that the soul of the stone or the mountain? Is it the spirit of that place?

Something has reached out and touched us despite our hurry to get somewhere. And what in us is responding to such spectacle, to such a mystifying feeling? When we stand in an old-growth forest, amid giant redwoods and thousand-year-old trees, what is happening in the silence of the forest that can humble us to tears or raise the hairs on our arms? What happens inside us when a tree we planted as a sapling and watered, nurtured, and loved is suddenly uprooted by a storm or taken out by fire or a neighbor's chainsaw? The part of us that bonded with the tree is deeply affected, changed by its absence; we've lost a dear friend to death. Something invisible is presenting itself to our senses, to our feeling body. Something bigger and outside us, some self-organized whole that cannot be found in its parts has stopped us in our tracks.

Michael Perlman describes the impact trees have on our psyche, our soul, as "[t]he reforesting of the soul."[1] When we sit with a favorite tree or walk in the forest, the impact on our soul is a sense of renewal and of deep connection with someone more than human. I've seen students sit with trees and witnessed the transformative powers trees have on their psyche. The erect straight trunks of pine trees infuse our souls, causing us to stand more erect and treelike; we develop a more profound sense of ourselves, of our boundaries, and feel stronger. Alligator junipers that grow in the high deserts of the Southwest lift our spirits to greater heights, bringing a sense of hope and a feeling of falling in love with all of life. Trees are erotic and sexy; it's not an accident that while walking in a forest with your beloved you are often moved to make love on the forest floor, immersed in the fecund, musky smell of leaf litter and pine needles, beneath a great towering canopy. Pine trees produce a great deal of pine pollen, one of the most abundant and ready sources of testosterone. It increases testosterone in the body and balances the androgen/estrogen ratio.[2]

The animistic worldview asserts that everything is ensouled, alive with energy. *Anima* is Latin for "soul," thus *anima mundi* is the world soul or soul-infused world, a mysterious life-force energy ensouling all that is created. From archaeological reports, we can surmise that so-called primitive peoples not only believed in an ensouled world but also saw the energies, souls, and spirits of things. They left a visible record of their encounters on cave walls and rock faces and erected monuments to the unseen, yet ensouled forces of the Universe.

> *The soul should always stand ajar, ready to welcome the ecstatic experience.*
>
> EMILY DICKINSON

> *Good for the body is the work of the body and good for the soul is the work of the soul, and good for either is the work of the other.*
>
> HENRY DAVID THOREAU

I have a sense of what soul is in me, in others, in animals, in plants, and in ecosystems. I cannot definitively define and point to it, nor has science been able to dissect it. I do believe that some things are meant to remain indefinable and mysterious. We understand very little if we can only understand what can be explained. Perhaps soul is one thing that we are not meant to fully grasp, though I think my theory and understanding of it is as workable as anyone's. We are each in our own private, trembling lives, fumbling toward understanding mystery and the mystery of our lives as much as possible.

I believe soul to be the accumulation of all the parts that make up the "I" of us.

[T]he absence of the soul is far more terrible in the living man than in a dead one.

CHARLES DICKENS,

BARNABY RUDGE

The Oxford English Dictionary (OED) defines soul as "the principle life in man and animals; animate existence; the principle of thought and action in man commonly thought of as an entity distinct from the body; the spiritual part of man in contrast to the purely physical. Also, occasionally the corresponding or analogous principle in animals; the personification of some quality; the inspirer or leader of some business cause, movement, etc. The chief agent, prime mover or leading spirit."

Soul has gone through some interesting semantic evolutions. From the Greek, Psyche is soul. It is through trials and tribulations that we are forced into the arena of psyche to craft responses and build character. In love relationships, Eros is a prime mover creating chaos in our interior world, forcing us downward and into the ground of our psyche. The Celts have defined spiritual wholeness by three conditions. According to the Encyclopedia of Celtic Wisdom, *cra'bhadh* is the trust of the soul, or devout observation; *creideamh* is the heart's consent, or belief; and *iris* is the mind's pledge, or faith: "When these three are as one, then there is true strength and power within the *coich anama,* or the soul-shrine, as the body is termed. The body is like the cover of a triptych which unfolds its panels to reveal a landscape full of wonders."[3] *Anam,* Gaelic for soul, insinuates life's vigor and strength of character and is related to *anal,* the breath of life. The soul weaves in and out of consciousness and wanders in and out of life. It is seen as dynamic, fluid, and flexible and can travel in and out of the body, and it is "intimately moved by the mind and the heart, and cannot often be seen as separate from either."[4] The Celtic soul is not seen as superior to the body or subservient to a divine master as in Christian definitions of soul. The soul is viewed as a personal responsibility; we are responsible for maintaining its wholeness and integrity.

Soul knowledge is the basis of all self-knowledge. It is intelligent, aware, mysterious, and fascinating, and it influences and shapes who we become. Soul has its own destiny. Soul seeks to know the truth of itself and strives to have meaning, has will toward meaning.[5] When we are unable to find the meaning of our lives, when there is meaninglessness, we do meaningless things, and it is in the midst of meaninglessness that people resort to violence. If we feel our life has no meaning, then what we do—the choices we make and what we think—does not matter.

Viktor Frankl articulated three drives, or wills, to meaning in our lives, and two of them occur when the basic will to meaning is frustrated. The will to power and the will to pleasure are "substitutes of frustrated will to meaning. The search for meaning is our basic concern. Only a man who has been frustrated in his basic concern resorts either to will to power or will to pleasure."[6] Living out a search for power ends in violence. The will to seek pleasure or the pursuit of happiness is self-defeating in that it is the very pursuit of happiness that derails us. We think that we can find happiness if we have enough money, enough things, enough love, enough security, and then we won't be afraid or sad any longer. Happiness is a by-product not an end in itself. Happiness is the effect of finding meaning in our lives, though it is related to happenstance; it comes and then it's gone. Joy, however, endures. It is the payoff, the effect of being in love, of loving another human being, of understanding the meaning in our work, our relationship with Earth, and in the experience of being alive. Plotinus asserted that happiness could not be found in the physical world, but that even daily, physical acts were determined by the "higher phase of the soul."

Our lack of having a sense, and an understanding of what soul is in ourselves; what its function is, its role in who we are and what we are drawn to, and what the soul is in all living things means we live in a world with no intimacy. Everything then becomes cold, dead, lifeless material to be used or consumed. Living an ensouled life is to have a relationship with not merely the physicality of Earth, with wilderness, and with sex, but to have joyful interrelations with the livingness of each, with the differentiating soul of each. It is a lack of understanding and intimacy that causes us to fear things we don't understand that leads us to clear-cut forests, to dominate and have power over what we do not know intimately.

Sex is not merely some thing or an event in the midst of a circumstance. It is a primal, life-force energy that happens in a soul-filled sea of details—of wants, desires, and hormones. Sex is soul driven to connect with the ancient powers of life, death, and procreation. Owning our wild sexual natures involves self-understanding: bringing our faintly appreciated feelings to full consciousness and becoming more aware of how we individually and as a species are related to other species.

> *There is no easy or quick plan to happiness, there is no single spot where you can start. Where you are right now is the best place to begin. Be careless in your dress if you must, but keep a tidy soul.*
>
> MARK TWAIN

> *Through soul you build your own world.*
>
> JOHANN WOLFGANG VON GOETHE

Only what you know to be true from your own experiments, feelings, and perceptions has value to your current life. The soul is always seeking to be expressed—that is its goal. It responds in each moment to what is presented to it. As you respond newly in the midst of old, familiar situations, new patterns are laid down, patterns that verify, ascertain, and reveal the soul's true essence. With each pattern, like setting mosaic tiles, the soul becomes ever more sophisticated and true in itself.

The soul is shaped through life experiences, difficult and challenging family and work relationships—seemingly dead-end jobs or demanding and fulfilling jobs and the trials and joys of marriage and raising children. It is educated in the fabric of life experiences, whether on solitary treks to the wilderness or on crowded subway trains. Through conflicting demands, illness, contrasting experiences, and accidents that when rightly seen may not be accidents at all, the soul discovers what its own values and belief systems are. It is through these life experiences that the soul knows what feels good, right, and true and what is not supportive to its life force and destiny. It is being in the world and through the world that our soul takes on its own unique shape and character. It is helped along if we are present in its making, home in our bodies using our internal sensory guidance system.

The more our soul, the I of us, is taken into account and accounted for, the more we are able to hold ourselves responsible. The little or large indignities that we at one time accepted become insufferable, and we are moved to respond to restore and maintain our essential dignity and character, to keep our soul intact, so that we are no longer the enemy of ourselves. With the OED definitions we can extrapolate that the I of our soul is the "chief agent or prime mover." The soul is the "leading spirit" of our lives, always moving in the direction to complete its wholeness. Ultimately, when we reach the end of our Earthly days, will we be able to face ourselves and answer "yes" to the questions: "Did I become myself?" "Did I live my own life?"

WHO IS "I"?

Take a few, slow moments to ponder the following questions. Do you ever eat in secret? Are you afraid to ask for what you want? Does your partner know you masturbate? Do you know what you want? What inspires you? Are you afraid to ask for help when you need it? Do you feel guilty when you ask for help or get what you want? Are you afraid to let your lover see you naked? Are you uncomfortable with your sexuality? Does sex scare you? Have you been waiting for someone else to make you happy? Are your other relationships the primary source of comfort and security? Do you treat yourself often with massage, hot baths, a day off in bed? Do you give yourself what the Italians call the sweetness of doing nothing? Do you enjoy your own company or do you avoid being alone? Do you hide yourself or practice invisibility to feel safe? Have you ever looked at photos of naked women? Naked men? Do you enjoy it? Does anyone else know? What's your favorite type of nude photo? How do you feel about masturbation? Are you comfortable walking around your house naked? What excites you sexually, passionately, gets your juices flowing? Are you pleased with your answers?

Who inside you answered these questions? Did you answer with your head or your heart? Were you honest with yourself? What will you change so you'll feel good about your answers and yourself? What will it take for you to be autonomous, self-ruling, and free?

Asking yourself these questions and others initiates the process of getting to know yourself. We take ourselves for granted and operate unconsciously on autopilot a good bit of the time. We have a surface relationship with ourselves, one that gets us from home to our jobs and back home again. The labor involved in getting to know ourselves is not unlike peeling an onion, one layer at a time. The onion is not really the best metaphor because our psyche is not organized in neat, peel-away-able layers. Though there are tears. The way I work with the parts of me is more like a model of the Native American Medicine Wheel with the I that is I in the center. All the other parts of me, my ego states, are around me like spokes in a wheel. That was my basic working model to begin with, but over time as I worked to integrate and harmonize my fragmented selves, the relationship between my different selves has become a more free-form, organic, and spontaneous working/playing relationship. Krishnamurti talks about it as the center and says:

> The centre is a bundle of memories, a bundle of traditions, and the centre has been brought about by tension, through pressure, through influence. The centre is the result of time, within the field of culture—and so on. So that is the centre. Now that centre, because it is a centre, has space outside it, obviously. And because of the movement, it has space in itself. If it had no movement it would have no space. So there is space, outside the centre and in it. And the centre is always seeking wider space, to move more widely. To put it differently, the centre is consciousness. That is, the centre has the borders which it recognizes as "the me."[7]

To get to the center, to the I, we begin to look at how the scripts we were given and the ones we made up for ourselves as children are part of our programming; they've become beliefs about how to act and think and what sort of person we are. They are not subconscious in the clinical sense of the term, but they do run our show without our awareness much of the time. Our subconscious has been running on autopilot for thousands of miles over many years. The conscious is the creative, thinking part of us, as well as the part that can notice what the subconscious is doing and saying. When consciousness is active, we say we are aware or awake. We are actively noticing. When we go unconscious, our default mechanism is to act out the old programming, often with detrimental, unpleasant effects.

When the conscious, aware part of you quits paying attention, you stop thinking and essentially go to sleep, then the unconscious and unintegrated parts that have been storing up feelings of mad, sad, scared, and enraged use your mouth to form words that fall out like glass marbles tumbling to the floor. Noisily at that. If we are unconscious, it's nearly impossible to stop it from happening. Then you have a relationship mess on your hands to clean up. If you're very lucky nothing gets broken like pottery or glass or trust.

Consciousness is the interaction of physical and cognitive processes, the faculty of perceiving. Ayn Rand wrote, "A consciousness conscious of nothing but itself is a contradiction in terms: before it could identify itself as consciousness, it had to be conscious of something."[8] Consciousness is a degree of awareness as opposed to alertness. For example, we've all had the experience of driving along in our car and then realize fifteen miles of road have passed under our wheels without our conscious awareness. Suddenly we "come to" and realize we have no memory of driving the car, but we were driving the car. Often we don't remember what we were thinking or where our minds were during the past fifteen miles. Something, or some part, drove the car; some part of us that knew how to drive the car got us safely along the miles that are now behind us while we were doing something else. Were we conscious while we were driving the car as our "minds" were someplace else? Were we simply alert enough to prevent an accident? The witnessing self, the I, went someplace else, took a nap, perhaps, or traveled to some distant planet to gather inspiration or work out a problem we've been having. That part came back just in time, and it was the reentry into our bodies that jolted us to awareness of our circumstance and, as it were, good fortune. Maybe we were daydreaming. The point is that during those miles, we can say that we "went unconscious." Our awareness took a detour while we mundanely operated a motor vehicle.

A solid foundation of intimacy with another person begins here, inside yourself, the I that is I. The work is difficult and challenging, and through it you'll confront hidden value systems and beliefs about yourself, about sex, and about how your world and the larger world works as well as your beliefs, values, and relationship with Nature. You'll meet yourself face-to-face, one-on-one. As one of my apprentices has often said, "This work is changing me." Indeed, it does change you; it is a transformation of character. And it is work. It requires making time in your life for you and for any sequestered parts of you to become unsequestered and in the open so they can have a life with you and through you. It is the work of what Jung called making the darkness conscious; bringing into conscious awareness those aspects of ourselves that have been hidden. It is bringing all that has been unconscious into our full awareness.

FILLING THE LONG BAG

Each human being is a complex, interesting, multifaceted system with a multiple personality. As infants, we come into the world as a vortex of energy, unabashed and unrepressed. All our basic needs for survival get met, and if we are lucky, our innate need for love and bonding are met as well. As we grow, we learn to get most of our wants met. As children, we know very well what we want and that we want it now. And we say no to what repels us.

But it doesn't take long for an infant to discover how to fit into her family or social environments. Between birth and six years old, we are most impressionable, and a great deal of the programming of our subconscious happens between these years. During these early years, we start accepting things that aren't true. This is how the child of us becomes corrupted. We're programmed to devalue and disempower ourselves. By the time we are two or three, we have a growing list of what we are to do to fit in—brush your teeth, eat all your food, pick up your toys—and an even longer list of what not to do—don't eat the dirt, don't hit the dog, don't cry, don't talk in church, don't ask questions, don't play with yourself, don't color outside the lines, don't hit your brother, don't be noisy.

Slowly, the vortex of energy we once were begins to lose vitality as parts of us are put in a bag. The young child learns quickly that parts of her personality are not acceptable to those who love her, so she puts the unlovable or inappropriate parts of herself in a secret room inside her, or they get put in what Robert Bly calls the long bag. In *A Little Book on the Human Shadow,* he says, "We spend our life until we're twenty deciding what parts of ourselves to put into the bag, and we spend the rest of our lives trying to get them out again."[9]

We learned to sequester parts of ourselves because they made others feel uncomfortable and were unacceptable in our family, in school, or in social settings. As we grow, we are socialized (made friendly or cooperative) to fit into the narrow definitions of what it means to be a human being, what it means to be happy, and what it means to be a contributing member of society. Often, part of that socialization means that we begin to believe what others say about us either explicitly ("You cry too easily" or "You're lazy") or indirectly through their behavior toward us.

> *Intimate relating begins with the self. It is a toxic fantasy to believe that we can be intimate with others when we have not learned (or are afraid) to be intimate with ourselves. Self-intimacy develops naturally when we have not been excessively poisoned by the toxic attitudes of others toward us or by toxic patterns that we inflict on ourselves.*
>
> JERRY GREENWALD,
> *CREATIVE INTIMACY*

Unfortunately, women and girls are too often told and trained to be nice and to look pretty. Unfortunate because inside those admonitions are messages that intuition is not to be trusted, that who they are and what they are feeling are not trustworthy and that anything besides "nice" is not acceptable and certainly wildishness is out of the quesion. They are trained to be powerless. Clarissa Pinkola Estés notes: "Women's curiosity is given a negative connotation, whereas men were called investigative. Women were called nosy, whereas men were called inquiring. In reality, the trivialization of women's curiosity so that it seems like nothing more than irksome snooping denies women's insight, hunches, intuitions. It denies all her senses. It attempts to attack her fundamental power."[10]

For men, as well, intuition is power, is genderless and a function of a healthy soul. Little boys are also given some version of these messages: be nice, tuck in your shirt, comb your hair, don't cry. With these messages planted, boys grow to mistrust their intuitive natures and are unable to discern what's real or what they are feeling and unable to say "the emperor has no clothes." Attempts to kill the willful, wild spirit in children are many and come disguised as teachers, parents, and religious leaders.

We'll be spending some time in the next chapter getting to know the parts of ourselves we've put in the secret room or the bag we drag behind us. Either metaphor can work, but Bly's metaphor of the long bag expresses how putting parts of ourselves away acts as a weight on who we are; it restricts our movements because often the creative parts, the predator, or the outrageous parts are in that bag. It's time for them to come out, to have a life and to be part of your life. It's time for you once again to be a vortex of energy, a spontaneous, 360-degree personality.

THROWING OUT THE OLD SCRIPTS

You can get a sense of how important it is to develop an intimate relationship with yourself if you begin to notice the internal self-critical chatter as you're tending to work or chores, as you interact with other people, as you walk by the mirror and see a reflection of yourself. Take note of how many times you hear a voice inside you that says "You're getting fat," or "You shouldn't have said that out loud," or "You're not smart enough to do that." These lines are scripts; that is, early programming that was given to us and internalized as truth. For some time you've believed the script, and it's influenced who you are and the choices you've made. Now, those admonishments are old, battered, overused; the expiration date has long expired, and they've begun to taste sour in your mouth. They no longer work, nor should they.

Eric Berne, founder of transactional analysis, defines scripts as lines and codes of behavior given to us by others, usually family members, but scripts can come from anyone whose authority we take more seriously than our own. The term *scripts* expresses Berne's idea that each of us follows personal life scripts from early childhood decisions and parental programming. Maintaining the scripts into adulthood restricts our movement and flexibility of responses.[11]

When I hear the word *script*, I have this image of standing on a stage and being handed pages filled with dialogue that is meant for me. I take a cursory look at what is written there and throw it back at the stagehand saying something to the effect of "Over my dead body I'll say these lines; give me some new ones." But there isn't time for anyone to write new lines for me, so I ad-lib (you must be able to improvise). I take a deep, inspiring breath that expands my belly. I inhale inspiration from the air spirit as the in-breath spirals in and down into my womb. A valve opens up, screwed open by the spiraling breath. Some old, ancient matriarchal energy begins to rise up from the primordial womb that connects all sentient, sacred, sexual beings and moves through my womb, up through my belly, dusting off the wild, instinctual, intuitive, truth-telling part of me. I laugh uproariously, a full-bellied, breast-shaking, table-pounding, tears-flowing laugh. I can't stop. Something has been set free, my voice has found its sound in the world, and I hear it echo off the theater walls. I fall in love with the sound of it. I have a vision of other women and children throwing their scripts off the stage or burning them. My soul begins to sing through the instrument of my body.

Throwing out old scripts is going against the unspoken rules of behavior set down by our family and culture. Breaking the rules, speaking out, doing something different, making noise is disconcerting at first. Notice if you feel scared after you've had an outburst of laughter, witticism, or anger, as if you have done something wrong. Estés writes about the meaning behind a sudden wild laugh.

> In the sacred, the obscene, the sexual, there is always a wild laugh waiting, a short passage of silent laughter, or crone-nasty laughter, or the wheeze that is a laugh, or the laugh that is wild and animal, or the trill that is like a run on the musical scale. Laughter is a hidden side of women's sexuality; it is physical, elemental, passionate, vitalizing, and therefore arousing. It is a kind of sexuality that does not have a goal, unlike genital arousal. It is a sexuality of joy, just the moment, a true sensual love that flies free and lives and dies and lives again on its own energy. It is sacred because it is so healing. It is sensual for it awakens the body and the emotions. It is sexual because it is exciting and causes waves of pleasure. It is not one dimensional, for laughter is something one shares with oneself as well as with many others. It is a woman's wildest sexuality.[12]

I think what a joy it is to be alive and I wonder if I'll ever leap inward to the root of this flesh and know myself as once I was.

FRANK HERBERT,
DUNE

Man's task in life is to give birth to himself, to become what he potentially is, the most important product of his effort is his own personality.

ERICH FROMM,
MAN FOR HIMSELF

RETRIEVING YOUR SOUL

This work, essentially, is doing your own soul retrieval. It is immediate, empowering, and rich and can ultimately bring renewed creativity and joy. The child parts of you that were put away, shut out, and marginalized are given a place to live inside you, an opportunity to be part of your daily life, and given permission to live loud and free and imaginatively. The door through which we wish to walk into freedom and into wholeness is not outside ourselves; we are the door. And once the door is found, one must then get up and walk through it. You may travel to faraway lands and seek a guru, but you will not find what you are ultimately seeking. What you seek is in a place that is too obvious and ordinary to consider: the soul that is called *I am*.

I don't need a minister to mediate between me and my gods or Creator or the wind or Mother Earth or my deceased grandmother or anyone for that matter. I go directly. I sought out intermediaries early on because they were the ones I found to talk to. Also, I was looking for someone else to make decisions for me or think for me. It felt important then in a distorted sense. In hindsight, I see how disempowered I kept myself. Until I found a spiritual path, I didn't know I could do it myself or how. On rare occasions now, I'll ask for external validation and an outside perspective, someone other than my partner or a close friend. Primarily, I go directly to the source, feel for the truth to sound its bell inside me. I no longer want anyone making decisions for me or telling me what to do. I believe in personal responsibility as a catalyst for deep and lasting changes that will echo into the larger society, one concentric ring of change at a time.

> *I believe that we are solely responsible for our choices, and*
> *we have to accept the consequences of every deed, word, and*
> *thought throughout our lifetime.*
>
> ELISABETH KÜBLER-ROSS

Having said all that, there are times we need someone else, another human being, to help us find our way. There are times when we are so deep in our emotional swamps of despair, grief, and fear that we are unable to see, think, or feel. In those times, by all means seek out someone to hear you and help you find your way. Be certain, however, that you are clear about why you are going to that person, what you are asking for, and what you need and that you are always feeling for the truth of it. Having clarity going into a situation can prevent drama and minimize the possibility of a disappointment or disaster.

Being vulnerable is the hardest thing of all. Sometimes the mere mention of a word brings up thoughts, feelings, and emotions that stop us in our tracks. We make a 180-degree turn and run as fast and far as we can in the other direction. Being vulnerable and self-revealing are tantamount to living an ensouled, intimate life.

> *As human beings our greatness lies not so much in being*
> *able to remake the world—that is the myth of the atomic*
> *age—as in being able to remake ourselves.*
>
> MOHANDAS K. GANDHI

> *We all walk in mysteries. We do not know what is stirring*
> *in this atmosphere that surrounds us, nor how it is*
> *connected with our own spirit. So much is certain—that*
> *at times we can put out feelers of our soul beyond its bodily*

limits; and a presentiment, an actual insight is accorded to it.

JOHANN WOLFGANG VON GOETHE

Being aware is one thing. Knowing what your options are in any given moment and circumstance is another thing. And choosing which of several options to act on from a place of wholeness is something else. The necessity for rigorous self-examination is not an academic exercise. You have to actually do it. No one can do it for you. It is the struggle for consciousness. It is a struggle because the parts of you that are invested in your being unconscious, in keeping a safe distance and maintaining old beliefs, will compete to maintain their reality; they will escalate, act out, and have temper tantrums. Those parts will offer you all sorts of justifications for maintaining the old beliefs and behaviors. When this happens, you must sit down with them and hear them out. Then you tell them all the reasons the old ways no longer work, how you want more from life and a deeper understanding of who you are. Tell them you want to be free. You must find inside yourself motivations for the change and hold on to that. Ultimately, you need their agreement, need to have them in alignment with your decisions for lasting change to take root.

Significant motivations for me are that I want to be free from reactionary, outdated beliefs. I want to create my own value system, not carry ones that belonged to other people who were afraid and didn't care to find another way. I want to know who I am and I want my soul to have its life in its most authentic, gratifying, passionate manner. I want to be honorable in word and deed. I want to live large, be outrageous, outspoken, defiant, incorrigible, irrepressible, unpredictable, creative, a force to be reckoned with. I want to know my interior world and all its inhabitants, all their gifts and virtues and idiosyncrasies, what moves them to tears and makes them shudder with joy and pleasure. These are things that motivate me, keep me going forward through the brambles, rubble and scree, and worn-out collections of cultural and familial scripts and values. These are the forces moving me onward toward clarity of understanding and freedom from habituated manners and fear of movement. I want to be called beloved by myself and to call Earth beloved. I want to feel alive. I want to be free.

Being intimate with yourself is the beginning of being intimate with another being. Not the new age rhetoric of simply loving yourself more or for the first time, though that is a small and beginning part of it. Intimacy is more than love, for love is never enough. Intimacy is self-knowledge and self-understanding; it is befriending yourself, companioning yourself, and caring enough to notice who you are, who you have been, and who you've always wanted to be. It is caring enough to get your hands dirty digging up the dreams you had as a child, those adventures you've always wanted to have, the projects you wanted to create, the books you wanted to write that have never left you. It is finding a way, if it's the last thing you do, to have them come alive in your life, in this lifetime, so the soul and spirit of you are awake and engaged with living.

It involves descending the treacherous steps downward into the basement of your psyche to find what makes your soul sing, to discover where your soul would have you go if you were to, at last, ask and listen for the answer that comes in the silent inner knowing deep in the intuitive heart of your child.

Intimacy begins in your inner world, between your legs, in those sensitive nipples, in your bedroom, on Earth—experimenting, exploring what is sexually exciting and pleasingly satisfying to you. It's discovering what makes your soul thrum, what inspires you, what holds you back. It is understanding the meanings in the stride of your walk, the carriage of your shoulders, the tilt of your chin, the look behind your eyes, and, more importantly, the who of you that is looking out of your eyes. This is the work of becoming conscious.

Making your unknown known is the important thing.
                                        GEORGIA O'KEEFE

Consciousness—that state of being aware of your internal world— begins the journey of becoming an integrated, whole human being from the inside out. It is being present with and aware of how you are feeling and what you are thinking in the midst of doing. Integration and coming to full consciousness begins with where you are. So, where are you right now? In your head? In your heart? Are you aware of your feet, your breathing, the aches and pains in your body? Are you happy, sad, mad, scared, pissed off, frustrated? Take inventory right now of how you feel. Go deeper inside. What voices are you hearing? What are they saying? Are they shouting, joyful, raging, whispering, whimpering? Not least of all: What are you seeing? And who is doing the seeing?

3

Getting to Know You

Without deviation from the norm, progress is not possible.

FRANK ZAPPA

I have been trained to use Eric Berne's Transactional Analysis model for identifying and gaining facility with interior ego states. Transactional Analysis is a modality that Berne, a Canadian-born psychiatrist, called interpersonal interactions. Berne described an ego state as "a coherent system of feelings, and operationally as a set of coherent behavior patterns; or pragmatically, as a system of feelings which motivates a related set of behavior patterns."[1] He noted that "[e]go states are normal psychological phenomena.* The human brain is the organ or organizer of psychic life, and its products are organized and stored in the form of ego states."[2]

---

*Berne viewed human beings as psychological phenomena, but ego states are really ecological phenomena because human beings have evolved within an ecological context. Every species has built into it a system of multiple ego states. Every species on Earth has an interior world that is a multiple personality where specific ego states emerge at specific times. Take, for example, cats. Everyone knows that a kitten has distinctively different energy than an old cat. The terms *kitten* and *cat* have inherently different meanings. Tree saplings have a distinctly different energy than a 100-year-old Juniper or a 4,000-year-old bristlecone pine. Further, there is a decidedly different *feeling* to the various ages of different species; how we relate to a kitten is very different from how we relate to an old cat, how we interact with a three-year-old girl is very different from how we relate to a ninety-year-old woman. When we see the parents of different species tending to their young, we instinctively understand the part of them (and the part of us) that nurtures.

Human beings are a kaleidoscope of multiple ego states. All of these ego states possess energy. Sometimes a great deal of energy. Have you ever seen a two-year-old having a temper tantrum? Comments Jungian analyst James Hollis: "It is not that we have a single child within, perhaps hurt, frightened, codependent or withdrawn in compensation, but a whole host of children, a veritable kindergarten, including the class clown, the artist, the rebel, the spontaneous child at one with the world. . . . Virtually all have been neglected or suppressed."[3]

Each ego state has a function, and each one will perform its function whether you want it to or not—or are conscious of it or not. It is crucial, over time, to be able to identify the ego states; free any that are repressed or locked away; understand their functions; and make friends with them so that you exist as a coherent, integrated whole. Robert Bly says in *A Little Book on the Human Shadow:* "But why would we give away, or put into the bag, so much of ourselves? Why would we do it so young? And if we have put away so many of our angers, spontaneities, hungers, enthusiasms, our rowdy and unattractive parts, then how can we live? What holds us together?"[4] And many of us are not held together very well, but we find ways to compensate and keep going. There is another way.

The goal is to have facility with interior ego states so that we walk as whole, integrated human beings in the world.

THE PARENT, ADULT, AND CHILD IN YOU

Berne thought of every individual as being three different people: a Parent, who is the moral consultant and who may be critical, sentimental, or nurturing; a rational, factual Adult who sets up contracts and commitments with other people and says yes or no; and a compliant, rebellious, or spontaneous Child—the instinctual, intuitive aspect of us, the one who "takes the trip" in sex and in life. In the sexual arena, her vocabulary consists of "Wow, that was great!" (The Child is a natural aphrodisiac.) And in some cases when the Parent or Adult has used bad judgment, "ugh, ouch, or yuck." When I use the term *Child,* I'm referring to any aspect of ourselves from infancy to about age twelve but truly, the Child never stops growing. It becomes more sophisticated in the world into the teens, twenties, fifties, and old age. I use the terms *ego state, aspect,* and *part* interchangeably.

The Parent ego state is the voice in our head, which also sometimes uses our mouth to say things out loud. It uses words and phrases such as "Well done," "I'm proud of you," "I'm sorry you got hurt," "You're the greatest." The Parent takes two forms, one direct, one indirect or one nurturing (natural) and one critical (adapted). The nurturing Parent is an actual ego state that is *cathected,* which means you put energy into that ego state so that a person becomes a nurturing parent. The critical Parent is a Child adaptation, not a natural Parent ego state but an indirect influence of the Parent. This one responds the way the real mother or father actually responded—"Do as I say, not as I do."

The Adult part of us is matter-of-fact and operates very much like a computer, calculating variables of speed, time, space, and outcomes. It tells you when to cross the street and how much speed is needed to cross safely, when to hold 'em or fold 'em, how to analyze outside data for optimum decision making, and how to operate an iPod and MP3 player. The Adult uses words such as *now, wait, need more information, in ten minutes*—factual statements. It has no interest in maturity but it is interested in accuracy. The Adult mediates objectively between the Parent and the Child.

There are also two forms of Child: the natural Child and the adapted Child. The Child personality of us is the little boy or little girl we once were. Each of us has a predominant child ego state; in some it may be the four-year-old, in others it may be the two-year-old or nine-month-old. Berne doubts that it is ever older than six years old. When the natural Child is cathected, we are spontaneous and childlike. The Child is the best part of us, the most creative, joy-filled, intimate, loving, just as real children are. The natural Child is best described as the little girl who has an energy coming off her that is magical and magnetic. When she walks into a room and your heart just goes out to her; you're naturally drawn to her. In men, it's the Child that makes them fun, witty, charming, charismatic (I love charisma), and playful. In women, the Child looks very similar: charming, witty, fun, and playful—these are sexy characteristics. It is the Child in us that loves Nature, loves the elements, loves socializing, loves to have fun, loves to feel, to be nurtured, soothed, held, and stroked.

When an adapted Child walks into a room, you immediately know there is something off-putting about her. Adapted Children react to their circumstances and their environment by withdrawing, whining, or pouting;

they are disagreeable to be around. They are complicit, behaving as mother or father wants them to behave so they tend to take on the voice of their real parents. This behavior masks painful or scared feelings and their inability to deal with the world around them. An adapted Child might say critical things such as, "You shouldn't have done that," "Stop being so immature," "That was childish," "Don't be ridiculous." Berne says, "The Parental influence is the cause, and the adapted Child the effect.

THE PREDATOR INSIDE

Another part of us, not specifically identified by Berne in his model, is the Predator. Human beings are a predator species with a capacity for unkindness, and cruelty. As Elisabeth Kübler-Ross was told by a young Jewish woman, a Holocaust survivor who had lost all her brothers and sisters, parents and grandparents, "The Nazis taught me this, there is a Hitler inside each of us, and if we do not come to terms with the Hitler inside us, the violence will never cease."* Each of us has a Predator living inside, a Mr. Hyde who is the worst in us, and until we face the predator inside, it will always lurk in the murky backwaters of our psyche planning a way out. There is a part of each of us that has wanted, may still want, to cause harm to something or someone. It has tremendous energy, often driven by unresolved anger about a perceived injustice, a discount to the Child, a recent lie told to you by a friend that you have stuffed inside yourself. Or this part may be driven by archaic rage—a deep-seated anger that has been fermenting and bubbling inside you while you've been holding onto something from the distant past. Rage is the kind of anger that the Predator can really sink its hooks into. When motivated by archaic rage, the predator may lob bombs at the person who originally caused you harm or at someone who in some way resembles the original perpetrator. Left unattended, either unresolved anger or archaic rage will result in bitterness, resentment, and soul sickness.

The human Predator takes two forms—the natural Predator and the adapted Predator—and comes in all sizes. The natural Predator has an ecological function within our structure. Its job is to be alert to danger that may

---

*As told to me by Stephen Harrod Buhner, who studied with Kübler-Ross. Her story of how she came to recognize the Hitler within is in *Quest: The Life of Elisabeth Kübler-Ross* by Derek Gil.

threaten its survival. When life is going along swimmingly with the current, everything seems to be in order, and the Universe is gracing you with relatively calm seas, the Predator relaxes its watch some. Then suddenly the winds pick up and the current becomes rough; the Predator is alerted to danger and engages its 360-degree radar for incoming trouble. Its function is to fight for your life either by hunting for food, a job, or a mate or by defending your life and property, your rights, and your dignity. It fights for what is rightfully yours. When we fail to integrate and work with our natural Predator we become easy prey, falling victim to crime, abuse, theft, financial scams.

Human beings are carnivores by nature, vegetarian by choice. We have pointed eyeteeth that we expose when we open our mouths to eat meat or vegetables or to smile. We are hunters of the animal order. We have an innate Predator and when that part is integrated its actions feel completely congruent and fluid, in the natural order of things.

The adapted Predator is another unfavorable adaptation of the Child. The threatened Child can take on and express adapted aspects of the Predator in the same way that a repressed Child expresses the critical Parent. The adapted Predator is the part of us that tears legs off spiders, clear-cuts forests, wages war, kicks dogs, or squashes bugs when there is another option. When given an outlet through hunting animals, whether for sport or food, the natural Predator (the hunter) is given release. When the Predator is afraid it lashes out in an attempt to protect itself. The adapted Predator is learned in childhood when our parents yell at us or strike us. The watching part of us wakes up and begins to look out for danger in the world around us. The Child learns how to attack when it's scared or mad. When our Child feels scared in intimate relationships it's apt to attack the other person in the way that it was attacked when young, which effectively shuts down intimacy. Often what happens is the Predator in the recipient attacks back. Then there is a real relationship mess.

Adapted Predators have not learned how to get their needs met without resorting to games or attacking others; they believe that the world is full of dangers and that people have ill intent. There are power issues involved; adapted Predators want power and control over others and over their environment, and they'll use manipulation to get it. Those who prey on the elderly or the poor for financial gain are expressing the adapted Predator. They'll engage in insurance scams and Ponzi schemes in a misguided effort to come out on top. This type of Predator has no sense of empathy, no connection between themselves and their prey. They see people only as an external means to an end. The adapted Predator is one who has not learned how to get its needs met without causing damage and feels there is no other recourse available when the Parent and Adult are not supplying critical information or tending to fears and terrors about survival.

Intimacy with self requires that we be willing to see each part of ourselves for what it is. Not just the bright, shiny, generous, loving, funny parts, but also the parts that have been hidden, denied, imagined not to exist, overshadowed, and, yes, especially, the parts of you that you have hated and come to resent and be fearful of. Being willing to see the goodness in me was almost as difficult as it was to see that I am certainly capable of being an asshole. We all have a part of us that has lashed out at a loved one or a store clerk or has had temper tantrums. When the pressure of stress builds to the boiling point, it's often the Predator that takes over. There are things that feed the Predator, that arm it with a sword or loaded gun or the verbal equivalent of each. Resentment, jealousy, unresolved anger, deep grief, and shame are some of them. Sometimes, it takes the form of the sexual predator. It prowls nightclubs and dance halls, hunting its prey. Sex isn't always its goal; the game of seduction is. Sex as the goal depends on how serious the player is.

We're all capable of it. It took some time, but I was finally willing to truly see that part in myself. Then to own it, make a relationship with it, and set limits on its behavior. I have been unkind, and I have hurt people I love and care about. A teacher told me once that there are two kinds of people: assholes and those who know they are assholes. I believed that was true. I also believed that I was a third kind—I wasn't an asshole. Eventually, it came time to own up.

I liked to think I was unkind unintentionally, but the truth is when the Predator is kept in the bag of shadow, it intends to cause hurt. Until I could come to terms with that truth, with the Predator in me, with this capacity to be unkind, I couldn't trust myself. Until I owned this part of me that was unclear, terrified, and strictly interested in survival, I couldn't stop watching, knowing that part could be let loose in the world.

We've all done something that inflicted some hurt on someone. My sister has a part that, when she was young, used to bite kittens' ears. Thankfully she stopped biting the ears of kittens, but whether she has acknowledged and integrated the Predator part of her is unknown to me. When my brother's girlfriend came to visit for the first time when they were sixteen (they've been married ever since), I, who was seven years younger, watched in horror as she delightedly pulled the legs off a daddy longlegs. This wasn't simply benign curiosity, I could tell by her skill and focus that she had done it before.

When my granddaughters at ages nine and six came to visit me one time, it took no time at all to discover their new catch-all phrase: "It was an accident." The first and second time they used it, I let it ride. When I noticed it was becoming a habit and realized they were using the phrase to conveniently excuse some behavior, I had to talk about it. Going unconscious is not an acceptable behavior for me. Nor, dear one, is hitting your little sister an accident. Words don't fall out of our mouths, nor do our hands of their own volition strike at someone accidentally or without intention. The words come out, the hand moves through the air because we've gone unconscious and some part of us that intended to say those words noticed that we went unconscious and took advantage of the moment.

Rudeness has become an acceptable violent behavior. We in the Western world seem to be much too willing to shrug off a comment, a behavior, ours or others, as accidents or "I didn't mean to" or "It wasn't my intention." This is a significant part of the problem in our world, in our relationships to others and to ourselves. Discounting a person's dignity and lying have become acceptable codes of conduct. Violence begins in our thoughts and is then is expressed in our speech. It escalates to behaviors. If you choose to take on this work and let it change you, you will be in a minority.

> [W]hat is imposed on you from outside is of no value whatever. It doesn't count.
>
> BERTRAND RUSSELL

Just because there is an invitation to incite a riot is no reason to incite a riot. Unkindness does not need to be met with unkindness. What happens "out there" is none of our business. What we do with external events that impact us on the inside is of consequence. How we respond, what choices we make, what behaviors we choose are, most certainly, our business. In spite of the circumstances we find ourselves in, we are free to act decisively one way or another. Ultimate freedom is reserved to each human being. How we respond to unchanging conditions and environments is the test of human character. When our soul is fragmented, when we have not found the meaning of our lives, we are powerless and unable to access what Viktor Frankl called "the defiant power of the human spirit."[5]

Gandhi had the Predator in him; the difference is he was aware of its existence and worked to keep it from acting out in a way that caused damage. He used its energy to effect change. He may have even given it a new job description, one that would support his work of *ahimsa*. Reading his autobiography, you hear the rage against injustices that he transmuted into a voice of authority to be reckoned with. And he was quite clear that nonviolence is not synonymous with passivity. To be nonviolent requires thought, decisions, and action. Just as there is a Hitler inside us, there is also a Gandhi; we have the capacity for great compassion, forgiveness, truth, and jusice.

> *Personal change and the ability to bring about social change are linked. There is no use striving to implement principles such as nonviolence or justice in public affairs as long as one neglects them in one's personal life.*
>
> GANDHI,
>
> *GANDHI: AN AUTOBIOGRAPHY*

ACKNOWLEDGING ALL OF YOU

Having a Predator inside does not make you a bad person. It's as much a part of your nature as the Child, the Parent, and the Adult. The degree to which you are unwilling to become conscious of the Predator and give it a new job description will determine how frequently and to what degree you let the Predator control your behavior. You cannot alter its behavior if you are unaware of its existence. It's really a matter of self-awareness and setting limits on acting-out behaviors. The Predator is activated when the grown-up or Adult part of you is not paying attention in situations that threaten the Predator's survival. The Predator is interested only in surviving.

These are not roles we play but ecological and psychological realities. The voices we hear in our head are actual people. It is in your best interest to cultivate relationships with these parts of you; acknowledge them or not, integrate them or not, they are with you for the rest of your life. Ignoring these parts or pretending they don't exist will cause you added grief, and the tremendous sources of energy, creativity, wise council, and personal power these states provide will be unavailable to you.

Everyone has a sense of these many states, but rarely do we take it much further and really look at what it means. We have all heard ourselves or a friend say: "One part of me wants to do this and another part wants to do this other thing." The meditations and exercises in this book will help you get to know who those parts are, and then how to work with competing wants and needs.

The crucial things in interior work are:

1. Identify the ego states. Who is talking, poking at me inside, trying to get my attention?
2. Free any that are repressed or locked away. We live in a culture that does not support being a fully functioning, self-possessed, confident human being. We live in a Prozac nation, a culture that bombards us from infancy with messages that tell us feeling is bad and talking about feeling is worse.
3. Understand their function. Each ego state may or may not know what its function is. Or its function may need to be redirected to another area, given a new job, so it has a place to put its energy into what supports all of you.
4. Make friends with them. This takes time and a commitment on your part to work with them daily. There will be parts of yourself that you do not want to see, do not want to even acknowledge exist, much less make friends with. All the more important to accept and befriend them.

[T]he child is the forerunner of humanity—forerunner in the sense that the child is the possessor of all those traits which, when healthily developed, lead to a healthy and fulfilled human being and thus to a healthy and fulfilled humanity.

ASHLEY MONTAGU,
GROWING YOUNG

◈ MEDITATION ◈
I've Been Waiting for You

Set aside about thirty minutes to do this meditation. Find a quiet place where you will not be disturbed; ask family members not to interrupt you during this time. Turn off your cell phone. Eliminate as many distractions as you can. Create a place with soft lighting and a comfortable place to sit: it's best if you're not lying down. Settle into an overstuffed chair or make a nest of pillows and blankets on the floor to support you so that you feel held and nurtured. Have a journal and pen close by, but not on your lap. (Note: You may want to first record the following instructions, allowing pauses between questions, and listen to them the first time or two you do this exercise.)

Now, close your eyes, letting them rest into the back of your head. Take some deep breaths: inhaling deeply, filling your lungs, your diaphragm, and hold it, hold it, hold it. Exhale completely. Again. And one more time.

See standing in front of you the Child that you once were. Just see her there. Notice everything about her. What is she wearing? What's her posture? Is she looking at you? Does she seem happy? Is she sad?

How do you feel seeing her? Will she make eye contact with you? Ask her if she has anything she wants to say to you. Is there anything you want to say to her? Ask her if you can give her a hug. If yes, then for real, reach out your arms and hold her to you. Bring her so close to you that your arms are wrapped completely around your shoulders. Hold your child and yourself close for a few moments. Notice how you feel.

When you are ready, thank your Child for coming to be with you. Bring yourself back to where you are sitting, pick up your journal, and write down everything you saw and felt and what she said. Do you like her? Are you comfortable with her? Uncomfortable? There is much information embedded in your response to seeing her. It will give you insights into how and why you have felt the way you have about yourself for many years.

BEGINNINGS ARE SUCH DELICATE TIMES

Anything can happen in this first meeting. You may see your Child clearly or just have a sense of her. For some, the first meeting will be easy. There may be a sense of homecoming, spontaneous joy, and love when you first meet. For those whose denied Child has been put away so deeply and for so long, the work will be difficult. She may be upset that it's been so long since you've spent time with her. She may refuse to look at you. She may have pain to share with you and stories to tell you, happy ones and sad ones. There may be a lot of energy in what she has to say as she's been waiting a long time for you to ask to see her. As well, the reunion may be genuinely joyful.

There is the story of Carl Jung as he was going through his middle years. He was sitting on the shores of Lake Zurich building sand castles and playing with toy figures, shaping stones, giving neglected regions of his psyche room to be. He knew that "when we are stuck we are saved by what is within."[6]

Beginnings are delicate times. Your Child will be watching to see if you will show up again and want to spend time with her. She may not trust grown-ups, and you are a grown-up. It's important to develop the relationship at her pace, and I suggest you do this work with her daily so trust can begin to be fostered. If she asks you to do something, take it seriously; do not make agreements you are unwilling or unable to keep. That will do more damage than saying, "I'm sorry, I'm unable to do that. Is there something else that would work for you?" Offer an alternative that will tend to her need or want. Learning the art of negotiation will be very helpful, for children will ask for things that in the moment you may not be able to deliver. Negotiate time frames or treats. If you ask her to do something she doesn't want to do, take into account that she may want a reward afterward. Ask her what she needs in return. Spending time with your Child and letting her have her wants and needs will bring you more joy and confidence than anything else you could do.

Intimacy depends on freeing up the Child, letting her have her voice and giving her a place to be alive and out loud in the world. To have true and deep intimacy with another human being, you must have true and deep intimacy with yourself. Get to know yourself, reclaim parts of you that have been shut away, repressed, alienated, and marginalized. This is the beginning of the journey to wholeness, of being an integrated, whole human being. This is more important than I can say. It's awkward, and in the beginning, it may seem silly or stupid, even. This work has the power to change your life, to heal wounds, to empower you to speak truth to power. This work—and it is hard work that takes a lot of practice—gets to the core of you, the truth of you, so you can live a life filled with meaning.

> *I wanted to change the world. But I have found that the only thing one can be sure of changing is oneself.*
>
> ALDOUS HUXLEY

From this position of empowerment and strength, no one can tell you what your truth is, or tell you to do or be anything but what you know is in you to do or be.

The child is the major source of energy. I have clients do this work and have seen physiological changes occur before my eyes. It's not unusual to feel different, feel happier, have more hope, and feel less alone even after the first meeting with your Child.

This relationship is real. The Child of you, the little girl of you is real, and she has been waiting for you to show up for her. It's important to talk over your goals and options with your Child. Include her in the process. If you make a relationship with your Child and then leave her out of your planning, she can and will likely make your life difficult and disruptive. If your Child is not aligned with your goals, you are going to have trouble achieving them. Children are clever at getting you to take notice. If the Child is not worked with consciously, she will break through; once she has tasted freedom, her only goal, if she is ignored, is to get out. She has no investment then in keeping your life orderly if you betray her trust.

*If you bring forth what is within you, what you bring forth
will save you. If you do not bring forth what is within you,
what you do not bring forth will destroy you.*

THE GOSPEL ACCORDING TO THOMAS

༄ MEDITATION ༄
Starting at the Beginning

Let's take this deeper still. Return to your sitting place as before and begin again with deep breathing and relaxation. This time, see lying in front of you on the floor, the Infant of you. How does she look? Is she breathing? What color is her skin? Is she moving? How do you feel seeing your Infant? Pick up your Infant, swaddle her in your arms at your breast, and let her nurse. Notice whether you held her in your left or right arm. Allow yourself to experience how the two of you feel being together. Really see her. How does it feel to feed the Infant of you? Let anything you feel rise to the surface. Wrap your love and caring around her as you nurse. Gaze into her eyes and notice the mothering instinct awaken inside you. Notice the degree of hunger she has. Tell her you are glad that she was born.

When you are ready, put her down and pick up your journal. Write down everything that happened and everything you felt. Many people feel a sensation in their breasts while nursing their Infant. It's extraordinary, really.

Both men and women are able to do this meditation. It is as important for men as well to nurse their Infant. Men have mammary glands just the same as women, and there are several instances, historical and recent, where men have either nursed their own children or become wet nurses for surrogate or adopted children.* The greatest, most immediate benefit to nursing,

---

*All male mammals, including humans, have rudimentary mammae, and the male nipple is nearly perfect in function. Prolactin, the hormone responsible for milk production, is present in both men and women. Evolutionarily, it makes sense that both sexes be capable of providing nourishment to the young to ensure survival of the species. Darwin speculated that among early mammalian ancestors both sexes may have nursed the young, but that over time the mammae in male mammals evolved to be inactive. Today,

for both men and women, is that it begins the emotional bonding of nurturing Parent to Infant, of you to yourself. Nursing your Infant is awkward at first, but it is imperative to bonding with yourself. Occasionally an Infant will look withdrawn, pale, even lifeless or blue. It can be alarming. Trust that you can bring more life to her. Breathe the life and love gently into her. Hold her near you as you fall asleep and again when you wake up in the morning.*

Who Makes These Changes?

Who makes these changes?
I shoot an arrow right.
It lands left.
I ride after a deer and find myself
Chased by a hog.
I plot to get what I want
And end up in prison.
I dig pits to trap others
And fall in.

I should be suspicious
Of what I want.

RUMI,
TRANSLATED BY COLEMAN BARKS

---

male lactation is found in at least one species: In an article in the 1996 issue of *Compleat Mother,* Patty Stuart Macadam of the University of Toronto states that male lactation "is somewhat common in Dayak fruit bats, a rare species found in Malaysia." In a *Scientific American* article (September 6, 2007), "Strange but True: Males Can Lactate," author Nikhil Swaminathan writes about several instances of human male lactation. For men to be able to produce milk, it takes strong desire coupled with nipple stimulation, with successful lactation happening usually within one to two weeks.

*When I work with women with disordered eating there is always a starving Infant inside, one starved for soul food, love, intimacy, being wanted and needed.

THE COUNCIL WITHIN

Ninety-nine percent of who you are is invisible and untouchable.

BUCKMINSTER FULLER

Working with our Child and Infant is the beginning of knowing the multifaceted personality that we are. There are many ego states and personalities inside of us. As human beings, we have been given an elaborate and fascinating inner guidance system.

☙ MEDITATION ☙
Meeting the Council Members

Begin as you did with the first meditation, getting comfortable in a quiet place with your journal and pen nearby. Go through a few cycles of deep breathing and relaxation exercises.

See yourself standing in a forest glade. It's a warm summer day, and there is a slight breeze rustling the leaves. Sunlight is filtering through the canopy, and you watch the dance of light and shadow on the forest floor. You notice a path beneath your feet, and you begin to walk along it. Eventually, the path leads out of the forest into a small meadow of wildflowers and grasses. Following the path down a meadow hill, you come to a stream. There are a few stones placed just so, and you are able to easily step across the stream to the other bank. You walk a few paces on the path along the stream and see just up ahead a one-room structure. Walk to the front door and step inside. Notice everything about this room. Take note of the round table in the middle of the room. How does the room feel? Is there a source of light? Where is it coming from? Take your time noticing; no need to hurry. It's taken awhile for you to arrive at this place. There are chairs, some around the table, some along the wall. Beings are there in that room. Some of them are standing; some are sitting in chairs.

Let your gaze travel the room noticing all who are there. How do you feel seeing them? Are they looking at you? How many of them are there? Do you recognize any of them? Ask them if they have anything they want to say to you. Pay attention to what they are saying to you and how it feels to hear their words. Is there anything you want to say to them, to the members of your inner council, in response?

It's nearly time to leave. Thank them for being here and talking with you. Do not make any promises or agreements unless you are certain you will keep them. They take these things seriously. Breaking agreements with any members of your inner council exacts a cost.

Leave through the door and step on the trail upstream to the crossing. Pick up the trail and head up the hill through the meadow and back into the forest to where you began. When you are ready, bring yourself back to the place you are sitting. Pick up your journal and write down everything that happened and all that was said.

Every age you have been and will be is inside you—the child ego state, the teenager, the young adult, the middle-aged adult. You also have inside you your own internal mother and father, your self-nurturing parents. The elder you will become is there too, as well as your future self. You don't have to wait to be that age to give them an active part and voice in your life. There are many times you may need to call on an elder from your inner council for the kind of grounded, mature advice only an elder can offer. We have nonhuman allies too. Some of us may have plant and animal allies. Anyone and anything can show up in our inner council. There are no rules here. Work with any of them individually as you need to.

Some people I've worked with had characters from *The Wonderful Wizard of Oz* and another from *Star Trek*. Some members are lifetime guides, and others may show up for a short time to help us through some growth period. I recently had the main character from an Elizabeth Moon novel spontaneously show up while I was in council. She's the captain of a space vessel. "Kylara Vatta, what are you doing here?" I asked, in surprise. "I'm your new captain," she announced, smiling. Indeed, I have called on her several times when in need of her particular strengths of quick analysis and decisiveness—strengths that only a captain possesses. If you need someone or a specific teacher to be on your inner council, ask that being from within your council if he or she would be willing to be a member, or call them in. They are similar in function to a board of directors in a corporate body whose mission ideally is the integrity and wholeness of the corporation. I've also enlisted single aspects, certain characteristics that I needed or wanted to have incorporated into my personality. I wanted Spenser from the Robert Parker novels to be on my inner council and Jay from Michelle West's *Hunter's Death* and *The Hidden City*. I have called on them at times when I felt their particular virtues were needed.

FINDING THE NURTURING PARENT

If you don't have a good model for a nurturing Parent, find someone you consider fills that role. We all need good models, mentoring in how to be a human being. As examples, Andy Griffith from the forty-year-old television series, the *Andy Griffith Show,* Jean-Luc Picard from *Star Trek's Next Generation,* and the most famous nurturing, wise, compassionate father of all (in my humble opinion), Harper Lee's Atticus Finch. He's strong, yet tender, and willing to stand up for what he believes. Richard Farnsworth in *Anne of Green Gables* stole my heart with the warm knowing twinkle in his eyes. My favorite has been Fred MacMurray who played Steve Douglas, the father in *My Three Sons.* I couldn't wait to watch that television show when I was growing up. For thirty minutes, several days a week, I would completely lose myself in that world. Mr. Douglas was my father—or the father I wanted. He was kind, funny, compassionate, strong in his values and beliefs, tender, and nurturing. Uncle Charley was curmudgeonly and scared me a little. He masked his nurturing side under the facade of tough love. Tough love is not nurturing; it's tough love.

As for female role models, it's been a challenge to find comparable traits in female characters, to find actresses who exemplify the combination of compassion, nurturing, and strength. I am tempted to call on Harper Lee herself and Ethel Barrymore. Aunt Bee in the *Andy Griffith Show,* was matronly, loving, and doting, though I prefer a little more softness and less "parent." And there was some attractive nurturing energy about Gloria Stuart when she played the elderly Rose in *Titanic* that made me want to be in her presence.

You can get a sense of what a nurturing Parent looks and feels like. Many of us grow up lacking a consistent nurturing parent. Most of the parents I know are critical; they mask their strength and compassion by being critical and stern. Nurturing Parent role models and the ones you create or call on inside yourself possess genuine caring. You must know yourself well enough so that anything hidden or repressed is cleared up, healed, and not left to contaminate the nurturing part of you.

RECOGNIZING AND INTEGRATING ALL THE PARTS OF YOU

Rigorous self-examination describes the process of interior work. You must be able to notice, account for, and be accountable to each part of you that lives within. The more you work with these parts, hear their voices, and understand each one's gifts and virtues and what each can bring to your life, the more whole and integrated you will become, the more alive you will feel, and the more mastery you will have over your life. When all of your inner council can make a decision together, in agreement with one another, the more ease and less drama you will have in your life.

Your heart must be in this—a deep desire and dedication to knowing yourself, to awakening your latent powers of intuition, motive force and creativity. You have a right to do this work, to be whole and happy in yourself and your relationships. And if there is to be any salvation for the human species, each of us must do this work. Now, without delay. Gaining facility with interior ego states takes time, devotion, and practice. But it won't cost you hundreds of dollars and time in therapy sessions, and the effects are immediate, the rewards innumerable.

All that we have ever been and all that we ever need to be is known in the eternal place inside ourselves where all is quiet.

RAM DASS

From this moment I am prepared to control whatever personality awakes in me each day. . . . Today I control my destiny . . . I will become master of myself. I will become great.

OG MANDINO SCROLL VI

The goal of this work is to exist as a coherent, integrated whole. Understand that any ego state can emerge at any time it is needed. In the interior world, all these ego states are interacting whether you are aware of them or not. Sometimes they interact well; often they are in conflict. In the exterior human world, people's many ego states are interacting with each other, sometimes well, often not so well. When they interact well, your life in those moments flows smoothly.

Culturally, pressure exists to locate consciousness in the brain and the adult ego state. In actuality, consciousness is limited to no particular part of the body and no particular ego state. Consciousness can become habituated to body location or ego state by restricting it to particular locations like the adult ego state in the brain. The most fundamental ego state is the Child.

Being a human being—in the sense of being born to the human species—must be defined also in terms of becoming a human being . . . a baby is only potentially a human being, and must grow into humanness in the society and the culture, the family.

ABRAHAM MASLOW,
MOTIVATION AND PERSONALITY

What is important to me is not the truth outside myself, but the truth within me.

KONSTANTIN STANISLAVSKY

DEVELOPING CHILD-TO-CHILD INTIMACY

All of this work with interior ego states is important in the context of sacred sex because of the nature of relationship and intimacy. The point of this work is to get to a place of actively noticing your interior world and to then be able to notice your partner's. The more elegant you become with your own interior world, the more intuitive you will become and the more present you can be with your lover. The Child in you understands the nature of sex; she has been pleasuring herself since she was developed enough in the womb to move her hands to her genitals.

Berne describes intimacy as "a candid Child to Child relationship with no games and no mutual exploitation." To get to the place of Child-to-Child relating, a sequence of things happens inside each participant. The Adult assesses the situation, reads the contracts, and commitments to each, and once this is all understood by the Child, the Adult retreats to the background yet continues to monitor the agreements and is in charge of keeping the Parent from interfering and spoiling the fun. Once the Parent is out of the way, the Child becomes freer to engage in spontaneous and fun-filled intimacy. Ideally, the Parent gives its blessing and encouragement, freeing the child of any fear of intimacy and reducing any possible feelings of guilt.

You can check this out yourself when you embark on an intimate relationship. Listen carefully to the voices inside you, and you will hear the Child exclaiming excitement at the possibility and the Adult reading over the commitments and any reservations or cautions the Parent may be inserting into the conversation. It can happen fairly quickly, so be attentive, but even after the moment has passed you can replay it and slow it down to see what took place.

As you become sensitized to subtle shifts in your interior world, you will become more attuned to shifts in your partner. You'll recognize the Child in him and be able to communicate directly with that Child. Just as you did when you began to work with the Child in you, there will be a time of trust building and finding your way together. It's quite natural for the Child in him to see the Child in you being happy and present in the relationship, even if on a conscious level he's unaware of it happening. You'll see the changes he's going through, the ego states he moves through, so you can match yours with his.

Remember when you were fifteen years old and you met a boy. The attraction, the awkwardness, the spontaneity, the giggles, the explorations, and the energy of that fifteen-year-old is still there and can be part of your current relationship. Use that energy to bring freshness to the relationship as you become good friends, exploring the world together with wonder and curiosity. Sixteen-year-old ego states are much more daring and exploratory with sex and each other's bodies. It's exciting and clumsy and potent.

It is vital to see that everything is attended to, lest something goes unattended.

The difference between sex and lovemaking is that in the latter, we tend to be the most unshielded, the most vulnerable and childlike. It is the Child who knows no distance, no space between desire and action. Sacred sex can be the catalyst for healing the wounds of our birth and our family of origin. It can heal sexual trauma, shame, and disgust. Because sacred sex happens in the arms of love, compassion, and intimacy, it becomes a portal, a threshold between what was and what can be. They don't have to be mutually exclusive. Sometimes I'll ask my lover to fuck me and make love to me at the same time.

Stepping through to the other side can be frightening.

It is the Child part of us who decides whether or not someone can be trusted. Respect comes from the Adult, after the Child gives her permission. The Child is always monitoring relationships and situations. She is the one who decides whether or not she likes someone, likes their smell and the sound of their voice. She is highly sensitive to the slightest perturbations, affronts, discounts, and all manner of meanings coming to her from the world; other people and relationships are part of the world.

When there is a strong foundation of trust between you and your Child and your Child and your partner, very young ego states may take the opportunity to emerge at will. For the health of that ego state, for healing to happen, it's critical to notice in yourself and in your lover when this is happening. Memories, pictures, visions, smells, and words—communications in various forms—will arise spontaneously to the conscious mind. Follow whatever is happening without censoring. Let them speak, cry, wail, laugh, ask questions. Inside yourself, have the older, nurturing part of you witness and be present with her without interfering.

That little one needs to know you are tending to her, companioning her, holding her, hearing her. She needs to know that the grown-up of you is with her and she is not alone inside.

As wounds begin to open up and the child shows herself—her fears, what she didn't understand long ago ("Why are grown-ups so mean?")— you do well to have answers for her. It's all right to not know all the answers; it's not all right to lie about them. Examples of responses are: "I don't know why grown-ups are mean. Sometimes people get scared, and they don't know what else to do and being mean makes them feel safe." "You know sweetie, your father was not a good person. And I'm sorry he was unkind, but he's not here now, and he can't hurt you anymore." "I wish I could shield you from all the ugliness of the world, but that can never be." If you know the truth, say the truth. Primarily, the Child needs to know that you are hearing her and that she can ask for and say what she needs to. Children are children, inside you or born from your loins. Answer their questions without evasion. Children can spot evasion faster than adults so don't confuse them.

As the Child emerges, there will often be subtle changes in voice, eye movement, word choices, or cadence of speech. It's not unusual for a two-year-old ego state, for example, to emerge. Remember having a conversation with a two-year-old you've known. They don't use big words. Often speech is rapid if there is excitement, slower if there is fear or shyness, and the voice may be nearly a whisper. The more you work with each one, the more you'll come to recognize who is presenting herself. The deeper you are willing to go, the more focused you can be in this work, the more you will come to know yourself, understand yourself, be intimate with yourself, and, thus, be intimate with anyone or anything you wish.

Before I was deep into this work on myself, I cherished early mornings together with a former lover. It was in those quiet, soft moments, as the sweetness of sleep is drifting away, before full alertness takes hold, when he wasn't fully awake and hadn't yet had time to put up defenses, that he had that little boy, sleepy look on his face. It was then that he was his most vulnerable, sweet, available, spontaneous, and natural child-like self. And so was I. The beauty of this work is that it allows you to enter those states at will at any time and in any place. One day, you'll be moving about your business and suddenly notice that it is the Child of you who is out in the world as the primary ego state.

And, ah, what joyful ease overcomes you.

You don't have to be a psychotherapist or a trained mental health professional to do this work. All that is required is that you *do* the work. We all walk around with unexamined beliefs, prejudices, and assumptions that impact our ability to be intimate, to be real, to be compassionate, to be free. Those unexamined psychological structures contaminate our reading of the map and ultimately the territory of the sacred.

It helps to read and have resources available. Children (I'm referring to the ones inside you in this instance) love having information; they are hungry for it. They need it to navigate the world, to help make sense of things. If I read a book that is helpful, I go immediately to the bibliography and order anything that catches my eye. I love books; the Child in me loves books. They are friends and teachers, bedtime companions, and trips to other galaxies, other worlds, and the world of fantasy.

I want to clarify a fine point in all this, and that is, if you were to walk around saying, "my child needs this, my child wants that," you may not get the outcome you're expecting. That's what dissociation is. The distinction is *you* are the one who is responsible for hearing what your Child needs and wants. It's up to you, to use your power to get needs met, to speak on her behalf; you do the work of integration. To use the above phrases as a habit diminishes your power, puts responsibility where it doesn't belong, and will likely irritate the people around you. It's fine to say "What my Child needs is . . ." in intimate relationships, especially if there has been a betrayal of some sort.

CROSS TRANSACTIONS

To understand how ego states interact requires an understanding of transactions. Spending a little time on this will help you understand how communications can go sour and how to avoid it in the future. Eric Berne describes this process in detail in *Games People Play* and *Sex in Human Loving*. They are worth looking at, if for no other reason than the clarity of the diagrams. As stated earlier, there are three main ego states in each human being: the Child, the Adult, and the

Parent. Healthy or straight-across transactions can be described as Child to Child, Adult to Adult, and Parent to Parent. Cross transactions occur, for example, when the Child in one person initiates a conversation or movement and the other person responds from the Adult or Parent ego state.

Initiator (Child): "I want to play the box drum. It looks like so much fun."

Respondent (Parent): "I'd be glad to buy you one if you agree to play an hour a day with me."

Child: "Um, OK. I can do that, that would be fun."

Parent: "I'm serious. I don't want it to sit in your closet like your guitar."

Uh-huh. Feel that? The Child feels chastised, shamed, and heartbroken. At once, all the fun, excitement, and anticipation of having a drum and playing music with her friend are dashed. She no longer has any interest in playing music with him in any way, shape, or form.

The Child's initial response of "Um, OK" indicated a thoughtful processing of the condition that was put on the gift of the drum: "If you'll play an hour a day with me." She decided that the one hour a day was agreeable and within her parameters of fun. Then came the critical Parent's voice out of her friend's mouth, sucking all the energy out of the room. The Child felt hurt, ashamed, and deeply disappointed: Her friend was mad at her for not playing the guitar and told her it was unacceptable behavior to let the guitar sit in the closet. But it wasn't her friend's voice she heard, it was her mother's voice, or it could be her father's voice—the voice of the Parent—telling her that her behavior wasn't acceptable and to be acceptable you have to do it this other way. To prevent an old pattern of responding with "Fuck you," or holding onto feeling ashamed and being mad at a betrayal of friendship, she went to her friend and still from the Child ego state said, "Are you mad at me for not playing the guitar regularly?" The friend is taken aback as he realizes what he had said and responds by saying, "No, sweetie, no, I'm not mad at you. I'm so sorry I sounded like I was criticizing you, and I understand why you'd feel that way, but no, I'm not mad at you. I'm so sorry, I apologize. It's your guitar; you can play it or not. I really want to play music with you, and I know how busy you are, and I would be heartbroken if we couldn't." He went on: "Are we OK? Do you need anything from me?"

The apology was genuine; the Child heard it and felt its sincerity. Moreover, the Child felt heard and cared for. Because the Child trusted her friend and wanted to feel close again, she went to him undefended. Disaster was averted, shame disrupted, and trust and intimacy restored.

When we are whole in ourselves, undefended, and willing to maintain trust and intimacy, then we are able to make decisions from a place of wholeness.

4

The Numinous

Numinous: of, pertaining to, or of the nature of a numen. Evoking awe or reverence, as the presence of something holy or divine. Irrational; mysterious, inscrutable. The numinous is the part of spiritual and sacred experience that is characterized by feelings of fascination and awe.

Sacred: set apart or dedicated to religious use; hallowed; pertaining or related to deity, religion, or hallowed places or things. Consecrated or dedicated to a person or purpose; entitled to reverence or respect; not to be profaned; inviolable.

THE READER'S DIGEST
GREAT ENCYCLOPEDIC DICTIONARY

In all Neolithic, Paleolithic, primitive, and indigenous cultures around the world, life was infused with the sacred, the numinous, a sense of other. Reality for those people, and for many modern people today, was a blending of the holy in all they did. What Western culture considers profane, daily acts—such as eating, having sex, preparing food, and building houses—were, for ancient, indigenous, and primitive peoples, enacted with a sense of the pervasive invisible world around them.

To them, the invisible world was sacred; spirit was revered, accounted for, and brought into daily acts.

The sacred in daily life was not a project, not a means to an end, but a pathway given freely from divine grace and a pathway, as well, leading to divine grace. It took into conscious consideration the intricate weaving together of human and nonhuman, physical and nonphysical, seen and unseen, soul and spirit. The life of the senses breathed the sacred into mundane acts, birthing a life inseparable from anything inside or outside us. The concept of outside was inconceivable as the sacred wove the physical and nonphysical worlds together into a cohesive whole.

SHAKEN BY THE NUMINOUS

In 1957 Mircea Eliade wrote *The Sacred and the Profane,* in which he described the world we now live in as having two separate realities. Religious people believe in, have experiences with, and orient their lives with a sense of the *hierophanies,* that is, the physical manifestation of the holy. "But for the primitive, such an act is never simply physiological; it is, or can become a sacrament, that is, a communion with the sacred."[1] Nonreligious people reduce daily acts as mundane and simply physiological. And the cosmos becomes a place to conquer, reducing life-forms to mathematical and scientific studies as well as a place for dissecting the parts in order to grasp the reality of the whole. But is it possible to live a life that is wholly and completely desacralized?

A lot has changed and transpired since Eliade wrote in 1957, and it would appear that, in fact, it is possible to live without a relationship to the sacred or a sense of anything manifesting holy virtues. Our world order, governments, and secular and religious institutions are seeped in deceit, secrecy, and abuse of power. But these things are nothing new; they have been happening since man created the state as an organizational structure. Eliade gives examples of "crypto-religious" behavior on the part of the nonreligious man.

There are for example, privileged places, qualitatively different from all others—a man's birthplace, or the scenes of his first love, or certain places in the first foreign city he visited in youth. Even for the most frankly nonreligious man, all these places still retain an exceptional, a unique quality; they are the "holy places" of his private universe, as if it were in such spots that he had received the revelation of a reality *other* than that in which he participates through ordinary daily life.[2]

I suspect, also, there are moments of profound, extraordinary sexual experiences that touch and move nonreligious people. The sacred and numinous know no boundaries conjured up by humanity's belief or nonbelief in their existence. The Earth quakes in laughter at our absurd religious doctrines and our tendency to draw physical and invisible lines. Lines that cut us off from sources of life-affirming mystery, from each other, from our birth-given, soul-charged experiences of intimacy. We humans have become our own sacred clowns, but we refuse to see our own joke. Listen closely in the still of the night; you'll hear coyote laughing.

Our world, the world of man and woman, of Homo sapiens, is a dendritic spiraling pattern weaving us in, around, and through the (mostly) invisible matrix that holds our very existence tenuously intact. It is arrogant to believe we can render the strands of connection nonexistent. It is possible for some to deny and be unaware of their presence. It is possible to live with no acknowledgement or place for them in one's life.

Even for the nonreligious man, an awakening, an epiphany occurs in desperate situations or during a crisis, altering the sense of reality at once. Times of feeling utterly helpless when our children are seriously ill, a parent is dying, or a life-threatening disease or accident befalls us. It is in these times that a door inside, a portal to the Great Mystery, is revealed, and we, by chance of circumstance, see the way through, see a new chance, a glimmer of hope, as we feel the influence of some invisible force at work in our crisis. A desperate clinging to life, ours or another's, aborts previously held beliefs, and we grasp for the nearest raft that may prolong life.

As if waking from a deep sleep or comatose state, we see reality with new eyes. What was previously hidden from view by our own making is present and palpable. At least for a while, if not permanently, the person we were has morphed into someone who has become aware of being woven into mystery. Whatever the reason, our prayers were heard, the medicine worked, the rescue workers arrived at the eleventh hour, and something has given us a chance for more time with life. The impact we feel of a life extended, of death averted, remains imprinted on our psyche. Even if, after the crisis has passed, we choose to return to an ordinary and mundane life, are tempted to discount intervention by the numinous, and with each passing day travel farther from the mystery, there has been inserted into the psyche the unexplainable, the nonrational experience that shook us aware for a few, brief moments. Where there was once irrefutable belief in a nonspiritual, nonsacred world, there is now a sliver of doubt; a questioning of attitudes and ideas has entered the mind and soul of the nonreligious. What remains is the impression of a map, delineating a new territory where the sacred has become part of our interior landscape. Whether we choose to pick up the map and rechart our life course or put the whole mysterious experience in a box and slide it under the bed in our interior house is our decision alone.

IN THE CHURCH OF EARTH

The moments of Spirit intervention are often too tritely called a religious experience, suggesting a philosophical conversion. The words *religious experience* are too simplistic and overused to describe what is often indescribable. It puts the experience into a category where it doesn't really belong.

Part of this is my own prejudice. The word *religion* leaves a bad taste in my mouth, left over from my experience with religions, particularly Christianity, and their public aspect of doctrines, hierarchies, and rules of conduct. Religion comes from the Latin *religare,* meaning "to bind or restrain," as in to be obligated. Religion is man-made, built on promoting the idea that God is "out there," outside us; furthermore, he makes an appearance in specific buildings at prescribed times and days, as set forth in the precepts of the religion's manifesto. The followers of the religion need a middleman to intercede on their behalf, to dictate how they should behave, to absolve them when they wander from the prescribed behavior, to bless, to give permission for marriage, to acknowledge life and death, and to be self-appointed determiners of life and when it begins.

I prefer *spiritual,* which is a private set of beliefs coming out of personal experiences with the sacred, with Nature, with the numinous. Those times of Spirit intervention, whether during a crisis or while walking through a forest, are spiritual experiences. My use of the word *religion* is personal and in the context of Cicero's etymology of the word, who traced it to *relegere,* which means "to read over again" or a "linking back." My religion is a spirituality that is by definition a relationship with the powers of the Universe, with incorporeal, immaterial, supernatural essences. When I work with Spirit, I am working with the vital powers and subtle energies that animate the material world.

I'm not religious in the sense of dogma or doing things according to an external authority. I link back and read over and over again the sacred texts or the original word inscribed on the land and in trees, in tracks left by animals passing, sleeping, and eating. The hierographology of pictographs, standing stones, cairns, pot shards or the way a sweat lodge fire is tended—all these speak of ancient relationships to the sacred, to the land, to Nature. I ascribe to no hierarchy in my personal cosmology; there is no overarching sacred leader. I am on equal footing with all that inhabit this earthly life; we each just have different job descriptions. That said, I am in service to something outside myself, greater than myself, and that is to be in service to the *anima mundi,* the soul of the world, to the Creator and Gaia. To do that, I must simultaneously remake myself into a whole human being.

My spirituality is not confined to a particular building, creed, or obligations to an organization. My church is the wilderness of southwest New Mexico, the Mississippi River, the forests, mountains, wild water—wherever I find myself. In this, I am of the Dionysian school of the madwomen, the maenads, who had no temples. Edith Hamilton writes about the Maenads and their worship of Dionysus in the wild outdoors.

> They went to the wilderness to worship, to the wildest mountains, the deepest forests, as if they kept to the customs of an ancient time before men had thought of building houses for their gods. They went out of the dusty, crowded city, back to the clean purity of the untrodden hills and woodlands. There Dionysus gave them food and drink: herbs and berries and the milk of the wild goat. Their

beds were on the soft meadow grass; under the thick-leaved trees; where the pine needles fall year after year. They woke to a sense of peace and heavenly freshness; they bathed in a clear brook. There was much that was lovely, good, and freeing in this worship under the open sky and the ecstasy of joy it brought in the wild beauty of the world.[3]

I take my communion with the plants, the green nations, the holy waters of hot springs, the sweat lodge. I engage in a dialogue with the spirit keepers of this land, or whatever land I sit on in a sacred manner to share the prayers and smoke of the sacred pipe. Sitting with my pipe, feeling the presence of the spirit keepers of the four winds, the ancestors and the old ones of this land, and my inner council that lives inside me, I am reminded of the mystery of all things. The Great Mystery, the numinous, the incomprehensible largeness of this immense, expansive, extraordinary, beautiful Universe. I am humbled at once by my smallness and my significance at the same time. Feeling them all come in to sit in a circle with me—invisible, palpable to my senses—to hear my prayers, to "break bread" together; this is my sacrament.

I am an ordained minister of the Church of Gaia, a nonprofit organization exploring and participating with the nonlinear intelligence of Nature. In the opinion of the organization's founders, "survivability of the human species depends on human beings once more reconnecting to the Earth. Without this rekindling of our ability to care for the nonhuman world from which we emerged, our behavior will continue to be careless of Earth and its preservation." This means that each one of us must learn to "reinhabit our interbeing with the world," as the rain-forest activist John Seed puts it. "This reinhabiting is essential, not an academic or rhetorical pursuit, and always a personal one."[4]

As a practitioner of Earth-centered spirituality, I continually expose and immerse myself in the numinous territory of sacred lovemaking and with the wild land of southwest New Mexico. Inexhaustibly, I look for novel and deeper ways to participate with life, to understand my place and my responsibilities, and to somehow speak on behalf of those who have no human voice. But to speak on others' behalf, I must first hear what they are saying not only with my ears but with my whole body—my skin, my hair, my feet, my heart.

They speak in vibrations, images, and feelings. Those forms of communication and expression are the many winds that breathe over the land: tree-bending gale-force winds; sand-blasting dust-storm winds; suck-the-moisture-from-your-skin winds; dry, hot, southwest June winds that take the water out of your lungs. The winds that come in July bring moisture and foretell of the monsoons near arrival, winds that carry a fecund, erotic smell of rain in the forest and release essential oils from the trees. The smell of piñon in the early morning air tells of humidity on the rise. The many songs and howls of coyotes tell stories of their lovemaking, their kill, their grieving, and their celebrations. Javelina tracks in red dirt and bites taken out of prickly pear cactus suggest migration patterns and movements. The voice is not solitary and cannot speak without some other: the trees speak through the wind; the wind speaks through the grasses; a coyote's voice speaks through a primordial echo in our soul; fire speaks through wood and air; rivers and streams speak through stones as water journeys off mountains and through valleys. They all speak directly to our hearts and imaginations through the invisible sea of energy we all share and swim in together. To think we can create and sustain a dichotomy, extract ourselves from this sea, creates a kind of insanity, a craziness, in our psyche.

Our own voices speak through vibration, air, breath, earth of our tongues, teeth, vocal chords, mouth, and fire of passion. I must listen attentively, objectively, as if for the first time. I must listen with my whole body, not a part of me, but the whole of me, hearing, feeling, smelling, tasting, touching, seeing. Only then can I begin to understand the meanings in the communications and how I can be in service to all those voices. Only then can I know if there is anything to translate or if it's time to simply listen, sit on Earth in a sacred manner, and take communion with them.

Unless we see or hear phenomena or things
From within the things themselves,
we shall never succeed in recording them in our hearts.

BASHO

WITNESSED BY SPIRIT

When I was searching for a spiritual path that felt right to me, I tried on the traditions that were available where I lived. For two years, I was a card-carrying, dues-paying, active member of a Wiccan church in the upper Midwest. After some truly mind-blowing psychic experiences with those women and discovering latent gifts of my own, I came to the conclusion that, that particular feminist path was not for me. I didn't like male bashing or even leaving out the male aspect of the Universe. I said thanks but no thanks, dropped out, quit paying my dues, and tore up my card.

After that, I talked to a friend of mine about his Buddhist practices. He invited me to join him at a Tuesday evening *sesshin* or *zazen* sitting meditation. We drove along the Mississippi River near New Albin, Iowa. As we drove the long, winding, and rutted gravel road through the sandstone bluffs and deciduous forests to the *zendo,* I felt a sense of something bigger than and outside of me getting involved in my life.

The first night of sitting was uncomfortable. I was fidgety, nervous, uncertain, and afraid of doing something wrong. The Buddhist monk gave a brief instruction on how and why to sit on the cushion so that our knees were lower than our hips, taking the stress off our lower backs and straightening the spine. He described how to hold our hands: left hand resting in the right palm with thumb tips lightly touching. He talked about watching our breath and letting thoughts that appear rise and float off like clouds dispersing. It was a very long forty minutes. I was shocked to notice just how much chatter was going on in my mind at any given moment.

Zazen agreed with me, and I loved it in return. I enjoyed the experience of sitting weekly with a small group of people, and I added it as a daily practice between the weekly sesshins. During a New Year's Eve sesshin, my experience radically changed. We sat in the usual manner for the prescribed forty minutes, after which there was a ten-minute *kinhin* or silent walking meditation followed by another forty minutes of sitting. This went on for three hours.

Sometime into the second hour, I found myself completely relaxing into the experience. All tension in my body had dissolved. I sat effortlessly as some invisible support held me up. I felt good in myself, almost happy, and quite calm. My eyes were softly focused on a point on the wall in front of me. It wasn't work this time to find the still, silence inside. Each breath took me deeper into being relaxed until I noticed something internally begin to shift. My senses became acutely fine tuned as my peripheral vision expanded. I noticed my skin begin to tingle. The point on the wall and the wall itself began to merge and expand; boundaries blurred. I noticed some new thing was happening in the area of my heart, and I felt something move out from and encircle me. I was acutely aware of being larger than myself. And, I was not myself. I sat still, breathing, soft focused, feeling, watching. The experience grew in strength. A lightness of heart and spirit overtook my senses, and I realized I felt happy, joyful. The physical elements of the room fell away, and I found myself in a strange and wonderful landscape. My body no longer had boundaries; no beginning, no end, nothing between me and the world I had just entered. Or had it entered me? The landscape was barren of any physical markers though there was a sourceless light that filled all space. I experienced a pervading sense of peace, calm, serenity, and an unexplainable, overriding sense of growing joy. Pure, radiant, blissful joy. And love. I was the only human being, the only being in that place, and I was overcome with tremendous, unconditional love. I felt loved. And I felt that I deserved this love. Nowhere inside me was there hesitation, doubts, or feelings of unworthiness.

It was my first experience of being seen, being witnessed by Spirit. And I was being loved. I held that ecstatic, mystical state, unwavering, for the remainder of the forty minutes. I didn't want to stop, not ever. My visible, physical world was being nourished by the invisible. From that moment forward, I tried to re-create that feeling in my life, and I found I could while I was alone in the woods or sitting along the river. Someplace inside me I knew I could have, was supposed to have, this feeling, this experience with another human being. Simultaneously, I knew this experience was available when connecting with Earth as much as it was here, in the sacred space of meditation, that this was a dynamic experience and as such, it was transferable to other places.

One afternoon, a few hours before I would be sleeping with my lover, I asked the ancestors if they would show me how to make love like a prayer. What happened was astonishing. As I lay down with him, I reached out my awareness to feel them with me. There was an invisible, palpable presence in the room, between us, with us. The room took on a soft, luminescence. It felt as if they became part of my body, they were so close. I was fully present, watching, participating, and aware of these magnificent beings in the room with us, wrapped around us, between us almost. I gave myself over to this ecstatic experience. It felt as though we were water, fluidly unencumbered by boundaries of any sort. As our two bodies were enraptured, our souls were ravishing each other, spiraling in and out, twining around, sharing fluids, memories, and DNA. All the while, being held in a numinous orb nearly floating off the bed.

Rudolf Otto in writing *Das Heilige* (The Sacred) in 1917 set afire schools of religious and philosophical thought. He set forth profound and, at the time, befuddling concepts of awe-inspiring mystery and human fascination with the mysterious. Otto frequently used the expression *the numinous feeling*. Though the phrase implies the subjective feeling, Otto was quite clear that numinous feelings were both subjective and objective realities.

> The word "numinous" has been widely received as a happy contribution to the theological vocabulary, as standing for that aspect of deity which transcends or eludes comprehension in rational or ethical terms. But it is Otto's purpose to emphasize that this is an objective reality, not merely a subjective feeling in the mind; and he uses the word feeling in this connexion not as equivalent to emotion but as a form of awareness that is neither that of ordinary perceiving nor of ordinary conceiving . . . The ambiguity attaching both to the English feeling and the German Gefuhl should not therefore mislead us. We do after all speak of feeling the beauty of a landscape or feeling the presence of a friend, and our "feeling" in these cases is not merely an emotion engendered or stimulated in the mind but also a recognition of something in the objective situation awaiting discovery and acknowledgement. It is analogously to such uses that Otto speaks of the "feeling of the numinous" or (less aptly) the "numinous feeling."[5]

PART 2

Earthly Sexual Body

5

Human Beings

The Ground Where the Gods Reside

The universe is dead for us, and how is it to come alive again? "Knowledge" has killed the sun, making it a ball of gas, with spots; "knowledge" has killed the moon, it is a dead little earth fretted with extinct craters as with small-pox; the machine has killed the earth for us, making it a surface, more or less bumpy, that you travel over. How, out of all this, are we to get back the grand orbs of the soul's heavens, that fill us with unspeakable joy? How are we to get back Apollo, and Attis, Demeter, Persephone, and the halls of Dis? How even see the star Hesperus, or Betelgeus? We've got to get them back, for they are the world our soul, our greater consciousness, lives in. The world of reason and science, the moon, a dead lump of earth, the sun, so much gas with spots; this the dry and sterile little world the abstracted mind inhabits. The world of our little consciousness, which we know in our pettifoggin apartness. This is how we know the world when we know it apart from ourselves, in the mean separateness of everything.

D. H. LAWRENCE,
"A PROPOS OF *LADY CHATTERLEY'S LOVER*"

We are so little at peace with ourselves and our neighbors because we are so little at peace with our place in the world, our land. American history has been to a considerable extent the history of our warfare against the natural life of the continent. Until we end our violence against the earth . . . how can we hope to end our violence against each other? The earth, which we all have in common, is our deepest bond, and our behavior toward it cannot help but be an earnest of our consideration for each other and for our descendants.

As long as man relates only to other men, he can be a specialist with impunity; . . . Once he is joined to the earth with permanence of expectation and interest, his concerns ramify in proportion to his understanding of his dependence on the earth and his consequent responsibility toward it. He realizes, because the demands of his place make it specific and inescapable, that his responsibility is not merely that of an underling, a worker at his job, but also moral, historical, political, aesthetic, ecological, domestic, educational, and so on.

WENDELL BERRY,
THE LONG-LEGGED HOUSE

Until I can know what other men know when they say, "this is where I live," I will know nothing of worth—and

when I can say that & feel it deeply, I'll know most of
what I'll ever be able to know. "This is where I live." What
a thing to know!

LEW WELCH,
QUOTED BY DOLORES LaCHAPELLE
IN *SACRED LAND, SACRED SEX*

If there can be such a thing as instinctual memory, the
consciousness of land and water must lie deeper in the core
of us than any knowledge of our fellow beings. We were
bred of the earth before we were born of our mothers. Once
born, we can live without our mothers or our fathers or
any other kin or friend, or even human love. We cannot
live without the earth or apart from it, and something is
shriveled in man's heart when he turns away from it and
concerns himself only with the affairs of men.

MARJORIE KINNAN RAWLINGS,
QUOTED BY DOLORES LaCHAPELLE
IN *SACRED LAND, SACRED SEX*
AND BY GABRIEL MILLER
IN *THE FILMS OF MARTIN RITT*

Indigenous and ancient cultures on Earth had, and still have, elaborate systems of ceremonies and rituals that revered the natural world as sacred. The realm of spirit, the invisibles, and the gods came to play and lived among them. These cultures engaged themselves in the changing seasons, made medicine with the phases of the moon, and created rituals to celebrate and mark transitions from one stage of life to another. During ceremonies of harvest and abundance, fermented plant brews flowed freely while the autumn air filled with songs and people danced. They made prayers and offerings to the spirit that moves through all things and to the souls of plants and animals for food, meat, and clothing so these things would continue to be abundant. They took care to maintain balance and harmony in all they did.

Time was set aside for thanking the gods for the growing season, for the stores of food for the winter. And it was a time of thanking Earth and plants and the spirits of growing. Prayers of beseechment for next year's planting season as well as help getting them through the winter months wafted up on spirals of smoke. A keen understanding and awareness of all the beings that were helpful and partly responsible for the tribe's well-being and failure, abundance and loss, health and illness were acknowledged and fed to keep them happy and nearby. It was understood that nothing could be done well without assistance and blessings from the unseen world of spirits and ancestors.

Central to indigenous cosmology is, naturally, the desire to maintain balance in all things to ensure a sustainable future for the generations to come. Ralph Metzner in *Green Psychology,* says, "Once we recognize that the human exploitation and destruction of the biosphere is related to a dissociative split within human consciousness between the spiritual and the natural, then the question becomes—how did the separation come about?"[1]

COUNSEL WITH THE STAR PEOPLE

The Inuit live on the treeless, windswept tundra of northern Canada, where the night sky is illuminated only by the Milky Way, far-off galaxies, and star formations whose ancient mythologies are expressed in their names. The Inuit believe in animism. All things, living and nonliving, have a spirit: people, animals, plants, material objects, forces of Nature, and the elements—fire, wind, earth, and air. As David Suzuki and David Knudtson write, "The heavens high above, they say, are the sacred abode of a mighty spirit. The *anatkut* (wise ones) say that it is a woman. To this place in the skies and to the potent feminine spirit, the souls of all who die are conveyed."[2]

To these Arctic peoples, the soul embodies the very essence of each form of life. They envision the soul as a tiny being, a minute version of the creature that it animates and transforms. Appropriately, they believe that the soul is located in a bubble of air in the groin, the same general anatomical area to which the modern biologist assigns the gene-laden germ cells, egg and sperm, bristling with DNA-encoded instruction for assembling a new life. Thus, the soul of a human being is a tiny human being, the soul of caribou a tiny caribou, and that of seal is a tiny seal.

DAVID SUZUKI AND PETER KNUDTSON,
WISDOM OF THE ELDERS

The sky ceiling in that part of the world is unimpeded by artificial light. There are places in the Gila Wilderness, where I live in southwestern New Mexico, that are completely uncontaminated by artificial light. Nights when the moon is dark, the sky people can be seen in their full glory. To plant feet on the ground, head tilted back, and gaze up into a night sky dazzling with trillions of stars and planets is to be humbled. It becomes glaringly apparent why ancient people called them Star People and their ancestors. Staring up at them, there is a sense of their sentience and a keen awareness of being watched and listened to. There is a wisdom there, an aliveness palpable to the senses, heart, and mind, and suddenly, feelings of being alone in the world dissipate into the evening air.

Human beings have a long history of living in harmony and intimately in relationship with the wild world. Francis Weller notes that "[i]t is the part of our psychic life that we hold in communion with the life that moves around us."[3] When we are in the wild, some primordial, elemental part of us awakens to this truth. Holding that truth, we are able to move from disingenuousness to authentic awareness of the life teeming around us. We become awakened to the innate need in us to recover our lost connections to wild things and places.

For I was born a thousand years ago, born in the culture of bows and arrows . . . born in an age when people loved the things of nature and spoke to it as though it has a soul.

CHIEF DAN GEORGE,
OPEN LETTER, 1975

We are biologically wired to communicate with, be in relationship with, and live harmoniously as equal members of Earth's species. Edward Goldsmith in *The Way* states that "it is part of that intuitive heritage that enables man to be cognitively adjusted to the world in which he lives. However, with the development of the world view of modernism, and in particular of the paradigm of science, the world became 'disenchanted,' secularized and mechanomorphized."[4]

For a short time after my son and I moved to Vernon County in southwest Wisconsin so that he could attend a Waldorf high school, we lived in a one-hundred-year-old brownstone house. We heated the house and water for cooking and bathing with wood. An artesian spring flowed year-round through a pipe under its own underground pressure about ten paces from our front door. The nearest town of two hundred people was six miles from our house. Neighbors were scattered over hills and behind small sections of old tree stands and forest remnants. I had been living in a college town for fifteen years before, and the move to the brownstone in Wisconsin, reawakened something ancient and primordial. Each night, I would unceremoniously bundle myself up in sweaters, gloves, and hat and go stand under the sky. Each night, I would gaze up at those Star People as if I had never seen such a sight before that night while simultaneously feeling an ancient kinship with them. I was awestruck, humility struck, and I prayed and prayed to those ancestors, my ancestors, the ancient ones who live there. Every night for the three months that I lived there, I would go out and talk with them, admire them, pay homage to them.

One night in the dream time, after weeks of talking with them, I was abruptly transported through a white cloud tube to the place where the Star People live. They were in council. They wanted to meet "in person" this being who was talking to them each night, and they wanted me to see them straight on. We held each other in high regard as I stood among them, motionless in the presence of such wise, magnificent, and luminous beings. I wasn't there long before I was ushered, or more like dropped, down a spiraling cloud tube again, and the moment I slammed back into my body, I was met with a raging, spontaneous, full-body orgasm jolting me awake. Spirituality and sex are intimately related.

The ancestors are real. And they respond.

ORIGINS OF THE SEPARATION

The Christian religion lost, in Protestantism finally, the togetherness with the universe, the togetherness of the body, the sex, the emotions, the passions with the earth and sun and stars.

D. H. LAWRENCE,

"A PROPOS OF *LADY CHATTERLEY'S LOVER*"

Sexuality is the sensation of Nature in one's own organism. In primitive and indigenous religions, religion and sexuality were one. When natural sexual expressions were repressed in the human animal during the development of religion and agriculture, this produced an unbridgeable contradiction between sexuality as a sin and religion as a liberation from sin.

How did we get so far from our relationship with and dependence on the natural world? David Suzuki writes about the origins of the mind-body divide.

> The movement away from the natural world was made possible by a quite remarkable train of thought—ideas that shaped our civilization. Today we take those ideas so much for granted that we see them not as ideas (which can be rethought, revisited, discarded) but as reality. Many thinkers trace the origins of our particular and violent fall from grace, our exile from the garden, back to Plato and Aristotle, who began a powerful process of separating the world-as-abstract-principle from the world-as-experience—dividing mind, that is, from body, and human beings from the world they inhabit. In the process they laid the groundwork for experimental science.[5]

The move from hunting and gathering to agriculture happened around 11,000 BCE, long before Plato and Aristotle. It began the long repression of sexuality in general and in women's sexuality specifically, which continues to this day, and directly parallels 10,000 years of abusive and oppressive environmental policies toward Earth, toward the environment, and toward wildness. The shift from hunter-gatherer to farmer—from wild mobility to agrarian domestication—changed the interior emotional and psychic landscapes as well as the physical landscape.

Once the reality of owning land was inculcated in the minds of over-lords, boundaries were set up and lines were drawn, and the struggle to accumulate property and material wealth was on. It didn't stop with controlling and domesticating the land; it seeped into the consciousness of our forefathers and spilled over to owning women and slaves.

With the advent of farming, women were quickly domesticated along with farm animals. Archaeologist Timothy Taylor argues that "[a] major event in the development of sexual inequality occurred when farming was invented, a system by which people could produce food when they wanted it rather than relying, like every other species, on natural availability."[6] Although women were central in the early development of farming, it quickly led to their oppression. With the increased availability of animal milk, along with breast milk, children were birthed more frequently. As sources of milk became more available, the ties that bound women to hearth and home also increased. And the economic value of women decreased as they were taken out of the labor force, unable to generate an income or sense of independence of their own.

My mother was a farm wife who much preferred sitting on "her" tractor and bailer or hayrake and feeding livestock to cooking, cleaning, and changing diapers. My younger sister (born eleven months after me) and I were primarily raised by our two sisters, eight and ten years older. By the time my mother was severely ill with emphysema, she was unable to get disability payments since my father never paid her as a wage earner, and therefore no social security payments were made on her behalf. It was a source of endless arguments and resentment between them.

How womankind, who are confined to the house still more than men, stand it, I do not know; but I have ground to suspect that most of them do not stand it at all.

HENRY DAVID THOREAU,

"WALKING"

Taylor, in *The Prehistory of Sex,* continues, "While hunter-gatherer sex had been modeled on the idea of sharing and complementarity, early agriculturalist sex was voyeuristic, repressive, homophobic, and focused on reproduction. Afraid of the wild, farmers set out to destroy it."[7] Paternity certainty has no value or importance in preagricultural cultures where concern over sexual fidelity was also relatively unimportant.

Taylor argues, "How a society treats the natural environment and how it views food are both closely connected to its attitudes toward sex and to the particular quality of the relations between the sexes. The rapidly expanding agricultural populations of Neolithic Europe swamped the hunting and foraging peoples who had lived there before by sheer force of numbers. Farming set in motion a cycle of ecological devastation—immediately connected with human sexual and reproductive aims—that seems set to continue until the world's last surviving forests vanish under the plow."[8]

An interesting concept worth pondering is that *fork,* an Indo-European word, was originally at one with *fuck.* Often the phrase "spreading my seed" is used to describe impregnating a woman with the male seed, as in planting seeds in farm furrows. Taylor notes that "[t]he idea of the female sex as a field into which grain is sown is common among farming cultures and can be found in Talmudic, Egyptian, and Vedic writings. The idea of the female earth mound being entered by the male force is startlingly embodied at Newgrange."[9]

> *Semen is Latin*
> *For a dormant, fertilized,*
> *Plant ovum—*
> *A seed.*
> *Men's ejaculate*
> *Is chemically more akin*
> *To plant pollen.*
> *See,*
> *It is really*
> *More accurate*

To call it
Mammal pollen.

To call it
Semen
Is to thrust
An insanity
Deep inside our culture:
That men plow women
And plant their seed
When, in fact,
What they are doing
Is pollinating
Flowers.
Now
Doesn't that change everything between us?

STEPHEN HARROD BUHNER,
THE TASTE OF WILD WATER

Newgrange at County Meath, Ireland, is a megalithic tomb built around 3200 BCE, about three hundred years before the pyramids. Construction of the Passage Tomb is estimated to have taken three hundred laborers at least twenty years to construct. The mound covers an acre of land. The inner passage is 19 meters long leading to an inner cruciform chamber. The mound is oriented such that at the winter solstice the sun penetrates the passageway illuminating the inner chamber. The sun was considered to have male penetrating and fertilizing properties.

In 1890, the massacre at Wounded Knee stripped native peoples of their myths and stories, turning them into property and their land into real estate to be parceled up. The lands conquered by the U.S. government were divided, bought, and sold as private property.[10] Detached from the spirit of the land, new rectangular boundary lines were drawn with no regard for natural landmarks, the sacred or holy. What was once commonly shared wildlands were plowed under, deforested, and desecrated. It happened in other places that European settlers came in contact with: Canada, Australia, Hawaii. In modern times, rain forests around the globe are being stripped of their power. The spiritual order, the ceremonies, the invisibles, whole native cosmologies have been burned, bulldozed, and paved over. We've cut down native trees only to name streets after them in some hollow attempt to immortalize what has been lost. It is a feeble attempt to assuage guilt and loss of something greater than the sum of its parts, as if a street sign serves as a monument to what has been lost. Taking it further, the roots of future generations of trees are sealed off in concrete graves.

Rupert Sheldrake writes, "The scientific and technological conquest of nature expresses a mentality of dominion that had been widespread in the ancient world but was vastly increased in power by technology and amplified by the mechanistic theory of nature has taken the place of Christian missionaries in justifying the dispossession of native peoples and the disregard of their sacred places. Since nature is inanimate, their animistic relationship to the living world around them must be superstitious, their attitudes backwards. They cannot be allowed to stand in the way of progress. And now, like the Buffalo hunters, we can hardly believe what we have done."[11]

There is widespread alienation from ourselves, each other, Earth, and the Spirit that breathes through and animates all things. We have severed the spirit from place, soul from body, sex from sexuality, and truth from power. In places where the wild is cut, mowed, and paved over, the soul of that place goes underground, waiting, while those left behind deal with the aftermath, inhabiting a soul-less landscape and suffering from diseases that arise from living on land that has no soul, that is empty of vitality and life-force energy, that is spiritually dead, where the livingness of the land is unavailable to infuse human souls and food that is grown there is devoid of the sustenance that can only come from ensouled landscapes. And underground is where the soul of place remains until the day when its rightful place is returned to it, until the day some person or peoples are willing to breathe and dance the soul to life once again, not unlike the Native American Ghost Dance of 1889.

When the soul of a culture is usurped, stolen, and marginalized, its soul undergoes severe distortions, showing up as diminished vitality, poverty, homelessness, mental disorientation, and dispiritedness. Loss of soul manifests as diseases of the spirit: depression, suicide, overeating, and addictions. In indigenous cultures, shamans, healers, and medicine people would be called in to restore the broken connections. The soul of a culture goes underground until the day of restoration and breathing it into life comes about, if it comes at all.

After hominids shifted from hunting and gathering to agriculture, from nomadic to settled, the wildness of life began to vanish. Christopher Ryan and Cacilda Jethá write about the effect settled life had on concepts of property and paternity.

> Once people were farming the same land season after season, private property quickly replaced communal ownership as the modus operandi in most societies. For nomadic foragers, personal property—anything needing to be carried—is kept to a minimum, for obvious reasons. There is little thought given to who owns the land, or the fish in the river, or the clouds in the sky. Men (and often, women) confront danger together. An individual male's *parental investment,* in other words—the core element of the standard narrative—tends to be diffuse in societies like those in which we evolved, not directed toward one particular woman and her children, as the conventional model insists.[12]

Not only did Earth need domestication in their view, but also women, wild and earthy, needed limitations set on their provocative sexual power, their sexual nature.

At the height of the witch inquisitions between 1550 and 1650, a paradigm shift took place. The move from an intuitive, magical, mystical, and visionary worldview to an objective, mechanistic, medical, and science-based view formed the basis for the hysteria and fear of Nature that followed. The shift coincided with the worst outbreak of syphilis in European history.

The epidemic was shocking. Scholars began to perceive Nature as threatening, no longer seeing it as the divine feminine soul of all creation, as Isis, Artemis, or Sophia. Nature was now seen as deceitful and dangerous. Sexual repression became epidemic as the new disease poisoned the innate trust between men and women.

When once the woman has tempted us, and we have tasted the forbidden fruit, there is no such thing as checking our appetites, whatever the consequences may be.

GEORGE WASHINGTON,
LETTER TO MRS. RICHARD STOCKTON, 1783

IT'S ALL FOR THE CHILDREN

Wilhelm Reich attained his medical degree in Germany and studied with Freud, becoming one of Freud's favorite students until Reich expanded on Freud's theories. His research on sexual repression was substantial and he wrote *The Sexual Revolution*. Reich was a pioneer in body psychotherapy, founded somatic psychology, and influenced, among others, Fritz Perls's Gestalt therapy. Reich traced civilization's suppression of biological (sexual) functioning and saw how it became perverted into social institutions: war, torture, racial hatred, and slavery. He believed that if "people were using their morality to repress their sexuality, but sexuality made life worth living—was in fact, life itself— then they needed to change their morality and have more satisfying sex; and psychoanalysis had to use whatever means were necessary to get the patient not merely to see this, but to live it."[13] Reich was a proponent of contraceptives, divorce, abortion, and the importance of economic independence for women. He believed that the split between mind and body causes us to destroy each other and the planet and allows us to go to war. He believed that we protect ourselves by "armoring" from expressing things society says we must not express. He went on to say that if men and women are unable to have orgasms it would lead to neurosis, anti-Semitism, hate, greed, racism and fascism.[14]

Sexual energy, like any energy, doesn't stop; it can't be stopped. It has to come out somewhere. It's like trying to keep steam in a boiling kettle. No matter how tightly you hold the lid, as the pressure builds, roiling steam always finds a way out. In the West, suppressed sexual energy is escaping to the tune of $200 billion per year spent on pornography, prostitutes. and Direct TV pay-per-view sex films.

When we look closely at the habit of Western culture to clear-cut old-growth forests, turn wilderness into open grazing and residential areas and deserts into gambling meccas, and build locks and damns to control rivers, you'll begin to see that it's not a far stretch at all to then institute laws and regulations that dictate and control our behavior around sexuality and the expression of it. It's not a far leap, hardly a skip, to book banning or the National Endowment of the Arts imposing a "decency standard."* It's not far from cancelling the homecoming dance at Vermont's Montpelier High School because of concerns about dirty dancing and student drug use.[15] In September 2010, CraigsList blocked access to the "adult services" section and replaced it with a black bar stamped "censored." Craigslist was criticized for allegedly facilitating prostitution and "sex trafficking" in the United States. In the summer of 2010, the organization Pornography Harms congratulated itself for being responsible for Facebook's removal of the "Our Porn Ourselves" Facebook page, claiming that the material was "inappropriate" and too easily available to children. Who's in charge here?

Of course, it's all for the children. We need to protect our children. Who and what are we protecting them from? I know the arguments: We're protecting them from pedophiles, axe murderers, mother rapers, father rapers, pornography, immorality, premarital sex, teenage pregnancy, sex trafficking, cults, drug use, and drug dealers—the arguments go on ad nauseam. As Marty Klein points out numerous times in his Internet newsletter, *Sexual Intelligence,* "And then we have completely bogus numbers (bound to be reprinted endlessly)—like the Rebecca Project's 'An estimated 100,000–300,000 American children are at risk for becoming victims of commercial sexual exploitation.' 'At risk!' Not in any way harmed, just vulnerable! The technical word for this is 'nonsense.'"[16]

Teens are being prosecuted and charged as adults for "sexting," sending sexual photos of *themselves* to their friends via cell phones. The laws designed to prevent exploitation of minors by adults are being used to destroy the lives of teenagers—the ones the laws are supposed to be protecting. A Michigan man is facing twenty years in prison for stupidly redoing a video of himself singing a children's song to a

---

*In 1989, as a result of the NEA being embroiled in the controversy between "freedom of expression" and the right of taxpayers to determine the use of public funds, Congress mandated the Decency Standard (public law 101-512), which has devalued freedom of expression in society.

group of first graders at their school, under the watchful eyes of their teacher. At his home, he took the video of the performance, spliced in shots of himself singing sexually explicit lyrics to the children. Then, he couldn't resist himself; he posted it on YouTube, disclaiming that "no actual children have been exposed" to the song. He's being charged with manufacturing child porn, even though he didn't actually manufacture child porn. He made it all up. No crime was actually committed (unless being tasteless and having a juvenile sense of humor is a crime), and no harm was inflicted.

David Sobel, talking about environmental education for second and third graders, writes:

> They hear the story of the murder of activist Chico Mendez and watch videos about the plight of indigenous forest people displaced by logging and exploration for oil. They learn that between the end of morning recess and the beginning of lunch, more than 10,000 acres of rainforest will be cut down, making way for fast food 'hamburgerable' cattle . . . In response to physical and sexual abuse, children learn distancing techniques, ways to cut themselves off from the pain. My fear is that our environmentally correct curriculum will end up distancing children from, rather than connecting them with, the natural world. The natural world is being abused and they just don't want to deal with it.[17]

The problems are not as simple or as superficial as we'd like to make them out to be. We are teaching our children to be disconnected from their feelings, from the ground of their own experience, to be afraid of Nature and the wild. We are giving them the right and wrong information at the wrong time or not at all. They are losing touch with what's real inside them and with the world in which they live.

The best way to protect your children is to empower them; give them good, true information and be their friend. Be honest with them. Children love having information, and only with good information can they can begin to make good choices. Be clear about not putting your insecurities and fears on them. Make certain that you do better than your best to keep their wild, intuitive, inquisitive, imaginative, and, yes, sexual selves intact. They will be exposed plenty to institutions, religious leaders, friends, schools, and governments that believe it is their duty to break a child's spirit and strong will and good heartedness. It's your job as a parent, guardian, grandmother, aunt, or uncle to nurture and feed their whole, wild spirit from the moment they take their first breath.

> *Children are educated by what the grown-up is and not by his talk.*
>
> CARL JUNG

QUELLING THE SONG OF THE WATERS

I grew up in the upper Mississippi River Valley of Northeast Iowa. My bones and blood were formed from farm soil and the waters of the Upper Iowa and Mississippi Rivers. My partner for five years before I moved to New Mexico was a raptor researcher along the Mississippi River, so over that time I logged a few hours in his boat with him as we trolled the lakes, backwaters, and islands of that part of the river in pools 9 and 10 (the river between locks are called pools).

On a quiet, early morning trip in late summer when the river was, what Mark Twain called, "a lazy river" and turning leaves of autumn were beginning to scatter across the surface and shoreline, I was becoming entranced by the gentle rocking of the boat against the slow, deliberate, current of the river. Just ahead in my soft vision was a lock, and in my entranced state, I could see how locks and dams act as river birth control, much like an IUD or a diaphragm. The river cannot flow freely, naturally, of her own volition. And there is a reason why so many of us have difficulty crying; our tears are dammed. Too often we feel unable to cry with abandon and without apology. Too often we become afraid of the power of our emotions to express them unrestrained. So, we dam them up; lock them away.

> *He gives water to the dead.*
>
> FRANK HERBERT,
> *DUNE*

This song of the waters is audible to every ear, but there is other music in these hills, by no means audible to all. To hear even a few notes of it you must first live here for a long time, and you must know the speech of hills and rivers. Then on a still night, when the campfire is low and the Pleiades have climbed over rimrocks, sit quietly and listen for a wolf to howl, and think hard of everything you have seen and tried to understand. Then you may hear it—a vast pulsing harmony—its score inscribed on a thousand hills, its notes the lives and deaths of plants and animals, its rhythms spanning the seconds and the centuries.

ALDO LEOPOLD,
FROM "SONG OF THE GAVILAN"

Built below the surface of the Mississippi River are structures called wing dams, which prevent the river from cutting a new channel. The Army Corps of Engineers controls the river—the river's habitats, ecosystems, channel depth, and island formations—via wing dams and locks, damming, and dredging—the process of digging out sand and silt that gets disturbed as tows move barges from city to city.

The increase in barge traffic on large rivers has nearly killed the Illinois River. One hundred years ago, it was as ecologically diverse as the Mississippi but is now considered "bleak" by the corps. The murky brown plumes seen trailing behind a barge in aerial photographs are the result of sand and sediment churned up from the river bottom. The sand, being heavier, settles quickly, but it takes two hours for the sediment to settle, and with anywhere from eleven tows a day near La Crosse to thirty-two a day at Alton, Illinois, the water never clears. Invertebrates are buried by the debris, and fish gills cannot cope with constant high concentrations of silt.[18]

In 1781, Thomas Jefferson wrote: "The Mississippi will be one of the principal channels of future commerce for the country westward of the Alleghaney . . . This river yields turtle of a peculiar kind, perch, trout, gar, pike, mullets, herrings, carp, spatula fish of 50 lb. weight, cat-fish of 100 lb. weight, buffalo fish and sturgeon."[19]

Carp, a hardy fish introduced to the United States in the 1880s, has dominated the commercial fishery of the Mississippi since the early 1900s. All others have declined, including buffalo, catfish, freshwater drum, lake sturgeon, and bullhead. Walleye, sauger, yellow perch, and white bass have disappeared entirely from the commercial catch.[20]

Sadly, the Army Corps of Engineers is under heavy pressure from corporations that use the river to transport coal and grain, making the corps blind to other solutions that would work with the river. Rather than shaping the river to suit barge traffic, imagine building barges and boats that fit the river. So much has been lost in the unwillingness to see the sacredness in the largest river on the North American continent and the third largest river in the world. As long as we continue to see Nature as something "out there," we will continue looking for solutions from the outside and from the top down—the reductionist's seat in the spectator's box. "Solutions" from this seat have no enduring qualities.

Jerry Mander in *The Absence of the Sacred* addresses this when he says:

> The assumptions have been gaining in strength for thousands of years, fed both by Judeo-Christian religious doctrines that have desanctified the earth and placed humans in domination over it; and by technologies that, by their apparent power, have led us to believe we are some kind of royalty over nature, exercising Divine will. We have lost the understanding that existed in all civilizations prior to ours, and that continues to exist on Earth today in societies that live side by side with our own; we have lost a sense of the sacredness of the natural world. The new technologies don't accept this notion; they live in a world that is removed from it; they themselves have lost touch with the source of that knowledge. They find it silly.[21]

There has been continual and growing exertion from governments, institutions, religious organizations, and lobbyists to suppress and control the wild in ecosystems and in human behavior. Diminishing biological diversity is analogous to diminishing diversity in human expression as our first amendment rights are undermined with each redefinition.

BECOMING WHOLE

I would like to recommend that in judging the rightness of our actions toward the natural world, we be guided by a fundamental respect for the dignity of wild Nature. Dignity is the intrinsic quality in all beings that we are morally obligated to uphold. If our behavior does not infringe on the dignity of animals, plants, rocks, rivers, and the relationships among them, our actions are proper and sustainable, both ethically and ecologically.

MOLLIE MATTESON,
"THE DIGNITY OF WILD THINGS," *WILD EARTH*

We all belong to Earth. We are of Earth, and Earth is inside each of us. Our existence depends on Earth and the elements. The separations we feel are man-made; we took ourselves out of the relationship. We invent labels and hierarchies, we draw lines of separation, and we even manage to separate ourselves from the ground we walk on, the trees we depend on for building our homes and cleaning the air and the plants we harvest for food and medicine. Separation is easy. But it isn't in the natural scheme of things.

The human predicament is that we can't seem to find the connection between ourselves and Earth. The predicament is that without that connection we are doomed as a species. If we were to know this connection in the deepest part of us, let awareness of that connection permeate and infuse every cell of our three bodies, we would necessarily have to make other choices; it would alter our entire orientation. The predicament continues—we are so deep in the quagmire we can't seem to imagine something else.

Unless you know that the ecosystem of you is intimately connected to the ecosystem of Earth, you won't be whole. Unless you are able to reconcile and integrate all the parts that make up your ecosystem, you will not be able to be integrated into the sensuous ecosystems of Earth. An ecosystem is a biological environment. It consists of all the organisms (ego states) living in a particular area (you or me in our body), as well as the physical components of the environment with which the organisms (ego states) interact, such as the air we breathe and the blood, sweat, piss, tears, light, and shadow in our bodies. *Biocoenosis* or *biocenosis* was coined by Karl Mobius in 1877. It refers to all the interacting organisms living together in a specific habitat. An ecosystem is not only the physical and biological components of an environment but also the mental isolates. Our histories, illnesses, and personal and family stories are also part of our inner ecosystem.

It is the collection of all the parts of us, physical, mental, emotional, and spiritual. It is the sum total of all our parts.

It doesn't matter if we are red, black, white, tall, short, Muslim, Catholic, pagan, Buddhist, communist, capitalist, or Rosicrucian, each of us belongs to Earth; we all breathe in the same air, the breath of the Great Mystery, and we *get* to live on Earth together. These words have no meaning without the experience of living on Earth, without "Gaiaphilia"—the feeling of love for Earth. Without the experience of belonging to the livingness of Earth, our lives become rhetorical and theoretical like environmentalists who never have dirt under their fingernails. We think that because we've said something, the problem is solved. The problem isn't solved; there are still problems, and we're still fighting, warring, and killing, mutilating each other and destroying other species. We still don't believe or act as if Earth is alive and sentient and aware. Nor do we act from the truth that we have emerged as a species from the womb—the soil and microbes, the water and air—of Gaia. Neither do we want to know that we are sexual, have sex; even as you read these words, someone is having sex, right now. Maybe it's your neighbor or your parents or your sister across the country. It could be your mail carrier, the clerk at the store, your children. It could be you.

A WORKING DEFINITION OF WILD

I've been using the words *wild, wilderness,* and *Nature* rather loosely up to this point. Before going further, I want to explore the meanings of each word. Our language lets us be lazy in our descriptions of things, people, and events. For example, to say "the wind blew wild" conjures up images in your mind. Other words that could be used and may be more accurate and for certain more descriptive might be: *tumultuous, ferocious, tempestuous, violent, furious. The Reader's Digest Great Encyclopedic Dictionary* gives the following definitions of the word *wild:*

> 1. Inhabiting the forest or open field; not domesticated or tamed; living in a state of nature. 2. Growing or produced without care or culture; not cultivated. 3. Being without civilized inhabitants or cultivation; desert; waste. 4. Living in a primitive or savage way. 5. Boisterous; unruly; unrestrained. 6. Immoral; dissolute; orgiastic.

It goes on to describe *wild* as, "originating violent disturbances; stormy; turbulent; rashly imprudent; showing reckless want of judgment."

Looking closer at the origin of the word *wild* in the Oxford English Dictionary, we find *wild* with intriguing, old English spellings that conjure up images and feelings about the word's origins.

The Reader's Digest Great Encyclopedic Dictionary defines *wilderness* as follows:

> Wilderness: 1. an uncultivated, uninhabited, or barren region. 2. A waste, as of an ocean. 3. A multitudinous and confusing collection; a wilderness of curiosities. 4. Wildness. Nature: 1. the fundamental qualities or characteristics that together define the identity of something; essential character. 3. The entire material universe and its phenomena.

Wildness is an idea that has moved immensely through time, notes author Robert MacFarlane. "And in that time, two great and conflicting stories have been told about it. According to the first of these, wildness is a quality to be vanquished, according to the second, it is a quality to be cherished."[22]

The etymology of the word *wild* is vexed and subtle, but the most persuasive past proposed for it involves the Old High German *wildi,* and the Old Norse *vilr,* as well as the pre-Teutonic *ghweltijos*. All three of these terms carry implications of disorder and irregularity, and as Roderick Nash has written, they bequeathed to the English root word *will* "a descriptive meaning of . . . willful, or uncontrollable. Wildness, according to this etymology, is an expression of independence from human direction, and wild land can be said to be self-willed land, land that proceeds according to its own laws and principles, land whose habits, the growth of its trees, the movements of its creatures, the free descent of its streams through its rocks are of its own devising and own execution. Land that, as the contemporary definition of wild continues, 'acts or moves freely without restraint; is unconfined, unrestricted.'"[23]

The basic definition of wildness has remained constant since those first appearances, but the values ascribed to this quality have diverged dramatically.

On the one hand, wildness has been perceived as a dangerous force that confounds the order-bringing pursuits of human culture and agriculture. Wildness, according to this story, is cognate with wastefulness. Wild places resist conversion to human use, and they must therefore be destroyed or overcome.[24]

The soul has a need for the wild. David Abrams in *Becoming Animal* says it this way:

> A calloused coldness, or meanness, results when our animal senses are cut off for too long from the animate earth, when our ears— inundated by the whooping blare of car alarms and the muted thunder of subways—no longer encounter the resonant silence, as our eyes forget the irregular wildness of things green and growing behind the rectilinear daze.[25]

The definition of that need is personal, but it is there, inside us. Jay Griffiths notes that "[t]he human spirit has a primal allegiance to wildness, to really live, to snatch the fruit and suck it, to spill the juice. We may think we are domesticated, but we are not. Feral in pheromone and intuition, feral in our sweat and fear, feral in tongue and language, feral in cunt and cock. This is the first command: "to live fealty to the feral angel."[26]

We get our need for the wild met however we can. Some of us go camping, hike hundreds of miles, go fishing, watch porn, or go to strip clubs. Eros is intimately involved in the ways we fill the need for the wild for Eros is the connector. We don't seek fulfillment from something unless there is a measure of attraction, need, or affection for the thing, whether it's camping, hiking, or sex.

Rupert Sheldrake explores the meanings of nature, from inborn characteristics to the wider natural world.

> One of the primary meanings of nature is an inborn character or disposition, as in the phrase *human nature.* This in turn is linked to the idea of nature as an innate impulse or power. On a wider scale, nature is the creative and regulative power operating in the physical world, the immediate cause of all its phenomena. And hence nature comes to mean the natural or physical world as a whole. When nature in this sense is personified, she is Mother Nature, an aspect of the Great Mother, the source and sustainer of all life, and the womb to which all life returns.[27]

Our concept of Nature is entwined with our concepts of and relationships between men and women, nature and humanity, humanity and animals. When we reject the idea of Nature as organic and motherlike and perceive it as cold and inanimate, our relationship to Nature becomes lifeless. But can we really claim Nature is inanimate and lifeless given all the research and writings on the teeming lives of bacteria and fungi, the studies on plant communication, the reproductive forces happening around us, and the mystical experiences most of us have had?

Every ancient culture on Earth had relationships with the animating forces of the Universe. Pythagoreans took into account the five great elements from which they believed all things were fashioned. The Chinese I Ching and feng shui, the system of ordering homes, gardens, buildings, are set on the foundations of the five elements. Nothing is built or undertaken without consideration of the elements and how they influence wealth, health, happiness, prosperity. Altars are erected to honor the ancestors and deities and to prevent misfortune from coming about as a result of dishonoring the dead, the spirits, and the elements. In Japan, mountains themselves are considered shrines connecting Heaven and Earth.

DEATH AND DISEASE THROUGH SEPARATION

Approximately one hundred years (depending on how you calculate it) of environmentalism and conservation have gone by, and things are getting worse. One hundred percent of the air in the Lower Forty-eight is now contaminated with eight cancer-causing industrial chemicals at levels that exceed safety standards. We are living with an epidemic of cancer, antibiotic-resistant bacteria, Lyme disease, and other debilitating diseases Rachel Carson warned of in her groundbreaking work *Silent Spring*. What does it mean when Monsanto sends thiram-treated tomato seeds (the EPA ruled thiram too toxic for home garden use and application requires the use of gloves) and Maxim XL–treated corn and vegetable seeds to earthquake-devastated Haiti? This "gift" of 60,000 hybrid seeds was distributed by a $127 million project funded by the U.S. Agency for International Development (USAID). The program, called Winner, was designed to promote "agricultural intensification." Monsanto, the same neighborhood corporation that brought us Agent Orange, recorded more than $11.7 billion in sales in 2009. They hold over 650 biotechnology patents, most of them for corn, cotton, and soy. In 2004, in Brazil, Monsanto sold a farm to a U.S Senator for one-third its price in exchange for his work to legalize glyphosate, the world's most widely used herbicide.[28]

Exporting hybrid seeds that devastate and toxify soil, water, and the bodies (human and nonhuman) that ingest genetically modified seeds creates a culture of dependence and sickness. "The genetically modified seeds, such as those donated and later immolated, cannot be saved from year to year. Some so-called terminator seeds—the DNA of which is altered so as to not drop seed after harvest—require the farmer to buy new seeds from Monsanto the following year in a legally binding contract, instead of collecting the seeds that would have naturally developed on the plant before its DNA was modified."[29] This increases poverty and indebtedness; legalized slavery.

Where there is no free choice, when our natural connections to the land that feeds our bodies and souls are severed, the soil is tilled for feudalism, imperialism, and fascism to emerge. On June 4, 2010, 10,000 Haitian farmers walked 7 kilometers to Hinche to receive the gift of seeds from their benefactor. Upon arrival, it was World Environment Day; the farmers took the 400 tons of vegetable seeds and burned them all. Sometimes you have to say *no*.

If you are unable to integrate and be in relationship with wild ecosystems, with ego states that naturally occur in Nature just as they do in human beings, with the aliveness and sexuality of Earth, you will never be able to integrate your own sexuality, your inner ecosystems.

Referring to Aphrodite, Michael Perlman comments:

> It is strange how rarely the Goddess of luxuriant sensuality and love is linked with the love of nature, with ecological concerns, with the power of beauty. Her world of sensual and erotic display, of night-club and bedroom, seems so distant from the backpack trail; we're not in the habit of juxtaposing thoughts of wild nights and the wildness Henry David Thoreau celebrates in his famous essay on walking. We don't generally think of ecological concern as having erotic and sensual power (even though the image of the woods as a sexy place is hardly confined to Greek myth), and recent ecological thought has begun to appreciate the loss in that omission. If, for instance, we are to talk about Greek mythological figures in relation to contemporary ecological concerns, shouldn't we be talking instead about Artemis, goddess of pristine wilderness and inviolate, virgin forest?[30]

As long as we maintain separation from all that is Earth and sensual, we will never know the kind of majesty and peace that comes from being whole and integrated as a sacred, sexual being, a playing member of the circle of life. And there will be continued assaults on Earth and continued sexual repression.

6

Finding the Wild

Now is the time for you to mark your entry through the spirited gate. You need to find your crossroads, the gateway that can take you anywhere in this world or in any other worlds.

BRADFORD KEENEY,
THE BUSHMAN WAY OF TRACKING GOD

Authentic tidings of invisible things!

WILLIAM JAMES,
ON SOME OF LIFE'S IDEALS

The great sun burning with light, the strong earth—dear earth—the warm sky, the pure air, the thought of ocean, the inexpressible beauty of all filled me with a rapture, an ecstasy, an inflatus.

RICHARD JEFFRIES,
THE STORY OF MY HEART

Our judgments concerning the worth of things, big or little, depends on the feelings the things arouse in us.

WILLIAM JAMES,
ON A CERTAIN BLINDNESS IN HUMAN BEINGS

A SACRED VOICE IS CALLING YOU

Abraham Maslow termed mystical experiences *peak experiences*. He said they frequently occur in well-integrated, mature people. Often a mystical experience results from a deep need to feel the numinous, to have an experience that transcends the understanding of the intellect. When we allow ourselves to fall totally, madly in love with the other, to give ourselves over completely to the feelings we have for him or her, the opportunity for the ecstatic to enter our lovemaking is increased. It's as if an invitation has been sent out for the mystical to enter the relationship. As we go deeper and deeper into feeling the love we have for the other, physical boundaries begin to fall away. Love in that deeply intimate place is the catalyst for the mysterious, ecstatic event to unfold between the two, and in our psyches.

James Hillman describes eloquently the *daimon* or *fate, genius, calling, soul, destiny* (he uses these terms interchangeably depending on the context), some invisible guiding force that is with us during our lifetime. Before we take on a human body there is a time when we sit in counsel with the Universe, with God, Creator, the cosmos, with Gaia and whoever else you might recall being there. In this counsel, before we make the journey to Earth, we make agreements about how we can best spend our time here during this chapter of the soul's making. At that time, we are each given a soul companion—a daimon—that guides us here to Earth. The daimon is necessary because on the way to becoming born, we lose our memory of the agreements we made. The daimon is a life companion, a soul guide who helps us navigate this life and to slowly remember why we've come here. Remembering those agreements; to become who we were meant to be, to make the soul's journey, to let the Genius out of the bottle, to enliven our destiny, to participate in making the world a better place, whatever our agreements are, our daimon guides us, pulls us here, pushes us there, brings that experience to us, helping us to be who we came here to be.

The daimon is alert to movements of our soul's purpose, and those early movements, intimations, can often be seen in early childhood.[1] Edward O. Wilson talks of it this way, "You start by loving a subject. Birds, probability theory, explosives, stars, differential equations, storm fronts, sign language, swallowtail butterflies—the odds are that your obsession will have begun in childhood. The subject will be your lodestar and give sanctuary in the shifting mental universe. . . . A man's work is nothing but this slow trek to rediscover, through the detours of art, those two or three great and simple images in whose presence his heart first opened."[2]

There has been a fairly obvious theme in my life of relationship experiences, sexual experiences, sexual abuse, sexual violence, sexual ecstasy, wilderness ecstasy, bonding with Earth, Earth sexuality that has undoubtedly helped shape who I've become, who I was born to be, and which has heavily influenced the writing of this book. I chose at each juncture to keep going, to say "yea" or "nay." And I am keenly aware of the touch of an invisible guide having a hand in my life and in helping me stay alive in dangerous situations.

> *Reason flows from the blending of rational thought and feeling. If the two functions are torn apart, thinking deteriorates into schizoid intellectual activity and feeling deteriorates into neurotic life-damaging passions.*
>
> ERICH FROMM,
> *THE REVOLUTION OF HOPE*

The ancient Greeks had a word (they had a word for everything) for making the invisible visible, *opathe.* We have a passionate desire to make what lies just below the surface of a thing visible to our senses, to our seeing, to our feeling. It is the work of the scientist to see the intimate workings of cells, mitochondria, bacteria, and organs and how all things are in relationship to each other. We need and want to feel the presence of the mysterious in our lives, inside our waking and dreaming. To know, without doubt, that which we came from is here around us and inside us, that we are not alone. We need a sense of mystery, of the unknown, yet we strive diligently to unravel, make sense, to prove or disprove the existence of spiritual forces, numinosity, invisible force fields. We want to know if our prayers and dreams are being heard and answered. We need to know this to have our lives makes some sense, have meaning beyond the mundane. If not, what has been the purpose for the inextinguishable existence of stories, legends, myths from every culture on Earth of gods and goddesses, spirit messages, trees that talk and walk about? We need the myths of old as well as to create new myths; those stories that are made up that have truth in them, help us find our own truths. We endeavor to unravel and unearth the magic and mystery of not only the Universe but, especially, our own humble inner and outer workings. As Richard Earnheart says, "It is the goal of every serious artist, scientist, and writer: unbridling the unseen, unearthing the undiscovered, unleashing a great tempest of the heretofore unexpected."[3]

It is through sacred sex and relationship with the wild that we strive to satisfy our deeply felt need for the numinous. These deep fully-present connections provide the moments when we glimpse the movement of some great thing inside us, or the movement of a barely visible form skittering past the corner of our eyes, seen but not quite seen. The moments when we feel so much love for a grandchild or lover that we are taken outside ourselves, moved in the core of ourselves. Feeling is at the core of becoming whole, is the center spiral from which sacred sex spins. It is the balm that heals the split between humans and Gaia, and it is this feeling that will repair damage done from the mechanistic, scientific worldview and return us to a state of wholeness. Sacred, ecstatic lovemaking is a gift from the gods; it is a portal through which we experience a spiritual reality, experience our lover as a sacred, holy being. It is in these sacred moments that our ordinary awareness becomes heightened, illuminated, and we experience the all-encompassing presence of spirit and our interrelationship with all beings.

If you cannot face directly into your sexuality,
You will never discover your true spirituality.
Your earthly spirit leads to discovering your heavenly spirit.
Look at what created you to discover what will immortalize you.

HSI LAI,
THE SEXUAL TEACHINGS OF THE WHITE TIGRESS

It is not just the moments after sex or, sadly, during sex that we often feel something is missing. Human beings have been feeling that something is missing for a very long time. Rather than try to name what it is, rather than turning to face the feeling and follow it back to its source, we turn to Prozac, television, and therapy and fill our homes with stuff. We think if only we have more stuff, the right stuff, then some psychological shift will magically happen, and we'll fill the loss with the meanings and connections we've been looking for. Stuff dulls our senses so we don't have to feel how much our life doesn't work while we're looking for meaning. What gives our life meaning is something invisible. But meaning doesn't happen in a vacuum, it comes out of being in relationship to the work we are meant to do—with our lovers, with ourselves, with the first plant that communicated with us.

Our relationship with the wildness of Earth is one doorway into the mystical experience. I had been walking the eighty acres of a friend's land for nearly three hours trying to find the right spot to put myself for my third vision quest, which I planned to begin a week later. I crossed the stream, hiked up the hill on the north, then meandered back down and back across the stream, up the southern hill, and around the forest edge. After a few hours, I made my way back to my van. Instinctively, I touched my left earlobe. Gasping in shock, I discovered one of my earrings was gone. It was a special pair, made by a friend who was a Mayan sculptor in the Yucatan. I was horrified and spent a few moments kicking myself in the ass for wearing them on a walk through the forest. I quickly gave it up as I decided that since I was asking a lot of the land and the spirit of the land—to hold me and guide me during my coming four-day fast—I was glad to leave the earring as an offering of gratitude. When leaving a gift for the spirits, it's good to give something that has value and meaning so it's not an idle gesture. I was happy to think of it being out there, somewhere, as one of my giveaways.

A week later, I returned to the land with my backpack, sleeping bag, camp pad, prayer pipe, and water jugs to fast for four days and nights. I began to walk toward the spot I had chosen earlier when I sensed it was now wrong; it didn't feel right today. I continued to walk, but as I prepared to cross the stream, I was stopped suddenly in my tracks, held still, prevented from moving by some invisible force. Instinctively I looked down as if to see what was holding me still. It took a moment for the reality of what I was seeing to register in my awareness. Next to my right foot was the lost earring. The impact of what was happening continued to move deeper into my interior world. Out of eighty acres, the earring could have fallen anywhere. I could have crossed the stream at any point, but here I was and here it was.

As I stood there feeling everything I was feeling, my mind whirling at the sight of it, an energy force seemed to rise up from the ground and stream, slowly wrapping around me a phenomenal sense of love. Oh, what a rapture to be in the midst of this experience—the numinous, the real, extraordinary. To feel unconditionally loved by the spirit of this land and the spirit of the vision quest. Certain my heart would burst, water flowed freely from my eyes. Something told me to pick it up, to take it back, and place it on my quest altar as a reminder during my time here, a reminder that I was not alone. I had invisible companions who loved me and this was a demonstration of their love and support for what I was doing. My four-day quest became a rich tapestry of meaning.

There was no doubt, to my way of seeing, that my daimon had a hand in that event. I have no doubt that Gaia, Earth, the spirits of place and of vision quest were instrumental in the confluence of that sequence of events.

The meaning of that moment when I was stopped in my tracks still percolates and affects my life. I needed that personal experience with those invisibles on that land at that time for my soul work and destiny. It may take years after such an event for the full meaning to come to fruition.

People are hungry for the invisibles. We are desperate to know they share our lives and to feel their presence. Note the popularity of the Harry Potter books and movies, *The Lord of the Rings* trilogy, *Stardust, Avatar, The Chronicles of Narnia, American Gods,* and so on. We are like Alice, of *Alice in Wonderland*. When a rabbit walked by as she sat under a tree reading, she knew by the waistcoat he was wearing that he was no ordinary rabbit; she could tell that he was intelligent and aware. She followed him down the rabbit hole into another world because the invisible had spoken to her.

The use of psychotropics such as marijuana, ayahuasca, peyote, or mushrooms is illegal but the illegality has nothing to do with addiction. These substances are illegal because they open the doors of perception, allowing us to see the invisibles underneath the form of the visible world. Publishers such as Inner Traditions publish New Age and esoteric books on subjects that mainstream publishers won't touch because these subjects validate the existence of the invisibles. The normal response is to deny their existence. As accounts of the invisible realm rise up from the underworld and from the dusty shelves of archaic libraries, they are being met by an equal force ready to discount, discredit, and censor them, as evidenced by the continuing war on drugs and the medical marijuana debate. In recent years there has been an increasing rise in the use of traditional herbal medicine, shamanism, energy work, and channeling and a resurgence of the peyote church and ayahuasca ceremonies as more and more people seek to meet needs that are not being met by allopathic medicine or pharmaceutical drugs. The degree to which people are willing to pay out-of-pocket expenses for non-Western medicine and healers, and risk legal recriminations to participate in "illegal" ceremonies speaks volumes of the need for invisibles. What if we actually lived as if the gods of Earth and myth lived among us? What would our life be like if we worked directly with our daimon every day and called on the invisible ancestors—spirits of place, of mountain, of ocean—to help guide us? What would our lives look like? What would it do to our level of hope? How would it change our orientation to Nature, to wilderness, to each other? How would we begin?

GOING WILD

We need regular infusions of the wild, of the numinous and the touch of the invisibles. We need to seek refuge or renewal in physical wilderness. We may need to smell the sweet vanilla scent of a pine forest or hear the waves rise and fall on the ocean. Wild is known through our senses. Going into wild ecosystems forces us to become aware; that's part of their function, to cause us to shift our focus from the prosaic and ordinary to the heightened, otherworldly, and extraordinary. Each of our senses becomes sharp, fine-tuned; we listen for the deep sounds, look for the unseen as our peripheral vision expands farther and farther out. Our nervous systems are heightened and each hair on our body acts as a kinesthetic radar receptor. We become acutely aware of our own sounds, our breathing, the heaviness of foot on the forest floor, the scratching sound of Gore-Tex, and the tension we are holding in our body. The primordial part of us knows that we are both predator and prey. There are bears, mountain lions, rattlesnakes, scorpions, and loose rocks to be mindful of. Before we even set foot in areas designated as wilderness or even go to a campground, some internal shift happens—we enroll the Predator part of us, the part that's interested in surviving. If we were to slow down a bit, we would notice that our concerns turn toward providing for what we were taught are the basic necessities for survival: food, shelter, water, and clothing. We begin by taking inventory of equipment and gear on hand. Is it in good working order? Do I need to replace or add anything? How will I protect and defend myself if a bear or mountain lion comes upon my scent, then my camp, then me?

We ask ourselves questions about the weather, about food and shelter. Do we need a tent or will a tarp be sufficient? Do we want to sleep on the ground sheltered only by the night sky? What if it rains or the temperature drops? Do we have rain gear, enough warm clothing? Is there potable water where we are going? Do we need to bring a purification system? What about food and cooking? The process of preparing for our trip increases our awareness; our senses become more acute. And once we've arrived, we need to know how to read the geography of the land to keep us from pitching camp in the middle of an animal path or in the floodplain of a creek.

As critically important as the physical needs are, we also need to know how to read the invisible geography of our chosen campsite. How does it feel? Is it benevolent, supportive, friendly, ominous? Some part of us is reading this landscape as that part is always looking for what feels good and avoiding places that feel funny, weird, or scary. We do it each time we go into a coffee shop or restaurant but rarely do we pay attention to what we are actually doing as we search the place to find just the right spot to sit, the spot that feels good. We actually imagine sitting there before our body arrives in the chair. Once in the wilderness, have we acknowledged that the wild has been called home by many others before we hominids showed up? Have we asked permission to camp in the middle of someone else's living room and has it been granted? Have we told the other inhabitants; the plants, the animals, the stones, the trees, the elementals, what we are doing there, how long we intend to stay? Have we asked them if they would grant us a drama-free stay? Have we regarded the spirit of the place and made offerings, or in some way reciprocated, given back in exchange for staying, as we would take a bottle of fine wine to dinner at a friend's house?

Despite our brilliance as a species, we still think the disharmony we feel within ourselves, with each other, and with Earth can be assuaged, ignored, or somehow altered by iPods, the Internet, instant messaging, and bigger, flatter, sharper television screens. Though I enjoy having those things in my life to some degree, none of them has been able to replace intimacy. None of them replaces my experience with the wild or the soul food I find there. The World Wide Web connects me to far-off lands, loved ones living abroad, hard-to-find books, new and old music and research papers. YouTube brings Viktor Frankl, Eric Berne, Virginia Satir and Occupy Wall Street into my office, but these things do not bring the livingness, the soul, of wild ecosystems into my home. They do not bring the scent of pine forest, the spontaneous call of a red-tailed hawk overhead, a lizard sunning itself on the rock in my path. They do not render me awestruck in the same way the soul of the mountains does or the experience of being seen by an ancient, invisible teacher come to walk by my side for a spell. And they certainly do not render my senses alert to the livingness of being immersed in changing landscapes and ecosystems.

> *But the Genius which, according to the old belief, stands at the door by which we enter, and gives us the lethe to drink, that we may tell no tales, mixed the cup too strongly, and we cannot shake off the lethargy now at noonday. Sleep lingers all our lifetime about our eyes, as night hovers all day in the boughs of the fir tree. All things swim and glitter. Our life is not so much threatened as our perception. Ghost-like we glide through nature, and should not know our place again.*
>
> RALPH WALDO EMERSON,
> "EXPERIENCE," *SELF-RELIANCE AND OTHER ESSAYS*

Our electronics keep our eyes engaged in looking while we lose our ability to see. We have become so geometrically single focused that when we look at the Müller-Lyer arrows pictured below, we can't tell whether one line is longer than the other.[4]

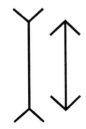

The Müller-Lyer arrows

The modern Western brain, has been trained by exposure to photographs and representational art and also by exposure to street corners, square rooms, and other "carpentered" features of the environment to see cues of depth and distance on two-dimensional pictorial surfaces. This training confuses the Western perception of the Müller-Lyer diagram. But studies such as one published by Philip L Kilbride and H. W. Leibowitz, "The Ponzo Illusion among the Baganda of Uganda," show that those living an indigenous lifestyle in the non-"carpentered" natural world are able to judge the length of the lines accurately. That is, they are able to see the lines as they are: equal in length.[5]

For the Western brain, the slope of the arrows in the Müller-Lyer diagram creates the illusion of depth. If you look at a corner inside your house you'll notice that the juncture where two walls meet the ceiling or the floor visually reproduces the Müller-Lyer line with the inverted arrows, or "V" shapes pointing in toward the line. When you position yourself across the street from the corner of a building you'll be able to see that the Müller-Lyer line with the arrows pointing out away from it is repeated where the vertical line of the corner meets the roof and again at the bottom corner of the building.

Many books have been written by people who travel to exotic lands, go deep into the jungle or to remote islands, to live and study with indigenous peoples. Overwhelmingly, they recount how they were transformed and their senses awakened, how they were finally able to see as indigenous people see. They saw minute details in butterfly larvae and in the patterns of leaves and tree bark. They were able to sense from a distance, when someone was approaching. Then they return to their ordinary life with the stories and myths that reveal some essential truth and even warnings, to write a book telling of their adventures benefiting all who read the accounts. I'm glad they are willing to be messengers.

It is helpful to travel to other countries and experience other cultures, to be offered a very different perspective. But not all of us can afford to take the time, commit the resources necessary, and then be lucky enough to be accepted into an ancient society that still has the old ways intact, unblemished by missionaries and Western culture.

What are we to do, those of us who are homebound, unable to travel? How are we to replicate and access the experience of restoring the indigenous way of seeing and feeling? We can do what indigenous people have always done: What they do is available to us, right here and now. There is not a single thing I can think of (short of being in a coma or a politician) that is stopping us from becoming indigenous to this place, the place where we are living in any given moment.

The knowledge indigenous people pass on is a wisdom that comes not from schooling, not from higher education, but from being intrinsically part of their habitat and using their heart field as an organ of perception. Indigenous people are as much a part of their landscape as the mosquito larvae, the mountain, the grasses, the uña de gato vine. It is wisdom, a body of knowledge that is dynamic and adaptable and transferrable and available. It is wisdom that is transmitted, if you will, directly from the jungle, directly from the mountain, from forests or desert mesas, from the trees and plants in the backyard, to anyone willing and choosing to be the receiver. The more time we spend in the forest, walking through streams and wild landscapes with a hungry heart, a desire to learn, and enough humility to allow ourselves to be educated, the closer we are to becoming indigenous. Humility must be part of the asking; the invisibles must feel, must know—for feeling is knowing—your desire to be touched, to be taught, to be shown.

In every walk with nature one receives far more than he seeks.

JOHN MUIR

The more time we spend in uncivilized landscapes, the more we know, the more intelligent we become, the more tuned to the life of the forest, to the intricate, delicate, minute breathing of the trees, the imperceptible movement of stone. It is unavoidable, then, to become aware of our own internal movements. And one day, when we're not looking, we realize we know things we didn't know we knew and have no memory of learning. It happens spontaneously as you move through your day. Interesting thoughts and insights are there, inside us, bubbling to the surface. We begin to see connections between and among things. We begin to sense and perceive things; we notice the smell of things and places and people. Authentic knowledge is percolating through gray matter. There is a noticed sense of calm that begins to relax our musculature. Our breathing deepens, our heartbeat regulates, and our peripheral vision expands more consistently. We may feel a sense of inner strength and a kinship with other life-forms. With each visit to uncivilized landscapes, we become more present in our bodies and more present with the experience of being there.

I am alarmed when it happens that I have walked a mile into the woods bodily, without getting there in spirit. In my afternoon walk I would fain forget all my morning occupations and my obligations to society. But it sometimes happens that I cannot easily shake off the village. The thought of some work will run in my head and I am not where my body is—I am out of my senses. In my walks I would fain return to my senses. What business have I in the woods, if I am thinking of something out of the woods?

HENRY DAVID THOREAU,

"WALKING"

Some part of us knows that to give life to that primordial, ancient faculty inside us, the indigenous heart of us, the part that knows how to walk silently through a forest, knows that we have to break a few rules of the culture we live in. "It's not polite to stare, dear." We're wearing a cultural "chastity belt," and I am quite done with the irritation and chaffing that it causes to my sensibilities and free will.

Dare to be seduced by the senses.

Cultures still living closely connected to nature, who depend on it for survival and livelihood, don't live in carpentered houses with square corners. Because they have not been schooled out of their native senses, their feelings not dulled or shut down, they are able to see when one line is longer than the other. Their seeing hasn't been adulterated nor their vision become pinpoint, forced into straight lines and corners.

> *The story of Romulus and Remus being suckled by a wolf is not a meaningless fable. The founders of every state which has risen to eminence have drawn their nourishment and vigor from a similar wild source. It was because the children of the Empire were not suckled by the wolf that they were conquered and displaced by the children of the northern forests who were.*
>
> HENRY DAVID THOREAU,
> "WALKING"

To reclaim the body's sensuality and sexuality requires reclaiming the body's sensory perceiving and feeling. Our senses evolved in concert with the wildness of the world. Sensory acuity is the ground where the wild is fostered. We are not encouraged to feel in our culture, to sense, to be sensual and full of sensations, or to find meaning in sexual experiences. Marjorie Hope Nicolson eloquently states it this way: "Like men of every age, we see in Nature what we have been taught to look for, we feel what we have been prepared to feel."[6] The experience of wilderness depends on, is fundamental to, and is accessed through our senses. The singularly most dissident, nonconformist, rebellious thing you can do and the most immediate entrance to the wild state of mind is to

come

to

your

senses,

now.

COMING TO LIFE

Wilheim Reich developed somatics, a system of body therapy used in conjunction with psychotherapy, to release held emotions and trauma. Reich wanted a full-body emotional response to life. He believed that if you covered yourself up, armored yourself, you could deaden pain, but you would rob yourself of a life full of joy. Reich asserted there was a direct correlation between aggression and body armoring. He held that the longer a person armors herself, the tenser the musculature becomes, the deeper the psychosis goes. Armoring leads to cancer, arthritis, and rheumatism and dulls awareness, intuition, and creativity. When emotions get backed up inside a person and the musculature becomes more tense and atrophied, the more likely it is for aggression to build and war to occur.

The armored body is not unlike an animal that has been taken out of its natural habitat and put into a cage. The animal paces back and forth, back and forth, getting more and more tense, feeling the bars of the cage getting closer and the space getting tighter. The animal's territorial rights have been usurped; it needs space to hunt and run. It needs to move, stretch, run free and uninhibited. But it is being confined, its movements restricted artificially against its nature, and it becomes, as a result, violent and rebellious. Krishnamurti describes it this way: "There is the desire to expand. And when society presses me in, drives me into a certain corner, I explode—which is again a revolt in order to expand. And when one lives in a small flat in a very crowded street and there is no open country to breathe in and no opportunity to go there, I become violent. The animals do this."[7]

Everybody wants to be more alive, to feel more alive, to thrive rather then merely live or survive. Psychobiologist Stanley Keleman writes, "Being more alive means being more sexual, more sensuous. To be more sexual is to broaden one's range of feeling and expressive action."[8] Eros, sexual energy, is life-force energy permeating all of creation and influencing our own creativity and ecstatic experiences.

Wild is sexual; we must become wild once again.

Wilderness is sexual. Jay Griffiths in *Wild* says, "[I]f you had to choose part of the human anatomy as an analogy for wilderness, you'd have to go for the loins—and we humans lose an acute and vital part of our sensuality when we ignore the wild world; the grinding of shoots thrusting up into the light; the hungry torsion as snake squeezes snake, birds flightily dipping as they twang an orgasm between wing beats, the delicate incipience of young sexuality in bud and blossom, lizards eyeing each other up for a darting lick of quick sex or basking with satisfied lust."[9]

When we exercise our senses, feeling into the world as we move through it, smelling, tasting, touching, hearing, we awaken the wild inside us. In *A Blue Fire,* James Hillman makes reference to this when he says, "When we move with senses acute, listening, watching, breathing in tune with the world about us, recognizing its priority and ourselves as guests, witnessing its 'God-givenness,' then we have made a wilderness area or moment. The restoration of the pristine stars in a fresh attitude toward what is, whatever and wherever it is."[10]

We take back the original meaning of the word *wyld;* that feeling that is out of the ordinary; that is fresh, unwearied and is present in old-growth forests, magnificent stone outcroppings, the sound of ocean waves cresting and crashing, and our sexual longings. We can be wild in any place or event, and when we do, we subvert the dominant culture's attempts to dwarf our senses and pigeonhole our feelings and colonize our minds. We come alive once again; we become the free, spiraling balls of energy that we were as young children, moving spontaneously and without hesitation through time and space.

Because the wild is dangerous to so many people's way of thinking (yes, eating the wild will change you), we are taught it must be repressed, suppressed, manicured, trimmed, tamed, cut, sprayed, fenced out, and controlled. The thing about fences is: when you fence something out, something else is being fenced in.

The soulful wild is a place where our soul can be reclaimed. Once you truly let yourself feel again after a few meals of the wild and sensuous Earth, a shift in consciousness penetrates the foundations of your beliefs and value systems—sometimes slowly and gently over time, other times an unexpected shift in principles and perceptions is thrust into your mind and all that you were before suddenly becomes pregnant with uncivilized thoughts unlike anything you've thought previously. That sudden shift is like that "aha!" moment that comes abruptly after you've been mulling over a difficult concept. One moment you're vexed by it, and the next you have clarity that rings pure like temple bells. When wyld inserts itself in our consciousness, a part of us that has been asleep is suddenly awakened. We begin to shift out of unconscious programming into conscious awareness.

> *You must get rid of what is commonly called knowledge of them [things seen in Nature]. Not a single scientific term or distinction is the least to the purpose for you would fain perceive something and you must approach the object totally unprejudiced. You must be aware that no thing is what you have taken it to be.*
>
> HENRY DAVID THOREAU,
> *TRUE HARVEST*

Our intuitions and perceptions become clear, and suddenly we are able to see why, for instance, we've had a particular, ongoing problem and why that person in our life has been such an irritation. You begin to see below the water's surface, beyond whatever sparkling reflections have been catching your gaze and distracting you. Moreover, the surface is no longer a satisfying place to be spending your brief life; a hunger for more begins to drive you now out of the familiar into deeper, darker waters. A willingness and need to explore and push the edges of conformity excites and animates your life.

And sometimes the shift comes with a painful, life-changing price, as it did with Aldo Leopold the day he killed a wolf.

In those days we had never heard of passing up a chance to kill a wolf. In a second we were pumping lead into the pack, but with more excitement than accuracy: how to aim a steep downhill shot is always confusing. When our rifles were empty, the old wolf was down, and a pup was dragging a leg into the impassable slide-rocks.

We reached the old wolf in time to watch a fierce green fire dying in her eyes. I realized then, and have known ever since, that there was something new to me in those eyes—something known only to her and to the mountain. I was young then and full of trigger-itch; I thought that because fewer wolves meant more deer, that no wolves would mean hunters' paradise. But after seeing the green fire die, I sensed that neither the wolf nor the mountain agreed with such a view.[11]

Many of us turn to writers and poets whose works were stimulated and inspirited while spending time in the forests, mountains, and deserts. They have taken into themselves some nourishment that kneads human souls and thus gives rise to the great works of the likes of Thoreau, Goethe, Leopold, Muir, Schauberger, and LaChapelle. They went into the wild to service an internal hunger and became servants to something outside and greater than themselves.

There are those of us who make a pilgrimage to a mountain, who need to feel the process of finding wilderness intensely in our bodies— legs pushing our weight up serpentine trails, lungs burning with the cold fire of clear, high air, skin flushing with the heat of exertion, as we ascend, laying this mile beneath our feet and then the next. Or we may go to the seashore for the spray of water as wave after wave is spent on stones. We may need the gentle, low, rhythmic tides on a sandy South Pacific shore. We choose places that fill a need, that match our psychological states or shake us out of them. We go to be stirred up, calmed down, soothed, inspired, renewed, healed. To make love, to be made love to, to be called beloved by Earth. Conversely, we may avoid places like deserts for their irrepressible ability to show us the desert that has for too long existed inside us. Taking the wild inside you, tasting the scent on your tongue, comingling your soul essence with the soul of Gaia, stirs primordial faculties, from groin to reptilian brain to conscious awareness, seducing the senses to shake off the stupor induced by the drugs called culture and materialism.

John Seed, the rainforest activist said, ". . . as the implications of evolution and ecology are internalized . . . we begin to identify with all life. . . . alienation subsides . . . 'I am protecting the rain forest' develops into 'I am part of the rain forest protecting myself. I am that part of the rain forest recently emerged into thinking.'"[12]

As your perceptions become acute and your seeing more clear, your sense of self grows more whole, sturdy, and potent. Your soul takes on larger dimensions, filling out, dropping baby fat, maturing and becoming sophisticated. You may even feel bigger, taller, taking up more space. You may find yourself changing the way you wear your clothes—tight-fitting jeans are replaced by garments that allow freedom of movement. Unwilling to be constrained, we choose clothes that are loose on our bodies, full of color, and outrageous. You may take on more affect in speech and behavior. Suddenly you notice your arms are moving spontaneously, your hands gesticulating. Your hips begin to loosen and sway, and there is an energy now, coming off your body, and your core scent has changed, becoming musky. You have more energy and improved memory. You shed the garments of civilization, and soon your favorite pair of shoes or your cool leather harness boots are squeezing and constricting your feet. You can wear those favorite shoes only occasionally now as your feet take on a hissing sort of dialect from walking naked between, up, over, and around the valleys and mountains of Gaia's bosom; feet skin touching Earth skin. And over time, we are able to bring life-giving water to our internal desert, transforming it into an oasis.

And speaking of shoes . . . The Mamas, or spiritual elders of the Tayrona living in the Sierra Nevada de Marta in Columbia, say shoes break the contact between people and Earth.[13] Walking barefoot in the forest or even around your home has psychological and physical benefits. It connects you immediately to the electrical energy of Earth, grounding you in your body, causing you to be more present. Life-force energy from Earth is directly transmitted through the soles of the feet, increasing awareness and energy. Walking barefoot reduces inflammation in the lower extremities, regulates thyroid function, and reduces stress, and since the bottoms of our feet are full of acupuncture points, the whole body is brought into alignment. Walking shoeless reduces the chances of sprains and deformed feet and toes, as well as strengthening the muscles in the feet and legs and increasing circulation. We are healthier physically, emotionally, and psychologically the more we move about sans shoes. In fact, there is no record of feet disorders before the Renaissance. The introduction of the elevated heel was a brilliant invention to depict wealth (Louis XIV had four-inch heels made for him) and to protect feet from the filth that plagued ancient Egypt and Rome. Butchers were known to wear heels to avoid the carcass debris that littered the floor.

Aside from their fashion and functional uses (keeps your feet in the stirrups), heels keep us off balance and insulate our naked feet from the sensual, erotic, wet, gritty, slippery muddy, warm, sandy, and rich soil of Earth.

A DICHOTOMY THAT DAMAGES

When the great crusade against sex and the body started in full blast with Plato, it was a crusade for "ideals," and for this "spiritual" knowledge in apartness. Sex is the great unifier. In its big, slower vibration it is the warmth of heart which makes people happy and together, in togetherness.

D. H. LAWRENCE,

"A PROPOS OF *LADY CHATTERLEY'S LOVER*"

Many spiritual traditions and religious practices have wrongly sought to separate the body and soul; the body is regarded as a place of denigration, an obstacle to enlightenment, while more value is placed on advancing and purifying the soul. Though we all seem to disagree on where exactly the soul resides in the body, or exactly what the soul is, it needs purifying whether or not it can be located.

Plato's philosophy was based on his theory of a soul divided into three components, reason, will, and appetite. He contended that one can identify the parts of the soul because they sometimes clash with one another. He regarded the body and soul as separate entities. As a dualist, he also posited an "unreal" world of the senses and physical processes, and a "real" world of ideal forms.[14] This way of viewing natural phenomena has had dire consequences.

Georg Feuerstein writes: "[Y]et how many spiritual seekers have struggled to realize truth, God or a higher consciousness by escaping what they called 'the prison of the body.' In treating the body as an enemy, that antagonist of the Spirit, they doomed themselves to experiences of an amputated God. They failed to see the body as part of the Great Mystery. We can learn from their mistake."[15] The body is the temple of the gods and the vehicle through which soul has life.

Bradford Keeney observes that "[c]elibacy makes no sense to a Bushman. 'You've got to be kidding! Are there really people who think that not having sex makes them closer to the gods? What god would want to hang around them? Maybe it's better if you don't go home. Your trick-ster gods sound boring because they don't know how to have a good time. Hang out with us and you'll learn that God loves sex!'"[16] The original cultures never had sexual hang-ups or phobias about touching. Keeney goes on to note that this mind-body schism is "a new development in the scheme of things, and it seems to have started as a word game. Mind got separated from body. Good was separated from evil. Mind married good, while body married evil. Thereafter, whenever mind experiences itself as inseparable from body, a sin of inappropriate union is declared. Being touched by God shifted to being heard by God. But God isn't listening to your words; God wants to be touched. The same is true for you, so go find someone to hug."[17]

I was between my fourteenth and sixteenth years. I was in a two-year love-hate relationship with Christianity and the Lutheran church I sporadi-cally attended a mile from our farm. There was something there that I was looking for, some need I had I thought could be met there. So many of the tenets and teachings were a source of rage for me, and still I returned hoping to find something to feed my unnamed hunger, which compelled me to attend. I didn't understand the reason for being born, for being dropped in this family in the middle of no-fucking-where.

Interesting to me was that the single most often misquoted passage from the book of Genesis is that human beings were "given dominion over all things." There was no room in the interpretation of the doctrines for Earth to be alive, aware, and sentient, yet that's how I experienced Earth. Everything, everyone, except human beings, was unfeeling and ignorant. It fell way short of answering how other life-forms were able to last and evolve for billions of years before the "superior" human species was created out of the genius of an oversixty, white, lonely, loving, upright, and vengeful god. Something was wrong with what I was being indoctrinated in.

Through the teachings of Christianity, only humans were created in the image of God, only humans have a soul. But prophetically it is written also in Genesis 9:2: "[T]he fear of you and the dread of you shall be upon every beast of the earth, and upon every fowl of the air, and upon all that moveth on the earth, and upon all the fishes of the sea; into your hands they are delivered." This is the passage from Genesis that is often underemphasized, the part that puts responsibility for caretaking the Earth in the hands of humans. It warns us that however we treat Earth and all that moves on Earth, we shall be treating ourselves for we are part of "all that moveth upon the Earth."

In whose image are the fishes, the seas, grains of sand, microbes, fungi, and snail made in? Why should human beings presume to think humans are the only species made in the image of God Earth-maker?

> *God Yahweh formed man out of the soil of the earth and blew into his nostrils the breath of life, and man became a living soul. And God Yahweh planted a garden in Eden in the east and placed the man therein . . . God Yahweh took the man and put him in the Garden of Eden to serve and preserve it.*
>
> DANIEL HILLEL,
> OUT OF THE EARTH

The word *animal* comes from the Latin *animalis,* meaning "having breath." Creator, Earth-maker breathed life into all beings. Can we extrapolate, then, that all animals are living souls, having breath? And further, *spirit* comes from the Latin *spiritus,* meaning "breath." All living things have a soul, and it is the spirit, the breath of life, that is given from the Great Spirit that animates and connects all living things. We all breathe the same breath, our inhale is that of the cosmic exhale. Each of us sit, lie, move, creep, crawl, live, die in the same matrix of spirit breath. When we feel *inspired,* we are filled, imbued with the spirit that moves through all things, and we are aroused to act, to do something with the inspiration. We know it is inspiration for it's as if we have been taken over by some benevolent force that insists we *do* something without a moment's hesitation.

It was in the middle of this time of my life that I would often ride my horse into the fields and open spaces behind our house. I loved riding my horse. It was one way I escaped the insanity of my family. I could breathe and smell the fresh air and think clearly without the contamination of our family psychosis.

I was indomitable and unconquerable with my legs wrapped around this magnificent, powerful animal, as mighty muscles, thighs, and shoulders moved and ass swayed beneath me with each stride. I became intoxicated with the primal scent of horse hair wet with sweat. And on one such day, as my horse was walking along with me on her back, the sun warm and low on the horizon on that late summer day, I was lingering deep in thought, as I often did when I was alone, when a peculiar feeling began to take over my senses. It touched the entirety of my body at once as if being bathed in it, a light touch at first, just light enough to get my attention. My skin began to flush and prickle, and I could feel the hairs on my arms and neck stand up. We walked slowly for a few more moments as the feeling got stronger and slid beneath my skin to my muscles, my bones, then each organ was infused with it; my blood took on its pattern until it settled into my bone marrow. I was utterly taken over by it, possessed by it. I stopped my horse. I was taken over by the potency of the feeling so much so it disabled me from movement. A sweet, unfamiliar exotic aroma filled my nostrils briefly. I became acutely aware of a presence near me. Slowly, and with effort, I turned in each direction fully expecting to see someone standing near me. I was surprised to see no one. I sat on my horse, still, and feeling this curious, unsettling phenomena.

From somewhere between my head and the space around me, not entirely inside me and not entirely outside me, I heard a voice. It wasn't my voice I heard; it was not any voice I recognized. It was strong and soothing, and in it I felt a deep sense of reverence and deep, abiding love. Like the sun on my skin, a unique warmth soothed my every cell. The words "I have given you all that you need" floated like ripe pollen finding ground upon my fertile, virgin consciousness. There was no doubt at the time that I had just heard the voice of God. Even now, decades later, I know it was the voice of God I heard that day, but it was not Yahweh, the standing, upright God of Christianity. My understanding of God is not a self-limiting concept, nor does it exempt me from taking personal responsibility as I'm waiting for the rapture. It is the God of nature, of Spirit; the One who weaves the matrix of life.

For thirty-five years, those words germinated, grew, composted, grew anew as I worked out various and possible meanings of it. I began initially to look outside myself, attempting to define at first what it was I needed. I had food, clothing, shelter, water, a dog, a horse, a farm, a family, schooling. I had a spiritual hunger; I needed food for that. I used drugs and alcohol in excess, attempting to understand the meanings of it. Later, I sought out teachers and ecstatic experiences until a realization that rang a brilliant tone of truth began slowly to emerge in my understanding. My body is the vehicle that enables me to have this human, incarnate, magnificent experience of being alive on Earth. Without a body, there are no senses, no feelings to get you to take notice, no feelings to follow, no anchor for the invisibles to touch you in their voiceless manner. Keeney writes "Your feelings must trigger the ropes to pull you in the right direction."[18] Feelings are our genius, our unique sensing apparatus that we use to find our way and follow what feels good and joyful. Feelings helps us know when we are in the presence of the Divine, the numinous, and the ecstatic. When we have a "funny" feeling, it informs us that something someplace inside is out of harmony. Feelings help us navigate life and the world around us and inside us. Without feelings we would be, what would we be . . . robots . . . a ship at sea with no compass or rudder.

The body is the vehicle for spirit and soul to have experiences, for them to evolve through a collective, intimate dance. Keleman says, "A person is not in or out of *touch* with his body. He *is* his body. We need to get rid of this crazy idea, 'I have a body.' It's the other way around. This is a fact we may not want to swallow, but the head is not the chief cook and bottle washer; the whole body is."[19]

Once you feel, and you must be in your body to feel, you are no body but yourself. No one can tell you what is truth and what is not; you feel it in your body. You feel truth in your body. Your body does not lie. It cannot lie. It doesn't know how to lie. And once you feel, behaviors are then invented out of imagination as a result of the feeling rather than an imitation or some archaic learned performance.

> *In my case Pilgrim's Progress consisted in my having to climb down a thousand ladders until I could reach out my hand to the little clod of earth that I am.*
>
> CARL JUNG

THE SENSING BODY

> *Sex is one of the nine reasons for reincarnation . . . the other eight don't count.*
>
> HENRY MILLER,
>
> BIG SUR AND ORANGES OF HIERONYMUS BOSCH

When I feel pain or stress, I feel it; I don't think pain or stress. Because I want to know and understand things, I trace the body feeling back to the first intimation of it, when the pain or stress were just hanging out on the periphery of my energy field before they became so engrained in my physical state, constricting muscles and causing one of my too-frequent tension headaches. I'm able to trace it back to a teeny, tiny, whispering voice and the beginnings of tension, which I recognize as irritation or a nagging feeling. Irritation begins like a breeze ruffling the surface of a still pond; it's just enough in the early stages to get me to pay attention, to notice that something is amiss and I need to tend to it, discover what it is and whether to do something about it or not.

One thing I hate most in my life is when my body is uncomfortable or restricted in some way, so I pay more attention to the early warning signs, those psychic pinches that, if unattended to, can throw me off my game. Paying attention to the subtlest messages sensitizes my nervous system to what and from where something is incoming, or if something is coming from my unconscious to the surface.

When the source of the feeling is coming from outside me, I feel it first in my body as the energy of someone's anger, or their fear touches on the electromagnetic field of my heart and causes an almost undetectable shudder as it continues on and penetrates my physical body. As fast as the speed of light, a psychological part of me feels it. If it's fear that is coming in, a deep part of me gets scared; I hold my breath and take care not to make sudden or large movements until whatever it is has passed or an older part of me takes care to reduce or redirect its impact one way or another.

We know when we are under stress because we feel it; our muscles tense up and get rigid. We know we are sick because we don't feel well. We buy just the right avocados and pineapples and melons by feeling their ripeness and sensing whether they are happy and alive. We choose activities and experiences that make us feel happy and good. We avoid as much as possible experiences that don't feel good. And it's the feeling of "doesn't feel good" that alerts us to look for something different to do.

We enjoy a cocktail or a glass of wine or a cold beer at the end of the day to unwind and relax after a stressful day at work. Sex feels good; it releases tension and stress. We feel close to another person, are held and loved, and often the afterglow can keep us going into the next day. We are hardwired to seek out what feels good, to repeatedly put ourselves in the company of good feelings.

Conditioning out of feeling begins early in life. Each time we tell a child that what she wants is bad for her, will rot her teeth and her mind, we are inserting messages that tell the child she doesn't know what's good for her, that her wants and needs are not trustworthy. When we dictate mealtimes rather than feeding on demand, we are sending messages that the feeling body is untrustworthy and not sophisticated enough to know what is best. Scheduled meals send messages that say natural hunger instincts are not important and they disrupt the orderly functioning of the family. We feel one thing in our body and hear contrary words coming to us from outside. Distrust of innate feelings, needs, and hungers are programmed into us by family, teachers, ministers, and friends who tell us "Don't be sad," "Don't be angry," "It's not time to eat yet," "You'll spoil your appetite," "Eat all your food," "Don't climb that tree," "Get over it," "Snap out of it," "Masturbation is bad," "Don't eat dirt."

*Our education from the start has taught us a certain range
of emotions, what to feel and what not to feel, and how to
feel the feelings we allow ourselves to feel. All the rest is just
non-existent.*

D. H. LAWRENCE,
"A PROPOS OF *LADY CHATTERLEY'S LOVER*"

From the first day of school, children are taught to sit still. The message is don't move, don't be noticed, don't feel (for if I feel, I'll have to move). We assume that children sitting still cause less disturbance in the classroom. But, there is more going on. In *Your Body Speaks Its Mind*, Keleman says, ". . . the stilling of the children's bodies induces individual patterns of alertness which enhance and sustain one another. The energy of each child's alertness can then be directed into forming the role of the ideal student."[20]

We have a spiritual imperative and responsibility to encourage ourselves and our children to feel, to trust in the innate wisdom of the body. Giving children time outdoors, in backyards, and in the forests around their homes, encourages self-confidence and trust in their growing intuition and natural instincts—things that cannot be learned in books or classrooms. We owe it to them to foster their innate instinct to bond with Earth in the most natural way inherent in them—play. They love finding secret spots or building forts where they are free to explore, imagine, and dream. They need contact with the real world around them and in their neighborhoods.

Children are naturally empathic with animals until some adult tells them that animals are dirty or that they have fleas and mites. We pass on our own fears of the outdoors, of ticks, Lyme disease, snakes, and falling from trees. By the time children reach six years of age and are in public school, they are afraid of their own shadows and of a little dirt. Trust in their instinctual movements toward wilderness, trust in their hungers and intuition are put in the bag of shadow.

We spend on average six hours[21] a day watching television or in front of a computer screen, on our iPods, with MP3 players, or with cell phones clamped to our heads like skull implants. We have instant messaging,

Skype messaging, text messaging, and social networks such as Facebook that give us the illusion of having deep, meaningful relationships. We no longer understand the distinction between friend and acquaintance or have real communication, real dialogue, as we become ever more super-ficial, our lives speeding up, hurling us toward death. Internet social net-works give the illusion of intimacy while we reduce ourselves to characters and caricatures. We become a data stream, links of superficial sound and data bites, like medical intake forms that tell a physician very little about the human being filling out the form.

After having thousands of images flit across our computer screens every day at an unimaginable speed, we then turn off the screens at some hour of the night for sleep and find ourselves in the midst of relative silence and a field of vision with no moving images. Everything suddenly is s l o w e d w a y d o w n. Then what do we do with ourselves? How do we sleep surrounded by silence? How do we sleep when our brain is pro-cessing all those images and information, our immune systems compro-mised by the nonstop bombardment of radiation from computer screens?

Our values and moral compasses were once formed from living in direct contact with the natural world and the world of invisibles and in tight-knit communities of cooperation and preservation. We understood the intrinsic, delicate balance of living in right relationship with all our relatives, not just upright two-leggeds but every created thing we could see and feel and sense and know.

We've created a world where our understanding of and relationship to the natural world is becoming squeezed into cubes and bites of informa-tion we can access from our homes, Blackberries, or iPads as we run from one mechanical place to the other. Nearly all we do is on the run; we eat on the run, talk on the run, try to keep relationships going on the run, have sex on the run. Slowing down is frightening, and we're not even cer-tain we know how to do it any longer. Jerry Mander says, "We hear people say that nature is boring, and it is clear why they say this. We don't know how to be with it. We are not slow enough."[22]

We seem unable to accept that we are part of Nature. If we could accept that fact, it would change our fundamental belief about ourselves; we'd realize that we are not special. We're simply an expression of Gaia, one species among approximately thirty million.

Being of the animal kingdom, human beings are not made to live on a diet of megabytes and gigabytes and artificial frequencies. We are at our best, calmest, and most creative, influential, self-confident, balanced, and healthy when we have regular time walking, sitting, hiking, and being in nature, especially wild ecosystems. Our brains and bodies evolved in the dynamic field of the natural world; it's there that we function at our optimum best physically, psychologically, intuitively, and spiritually. Our senses come alive when we are in natural and wild ecosystems; we are immersed in unusual sounds, interesting smells, and our bodies move differently across unpaved and uneven landscapes.

Denying our feelings, turning away from them because they are too painful or discomforting or we don't know what to do with them, desensitizes us to subtleties in feeling and the meanings they contain. We've been so conditioned to not feel. Lacking awareness of our feelings and letting them atrophy grows a kind of callus on our sensing body. If you've ever learned to play guitar, you know the experience of watching your fingertips get thick with layers of skin. Or have you ever had the experience of having Super Glue dry on your fingertips? Being taught at a young age that our feelings are not to be trusted or acted upon desensitizes our psyche in the same way that getting a little Super Glue on our fingertips dulls our sense of touch. Until the glue wears off, there is a numbness, a desensitization wherever it has dried. Feeling objects with those glue-muffled fingertips produces an odd sensation; feeling is there, but it is dull and distant, almost like a memory. A similar phenomenon occurs with our feelings over time. You sense something is there, but you can't quite put your finger on it. Emotions, which are not the same as feelings, get dumbed down as well, so much so that it takes focus of will to say what you feel. "I think . . . I feel . . . kinda . . . um . . . don't know . . . sort of . . . like, ah . . . oh, sad . . . I think I feel kind of sad."

When I work with clients and students, I often begin by getting them into their bodies. I had a student who was very intelligent and articulate, and when she talked, she was very animated. Her arms flew here and there, her eyes were often cast upward, and her chin tilted slightly upward as well. Her voice was high in her throat near her sinuses, and the authority of anything she had to say went drifting up and out of the room like a puff of smoke. She had interesting insights and valuable experiences to share, but when she talked from her head, it was difficult to take her seriously. She wasn't home to own her authenticity, her body of experiences.

I had her feel into her feet, without looking at them and then asked her to talk from her diaphragm. Her energy immediately and visibly shifted; her shoulders relaxed, her chin dropped, her cheeks flushed. She looked more present because she was more present; she was grounded in her body. Then I had her breathe through her heart and bring her breath all the way into her diaphragm. Her eyes grew a little larger and softer, and suddenly there was a beautiful, wise, mature ego state looking out of her eyes. She let go a long, deep sigh. When she spoke from that place, her voice came from deep in her belly (in the belly of Earth), as if the Earth herself were speaking. Through body presence, she brought an authority and aliveness to her life force and into the room. And when she spoke from that place, I noticed my own body shift in response to the power that was now there in the room. I felt her authority and the truth she was speaking. Once a person speaks from inside her own body, from her diaphragm, from her loins, there is sexual power attached to it that we call charisma. That is sexy.

Our sexual health and expression are woven into our hearts and our souls and are anchored through gravity and attraction in our body; the interplay of tension between Eros and Psyche. They touch and are touched by Earth and all beings who share this planet with us. To know we are touching and being touched, we must feel and be at home in our bodies.

Our bodies, our brains, every part of us was designed to be impressed upon by the natural world. We need immersion in the world of nature, the world of invisibles where *spiritus mundi* is easily and readily accessible. To come back to our sensing bodies, we need to return to the body the source of natural impressions, to have our souls imprinted with the visions of seeing butterflies alight on flowers in bloom, hear birdsong, drink from the deep well of direct knowledge that is found only in wild and natural ecosystems. But not just imprinted, our souls are taught, reshaped out of linear programming and technological programming into something more.

Simply living does not equate with being alive. In Hawaii there is a word for the energy or life force that activates all living beings and the elements and is true vitality—*mana*. Describing this force, Hawaiian musician Israel Kamakawiwoʻole says, "Mana is like an energy that you get. We believe we get ours from the elements first, the Earth, your sky, your ocean, your God, and all that is inside us. And when we open our mouth to speak, to sing, to play, that's what we let out."[23]

> *Freud and his psychoanalytic descendants are no doubt correct in their assessment that the search for ideal love— for that one perfect soul mate—is the futile wish of not-fully-developed selves. But it also seems true that the longing for a profound, all-consuming erotic connection (and the heightened state of awareness that goes with it) is in our very wiring. The yearning for fulfillment through love seems to be to our psychic structure what food and water are to our cells.*
>
> Barbara Graham,
> "The Future of Love," *Utne Reader*

The absence of experiential processes reinforces feelings of separation. It is not just another human being that we long to feel the touch of intimacy with. There is longing to feel a deep, innate, natural connection to the living Earth and all that we share our life with. There is a primordial need built into the human species for fenceless open country, for the musky, erotic smells of the forest floor, for the sounds of birds and insects, and for the sight of expansive vistas. In ancient and indigenous cultures, there was no separation, no divide between human beings and Earth. All was sacred, alive, intelligent, aware, and sensual. Plants, trees, stones, and the elements were part of daily relationships for food, medicine, and wisdom. Foragers of the Kalahari and aboriginal tribes in Australia are intimately connected to and have a deep sense of and relationship with the places they inhabit and hunt. They use song lines to connect and bind them to place and to non-human beings. As David Abram reports in the *Spell of the Sensuous,* "Language is inseparable from song and story, and the songs and stories, in turn, are inseparable from the shapes and features of the land.

The chanting of any part of a song cycle links the human singer to one of the animals or plants or powers within the landscape, to Crocodile Man or Pandanus Tree Woman or Thunderstorm Man—to whatever more-than-human being first chanted those verses as he or she wandered across the dreaming Earth. But it also binds the human singer to the land itself, to the specific hills, rocks, and streambeds that are the visible correlate of those sung stanzas."[24]

Far from our Western orientation of anthropocentrism, indigenous and aboriginal peoples tend more toward *Gaiacentrism*, if we must put a "centrism" label on the human/nonhuman relationship of those cultures. It is our anthropocentrism, the political philosophical mind-set that human beings are the center of all things, that is at the center of the separation. Human exceptionalism has various meanings in different contexts. To the ancient Athenians, the ability to reason distinguished humans from the natural world. For Christians, it has been spirit—the human spirit, the Holy Spirit, and the spiritual (Christian) life.

In modern times, human beings have created a Grand Canyon–size physical, emotional, and spiritual chasm that is growing deeper and taking us farther away from our bodies and Earth as holy places. Reclaiming the soul, our inherent, intuitive, instinctual nature, opens the door to remembering and reclaiming the body of Earth and our bodies as sacred, alive, aware, intelligent, sexual, and caring. The gravity of humility pulls us below superficiality, shedding our robes of grandiosity and anthropocentrism. Viewing ourselves as a superior species, for which we see the results of as we look around, has led us to the edge of the shaky precipice of becoming an endangered species. Dorion Sagan and Lynn Margulis postulate in *Dazzle Gradually* that the human mind is not as unique or special as we like to believe.

> Perhaps the greatest psychological stumbling block in the way of widespread scholarly acceptance of Gaia is the implicit shadow of doubt it throws over the concept of the uniqueness of humanity in nature. Gaia denies the sanctity of human attributes. If intricate planning, for instance can be mimicked by cunning arrays of sub-visible entities, what is so special about Homo sapiens and our most prized congenital possession, the human intellect? The Gaian

answer to this is probably that nothing is so very special about the human species or mind. Indeed, recent research points suggestively to the possibility that the physical attributes and capacities of the brain may be a special case of symbiosis among modified bacteria.[25]

Focusing on the deep ecology of Earth and our own deep ecology begins to uproot archaic beliefs and values that prevent us from living an inhabited, authentic life. Working directly with the intelligence of plants, with all the intelligence and graceful beauty of our bodies and through ceremonies, we begin to heal and reclaim the sacredness of Earth, our earthly sexuality, and the bond that has been severed.

How do we go about reclaiming an intimate connection with the wild Earth, with a stone, a tree, or the animals that live with us? We begin by understanding that connection is a feeling thing, not a thinking thing. Secondly, the mind cannot feel; the mind analyzes and categorizes data, and it interprets feelings. Our feeling sense is the instrument of true knowing. Whether we are creating intimacy with our lover, our children, our friends, or other animals or beings, intimacy begins by teaching yourself to see, to perceive, and to feel as we each did naturally as infants and young children.

7

Choosing Another Way

The earth does not belong to man; man belongs to the earth. All things are connected like the blood which unites one family. Man does not weave the web of life; he is merely a strand in it. Whatever he does to the web, he does to himself.

CHIEF SEATTLE,
LETTER TO ALL, 1854

The language of the body is the key that can unlock the soul.

KONSTANTIN STANISLAVSKY

If you understand what is being said and live it then you will be in a totally different world. But if you don't live it, daily, then you will just be living as you are. That's all.

J. KRISHNAMURTI

None of us ever truly forgets the nurturing, warm comfort of the womb. We spend our lives trying to re-create that feeling of being held and protected from real or imagined demons and threats. We yearn to be fed all the food that sustains our three bodies. Nor do we forget the pain of individuation, of leaving Mother and home, peers, and social circles. Individuation causes a pain of separation, and we seek throughout our lives to have the separation and the resulting loneliness filled with meaningful relationships. We seek to fill our need to have purpose and significance in our work and meaning in our lives. If we succeed in finding those things, they hold little meaning without someone to share them with.

This desire for intimacy with lovers and friends, to feel that we are not alone in the Universe, is innate in each of us. I do still feel lonely at times, but never alone. If I feel alone, it's simply because I've shut myself down and have not called on the powers of the Universe. They never abandon us; it's we who take ourselves away from them.

There is a cost, however, in choosing to do and be something different. A willingness to give up whatever the gods ask of you is integral to having a new life. Sometimes their asking is a demand.

Friends may drop away, go away emotionally, or start a fight to create distance when the fingers of intimacy reach beyond their comfort level. Maybe you feel a need to move, one that painfully takes you away from children and grandchildren, the geography that shaped you during your formative years, and all that is familiar.

One of my lovers told me he was afraid of me. Another said that he didn't know what to do with me. Those statements feel funny, don't they? They meant that I was different; I wanted things they did not. They sensed a thing in me that set me apart from them, and it was that thing that I followed even as I left the relationships and moved 1,100 miles away from my granddaughters and the Upper Mississippi River Valley. Regrettably, at the time I was still young in my learning and becoming aware. I did not know what to do with those statements. I felt alienated and alone in my need. I didn't have the skills then to talk about it, to open up a dialogue to begin to bring the other into my world. What I was certain of then, and still am, is that they did not want the discomfort that depth of intimacy brings. One of my lovers had a habit of losing his cell phone when intimacy began to stretch beyond his comfort level. I had my own habit of distancing: I'd start a fight. My family fought; it's what I know how to do. It's what I did when I was afraid. Fights release pressure that's been building from too much or too little intimacy, not getting our needs met. The aftermath creates space and time. Berne named this game uproar. It's a dance of getting close, fighting, creating distance, getting closer, fighting. Nothing was ever resolved. We didn't have the skill or willingness to analyze what had happened, why it happened, or what to do differently to get to the next level, to deepen our relationship. We painfully maintained the status quo. I painfully left the relationships.

These relationships could have grown, become more intimate, if I had been able to say: "When you lose your cell phone I feel abandoned and hurt. I get afraid that you will go away forever, so I do what I know how to do and that is argue." He could have said: "I've always run away, that's why I chose a career that kept me moving for long periods of time." Or, "You're really strong in yourself and I get afraid that I am going to be a disappointment to you so I go away." Willingness to self-examine to root out the source of the behavior and willingness to apologize, and mean it, are vital to a healthy relationship.

It is important to know what you need in a relationship. Is the person able to give you those things, meet your needs? Is he able and willing to go to the places you need him to go to? If not, you're headed for a heartbreak or drama or both. Are you willing to compromise, take what you can get, and still maintain integrity with yourself?

Filling a role for another person that is not the truth of you betrays who you are, your authentic self, and creates a wound in the child of you. The wound that is created takes significant work to mend. Your child self feels you have abandoned her needs, put her back in a bag, and sent the message that it is not acceptable for her to be out in the world. The trust the two of you had will be ruined, and that is difficult to repair. It can be mended over time, when she sees that you will fight for her right and need to be alive and have a life with you. This is one of the basic, most necessary aspects to healing old wounds. Apologize, negotiate, and hear her voice, listen to her needs and wants. Trust can be mended.

When it comes to the wholeness of the relationship or the wholeness of self, fight for wholeness of self first. You are your primary relationship, and wholeness in yourself is your primary responsibility. You cannot have a healthy relationship with other people or any aspect of Gaia if you have no internal integrity. The need for rigorous self-examination is of utmost importance. Being honorable with yourself leads to becoming honorable in other relationships. Intimacy begins with being intimate with yourself, all parts of you, and, most especially, your deep self. Self-examination—being attentive to the voices inside, articulating your needs, finding ways to get them met, speaking on behalf of your child—is ecological reclamation of the soul. This work is, in reality, doing your own soul retrieval. It's simply accessing and integrating parts of you that have been marginalized and put, as Robert Bly writes, "in the long bag of shadow." The work is to reclaim the child without destroying the child. Thomas Patrick Malone writes about the importance of the unconscious in establishing intimacy.

"Unconscious" is not really a useful or descriptive word. It simply means "that which is not conscious," which really tells us nothing about what it *is*. The negative term belies the power of the concept. Perhaps "unconscious" should be renamed the "intimator," the natural connector, the natural spirit, the nexus, or perhaps, in Paul Tillich's phrase, the "ground substance." Whatever it is, it is a universal natural constant, not an absence of something else. Movement into the unconscious while you are awake is intimacy. Without the unconscious, we cannot have intimacy, only knowledge. Only in the intimate, unconscious experience can we know our true ecology, this is the intimate self.[1]

HEALING OURSELVES, HEALING EARTH

After I left therapy and counseling, I became captivated with indigenous teachings at about the same time I began working more fully with plant medicines. Something powerful tugged at my heart and mind, something familiar and resonant. I went from one workshop and intensive to another, gathering pieces that worked for me, inspired me, and fueled me until the next one. But always I had a feeling that something important and integral to where I wanted to go was missing. Finally, I heard a teacher speak about the spirit of plants and how to work with them beyond the physical. I wrote to him, and the following year I flew out to spend a weeklong intensive. It was my introduction to the work that has shaped my life and, eventually, this book.

During that week, the six of us were introduced to the exercises presented in the following pages. I hated the exercises at first and didn't really believe in them. The last thing I wanted to do was fucking inner child work. I had gotten so sick of hearing about "my inner child" from my sister I wanted to projectile vomit on her if I heard it one more time. I went into the work kicking and screaming. But like other therapies and workshops, my bottom line was, "Well, hell, I've traveled all this distance and paid all this money, I'm going to get my money's worth." I would take all the teachings inside me and do what I could with them later. If they stuck and felt right, I'd keep working with them to more or less degrees. If not, they got shit canned.

Here I was, in a small room with just five other people, strangers at that. Intimate? Hell, yes. It was uncomfortable, vulnerable, and emotional. I did the exercises, spent the week giving my all to it, and flew home. I continued to do the work half-heartedly for a few years until I began to see and experience the value of it and the changes I was making—deep, lasting changes. My intuition and senses became sharper, my thinking quicker. My ability to analyze interactions became more elegant. I felt more confident, self-assured, and aware. After some years, it went from being second nature to first; in a healthy family environment, it could have been first to begin with. I can't imagine doing anything different again. It would be impossible to do anything different.

I teach it to my students and apprentices and some clients. It's astonishing to see the changes it makes in people, instantaneously. The goal is to integrate it, let the work change you, take you on, shape the truth of who you are, and bring you into sexual loving. Ultimately, you become the author of your life through this practice. And it does take practice.

Much of our current dysfunction, lassitude, and discomposure is the result of and can be attributed to the loss of our connection with Nature, with old-growth forests, wild streams, and mountains. And it is the result of the loss of our connection with our own nature, our sexual nature, and our bodies—that sensate, sensing organ of perception. Will Johnson talks about this when he says, "By losing touch with the energies and sensations inside our bodies, we've severed our connection to the greater world of nature of which we're so intimately a part. The domain of union that spiritual seekers strive to contact is not some kind of exotic or esoteric condition. It is our simplest and most natural state; but we need to be here, fully in our bodies, and we need to heal our alienation from nature, both within and without, in order to experience it.[2]

The more we take ourselves out of the ecosystem, distance ourselves from Nature, and from our own nature, the more unstable we and our culture become. If some part is cut off, or alienated from the whole, it is no longer whole. When our sexuality is cut off from the body of Earth sexuality, we are unable to function as whole beings; one part does not contain all the parts of the whole. Earth is unable to function and produce as a healthy organism because our relationship is dangerously out of balance. If we are going to live on Earth, then shall we be alive and *live* on Earth? As long as we live on Earth, we need to be whole; a complete, fully functioning whole.

Many people and environmental groups insist Earth needs our help in healing. What Earth needs from us upright two-leggeds, if anything, is for us to be whole, to own every part of what it means to be part of the biota. That means the feeling aspect of the human species. And sex is a feeling thing. Sexuality, sensuousness, erotica are feeling things; when we allow ourselves to feel, we feel more alive, ensouled. It is a cruel disconnect to deny our innate feeling function. We are sensate beings. We cannot live healthfully denying our feelings.

If human beings didn't exist on Earth, all species, all life on Earth would do remarkably well without us. How would we do without other species? Where would we get our inspiration, our medicines? Where would we get our air? Our food? Our houses? We could not live at all.

Feelings are not socially constructed; that is, we were feeling the world before we began to think. While we were in our mother's womb, we could feel if we were loved and wanted, or not. Thinking our way through life without feeling cuts off part of our innate intelligence. Our imaginations and feelings have been stifled and subdued. Let's bring them out into the world, shall we? Set them free in the world, let their fingers reach out and touch the other, out there, and watch what adventures rise up to meet you.

> *If I spent enough time with the tiniest creature—*
> *even a caterpillar—*
> *I would never have to prepare a sermon. So full of God*
> *is every creature.*
>
> MEISTER ECKHART

RECLAIMING THE BODY'S SENSING:
THE HEART OF THE MATTER

Most of us are more or less aware of invisible energy fields. We feel it most when someone walks up to meet us. There comes a certain point at which, as he gets closer in physical proximity, you begin to get a little uncomfortable, when you feel he is now "in your space." You feel a little invaded; he is too close, and it's a discomforting feeling. You may even pull back a bit, stepping out of and away from that space. Often when someone, especially someone we don't know, gets too close, we stop breathing a bit. Once a "safe" distance has been reestablished, we can breathe normally again.

The ancients knew that the organ of perception is the heart. It is through the heart that we are connected to things by means of the senses. Apprehending images is the role of the heart. James Hillman says, "But the heart's way of perceiving is both a sensing and an imagining: to sense penetratingly we must imagine, and to imagine accurately we must sense."[3]

With each beating of our heart, electrical and magnetic energy is created, and it radiates from our body as the electromagnetic field of the heart. There has been much scientific evidence of this over the past fifteen years. Stephen Buhner writes that the "electromagnetic field that the heart produces is some five thousand times more powerful than that created by the brain."[4] The field of energy that is emitted is measurable with the use of magnetic field meters and is strongest in most people at the surface of the body to about eighteen inches from the body. Even the most sensitive electromagnetic measuring instruments can still detect the field up to ten feet from the body. Being an electromagnetic field, there is no way to determine just how far the heart's electromagnetic field actually extends or whether there are limits to it.

Everything emits a field of energy. What that means is that we are literally swimming in fields of electromagnetic energy. These fields of energy are transmitting meanings to us via our own heart field. The heart perceives the transmission and immediately images appear on the screen of our vision. The soul of the world, the soul of our lover, is not perceived if we are unconscious to our heart as a sensing organ. Keeping the heart in the reductionistic model as a pumping mechanism dooms us to a life of unconsciousness. It's important to begin to work consciously with the energy fields and, more importantly, with the heart as an organ of perception and imagining.

When we are in the depths of sacred sex and sexual loving, we are in an ocean of senses, images, and meanings. These images and meanings are communications that flow between two lovers, between human beings and Earth. Because everything in Nature gives off electromagnetic frequencies and Nature is having sex all the time, the sexual energy of Earth is part of the sea of communications, the linguistic medium and meanings we live in every day.

Let's begin to play and work with the heart field that each of us possesses.

ஓ EXERCISE ஓ
Expanding the Heart Field

Get comfortable in a cozy chair, feet on the floor, and take some deep, relaxing breaths. Now, bring your awareness into the area of your heart. Let your breathing move into your heart, as if you are breathing through your heart. In the beginning, it may feel a little tingly in that area, which is a good indication that you're there. If you don't feel it the first time, don't panic, just keep breathing through your heart. You're using a new sensing awareness, one that has been dulled through a lifetime of atrophy. When you feel that you can hold your attention in your heart, stand up and notice how you feel. Do you feel more present, grounded in yourself? Notice that your peripheral vision is expanded; that is, as you look straight ahead, you can see things to your far left and far right. With practice, you'll be able to feel your awareness move into different parts of your body.

Take a walk outside and find a tree that captures your attention. Sit down beside it and take a few deep breaths, relaxing more fully with each one. Let your eyes become soft focused on the tree you've chosen. Notice everything about it: its colors, shapes, textures. Now, ask yourself, "How does it feel?" What's the first thing that comes to you? Where do you feel it in your body? Are there any sensations, images, words that accompany the feeling? Sit with the feeling for a moment.

Stand up and walk away from the tree about twenty feet. It's helpful to pull your shoulders back and hold your arms straight out at your sides. When you do this, you may feel vulnerable and exposed. You are, that's why many of us become habituated to rounding our shoulders and slouching so we feel that our chests, our hearts, are protected. It's also a way to feel less noticeable. Pulling your shoulders back and up really opens up the heart and lungs and can release emotions we've held there. As you hold your shoulders back, with your heart open, slowly begin to walk toward the tree with your heart field extended. Pay particular attention to the moment your heart field and the "heart field" of the tree touch. This is nonphysical kinesthetic touching; touching with the invisible, nonphysical field of the heart. Pause there for a moment and notice how you feel to be touched this way. Continue on toward the tree, noting if the field grows in potency as you move closer to it.

Now, ask your Child to come and sit with you. As you keep your eyes soft focused, ask your Child to tell you everything about this tree. She is the one who has direct access to everything she comes in contact with and to the world trees live in. She knows how to talk with them. Notice, as well, any feelings or emotions in your body. How do you feel doing this?

Next, ask your Infant to be with you and hold her in your arms or on your lap. Infants have no language, but they perceive the world directly. Notice everything your Infant does. If you need to, ask your Child if she would translate for you. Children often translate for preverbal infants; they understand that language. Whatever movements, faces, or changes in color the Infant makes are all communications to you about the tree and its medicine or teachings or power.

It's helpful to keep a journal of your experiences, your "readings." Just when you think you're not becoming more sensitive, you can compare earlier entries and see how much more keen your perceptions are getting.

You can do this with anything, but trees are so generous, have potent energy fields, and love to play this way. You may find if you do this with trees of various ages, saplings to very old trees, and of different species, that each has a very different feeling to it. Everything in Nature has it own intelligence, sexuality, and personality, and each moves through ego states just as human beings do. Some trees are sexier than others, just like humans.

There will come a time when you suddenly realize that this way of feeling and seeing has become a part of how you move in the world. You no longer have to think about it; it just is, you are. Occasionally you'll notice that you are moving too fast, getting wrapped up in and consumed by some mundane event or deadline, and a soft voice inside will whisper to you or somehow make noise or a movement to remind you that you know how to feel better, different, more present, and you'll just make the shift then, in that moment, to breathing through your heart. Once you do that, you'll be in your body again, aware of your feet and surroundings, hearing birdsong and wind.

In the beginning, you will want to stop soon after you start as it can be unsettling. It just takes practice. You are using sight and sensory feeling that has been malnourished. It's never been completely gone you know. We use this every time we walk into a room or walk in the forest or talk with a friend on the phone. There are immediate psychic "hits" we get, but we have learned to ignore them, to let them stay below conscious awareness. With practice and patience with yourself, you will be able to understand just what those hits mean. You'll begin to decipher the meanings in them.

I am the wind that breathes upon the sea,

I am the wave on the ocean,

I am the murmur of leaves rustling,

I am the rays of the sun,

I am the beam of the moon and the stars,

I am the power of the trees growing,

I am the bud breaking into blossom,

I am the movement of the salmon swimming,

I am the courage of the wild boar fighting,

I am the speed of the stag running,

I am the speed of the stag running,

I am the strength of the ox pulling the plough,
I am the size of the mighty oak,
And I am the thoughts of all people
Who praise my beauty and grace.

THE BLACK BOOK OF CARMARTHEN

EXPERIENCING THE INTERWORLD

You will be astonished to find what happens when you comingle your attention, seeing, and feeling with another living thing in nature. Repeatedly, I feel the thing I'm gazing at in this way responding. They are as equally responsive to this touch, to this silent communication, as we are hungry for it. It is their adventure too, you know. They need us to be part of their life experience. When I sit with a plant and ask it for its body to make medicine and then administer the medicine to myself or to a client, the plants are able to do their work in the world. We have an obligation to do this work, to reclaim our place in the scheme of the natural, wild Earth and the place we call home.

One fine day, without expectation, something from nature touches you back. You feel a "hi" as you walk by the plant. The blue boulders shaped and softened by water spiraling through the canyon touch you like a lover and ask you to lay naked on their cool bodies. Walking through my house, I feel the plants communicating their thirst and hunger, that it's time for watering and feeding.

You'll be walking along, and suddenly a tree will reach out and touch you. Maybe it's not even a tree in your field of vision, but you know that what is touching you is a tree. As you are touched by the invisible energy of that tree, a rapid series of things happens without you being aware of it. Some invisible part of the tree touches an invisible part of you, and a memory, recognition, and perhaps even a picture is formed in your mind's eye, and you see the tree you've sat with and talked to and wrapped your arms around. All of the feelings and experiences of being with that tree flood your entire being at lightning speed.

One day, you decide to take an alternate route that bypasses the tree by a hill and dale. You feel the touch of something, and you know in your most earnest self that it is that tree, not just any tree in the park. And something inside switches on automatically, a subconscious decision is made, as if some large hand reached out from the Universe to pivot your body, and you turn, change your direction and plans, and make tracks to that tree. The touch grows in strength and the pull on you stronger, more insistent, and you pick up your pace, and ah, there she is, a magnificent, large, old red oak. As you approach the tree, you feel her move inside you. Her strength touches a primordial and infantile part of you, and tears of reunion and more fall out the corners of your eyes for that love is touching places inside you that need this medicine, medicine you didn't know you needed until it finds a resting place inside, and it's there inside you now because you've been sitting with this tree, getting to know it. Unbeknownst to you, it was getting to know you, see you, all of you, what you have, who you are, and what you need to be whole or to do your work in the world. And for the love of sharing this way, of going to the tree with childlike curiosity, a bond of intimacy was formed, and the tree reciprocated by touching you back. As you feel this awe and wonder overtake you, you say thank you, and you raise your face to the sky and say, "Yes, I want more of this in my life." You affirm the experience and anchor it in this moment by saying yes and thank you out loud.

This is what an intimate meeting at the interworld between the human world and the world of trees feels like. I was touched by something invisible, yet palpable, and of the ground I stood on beneath that great, sheltering canopy. The mythic power of trees shows up in cultures the world over; the Bodhi Tree, the Tree of Life, the tree that connects the underworld of legend to the upper world of the gods. And we humans are in the middle of those worlds, as they pass through us, calling us to take our place in holding the balance between worlds, to hold the balance of human and nonhuman, between caretaking and dominion. We are not smart enough to walk this world without the intermediary help of those who abide in the other worlds. We pass by, casually taking in the scenery, but do we stop to acknowledge the ancient voices whispering to us as leaves rustle on a wind-less day?

As Michael Perlman says, "The trees are psychological presences that move the soul—sometimes to right them, sometimes to cut them down, always to somehow imagine them. So it is misleading to speak of 'animism,' or the projection of human qualities onto trees. To speak of 'powerful trees' means addressing the ways in which trees animate the human."[5] Nature is ensouled, filled with an aliveness, intelligence, and consciousness. That knowledge has never left us; it's just been buried deep in our subconscious under layers of false information and schooling, religion, the work of putting food on the table, and unsupportive family scripts. We live in a culture that puts very little value on living an inhabited life. And the practice of seeing and feeling in this way is the root of living an inhabited life, a life of purpose directed by soul. It is the beginning of interbeingness, of mutually weaving your being with another. Doing this with parts of Nature starts the process of growing intercommunities. You are engaging in an ecological reclamation that our ancestors never forgot or buried. It is a simple wisdom addressing the heart and of recognizing our kinship with all of creation. And it is paramount to our survival as a species and to the survival of Earth as we know her.

According to William Blake, the move to abandon the polytheistic animism of antiquity, what was at the time seen and experienced through the lens of spiritual perception, came about when a system was formed that "enslaved the vulgar by attempting to realize or abstract the mental deities from their objects: thus began priesthood."[6] In other words, Ralph Metzner extrapolates, "the loss of direct perceptual communion with the spirits of nature was brought about by a political move—the institution of priesthoods as intermediaries between the human and the divine."[7]

Right now, where you're sitting, look around you; what is the part of Earth that is nearest to you? Some people will get a confused look on their face and uncomfortably look around the room. Perhaps it's the clay pot on the bookshelf? The potted plant sitting on the windowsill? The wood stacked neatly near the fireplace? Maybe it's the beam in the ceiling? These are parts of Earth. But, did you touch your own skin, your own sweet face? That is the part of Mother Earth that is nearest to you. It doesn't get any closer or any more intimate. Touching our own skin and realizing that we are able to do so because we are Earth; we are the pulsing, moving, sweating, shitting, crying, laughing red-blooded, breath of air, fire of digestion and passion, and bones of long dead human, plant, and animal ancestors. Each of us is a microcosm of the macrocosm. Everything that makes up Earth makes up us; we are made of the same substances.

We are all made up of the soil, rocks, minerals, plants, air, water, and animals that share Earth with us. It's an intimate thing to take into our bodies the bones of our ancestors whose bodies have become part of Earth in the plants and animals we eat and the water we drink. Because of this, we have an evolutionary connection to everything that has been created.

Now, touch your hand to your cheek and hold it there for a moment knowing that you are the result of billions of years of evolution. How do you feel?

Gaia, Earth, breathes, reproduces, composts all manner of waste—physical, psychological, and emotional. We breathe oxygen created by plants' respiration. The water we drink sustains the water and electrical systems in our bodies. Going barefoot grounds us into our bodies. When we wear rubber soles on our feet, we are separated, insulated from the electromagnetic field of Earth. As soon as we kick off our shoes and walk barefoot on Earth, we are instantly grounded in ourselves and to Earth. It resets our circadian rhythms, mineralizes our bodies, and reduces inflammation in the lower extremities. The negative charge from Earth through our feet dissolves calcium buildup from positive charges in tumors, heart, kidneys, and gallbladder.

> *When we look at the world around us, we find that we are not thrown into chaos and randomness but are part of the great order, a grand symphony of life. Every molecule in our body was once a part of previous bodies—living or non-living—and will be part of future bodies. In this sense, our body will not die but will live on, again and again, because life lives on. Moreover, we share not only life's molecules, but also its basic principles of organization with the rest of the living world. And since our mind, too, is embodied, our concepts and metaphors are embedded in the web of life together with our bodies and brains. Indeed, we belong to the universe, we are at home in it, and this experience of belonging can make our lives profoundly meaningful.*
>
> FRITJOF CAPRA,
> "IS THERE ROOM FOR SPIRIT IN SCIENCE?"

With each turning of the seasons, we innately feel it in our bodies. As spring begins its stirrings from deep in the heart of Earth, we feel a renewed sense of hope, our energies rise with each young plant that slowly emerges from the warming ground. As warm spring winds cleanse the air of winter, we tend to do our own spring-cleaning of our homes and bodies. We change our diets to eat lighter foods, such as fresh spring greens, and we may be reinspired to start walking or running again. When we feel the first hint of fall in the air, we gather wood, store food, seal windows, and weatherproof our homes. The hunter-gatherer still lives in our DNA; it knows how to live with each changing season. We are influenced deeply by the cycles of Earth, the moon, the sun, thunderstorms, winds, and wild places. Inextricably woven into our DNA is the DNA of Earth and all life-forms that have lived and died.

Think how often we use images of nature to describe our sexual experiences, our orgasms? Try to describe these without metaphors from nature. It can be done, I suppose, but our natural inclination is to reach for the elements and raw elemental power to relate our experiences. Just think of Carole King's "I feel the earth move under my feet," or Barry White's "It may be winter outside (but in my heart it's spring)."

> *People like you and I, though mortal of course like everyone*
> *else, do not grow old no matter how long we live . . . for we*
> *never cease to stand like curious children before the great*
> *mystery into which we were born.*
>
> ALBERT EINSTEIN

Conversations between our bodies, the invisible field of energy we emanate and are immersed in, and the things and people we surround ourselves with are happening all the time. It doesn't stop; there are just gaps between words, sentences. Even the gaps, the rests, the pauses are rich in meanings and feelings.

> *Men of earlier times do not as yet separate their own soul*
> *experience from the life of nature. They do not feel that*
> *they stand as a special entity beside nature. They experience*

themselves in nature as they experience lightning and thunder in it, the drifting of clouds, the course of the stars or the growth of plants. What moves man's hand on his own body, what places his foot on the ground and makes him walk, for the prehistoric man, belongs to the same sphere of world forces that also causes lightning, cloud formations and all other external events.

RUDOLF STEINER,
THE RIDDLES OF PHILOSOPHY

I have lost, as I have said, some sense of myself. I no longer require as much. And though I am hopeful of recovery, an adjustment as smooth as the way the river lies against the earth at this point, this is no longer the issue with me. I am more interested in this: from above, to a hawk, the bend must appear only natural and I for the moment inseparably a part, like salmon or a flower. I cannot say well enough how this single perception has dismantled my loneliness.

BARRY HOLSTUN LOPEZ,
RIVER NOTES

❧ EXERCISE ❧
Heart Field Practice

Bring your breathing awareness to the area of your heart as you did earlier. Notice your peripheral vision. This immediately drops your sensory feeling into your heart, the organ of perception and communication. Physiologically, it is the fastest way to change your heart rate, breathing, and blood pressure, and it changes the cascade of stress hormones to healing hormones.

Choose some object to look at. As much as possible, stop thinking and simply feel, simply see. If thoughts try to lure you to an unresolved dilemma, return to looking and feeling. Notice everything about the thing you are looking at. How does it feel? Is it mad, sad, happy, scared, lonely? Do you like it? Do you like one part of it more than another? Can you articulate why? Can you see the hands that made it? How did they feel about making it? When we do this with anything, the touch of our heart field and caring begins to slowly awaken the sleeping spirit of the thing. Some things take longer than others to awaken.

Keep your heart wrapped around it. If you have a fondness or appreciation for this thing, you can send that to it. As soon as you do this, the electromagnetic field of the thing you are gazing at and the electromagnetic field of your heart begin to merge. Stay with this, keep feeling.

Before you know it, the thing you are seeing will begin to alter ever so slightly revealing itself to you in response to your heart. Its history, its medicine, its maker, its needs, if any, will appear on the screen of your vision, and you will feel it in your body. Notice everything that is happening; how you feel, where you feel it in your body, how your breathing is, how your heart feels. Pay attention to any attempt to censor or discount the information that comes to you in any part of you. This is how the thing is communicating to you, through your body. The thing you are seeing and you become intertwined, and the separation, the space between you and the object, has become filled with directed meanings. This is the ecstatic path toward revisioning and living an ensouled life. This is our birthright, and it belongs to everyone.

When my partner and I were building our house, each tile, stone, artwork, board, and beam that was brought in was worked with in this way until we could feel the spirit of it begin to awaken and come into the room. We prayed with, talked to, and brought Eros into each piece until everything in our home became alive, our home ensouled. In anything you undertake, you can direct the flow of heart into it.

> *This form of wisdom will enable the physician to discern the Unity of Nature and to recognize man as a faithful copy of the great Universe, governed by the same laws and expressing them in his own being. As this is a meta-physical truth, every physician must be also a philosopher. And as*

*true wisdom comes from within, the physician must posses
the faculty of intuition, the handmaiden of self-reliance.
Therefore the true physician is one who does his own
thinking and is not satisfied merely to repeat the thoughts
of others. As intuition and self-reliance are developed in the
physician, the secret doors of Nature will open to him.*

PARACELSUS

ᏒᎧ EXERCISE ᏒᎧ
Expanding the Heart Field with Your Lover

Ask your lover to sit with you so that you are facing each other. Breathe through your heart for a few moments. Release any tension you feel in your body. Feel your love for him. Let yourself be filled up with all the love you have inside for your partner. Keep feeling the love you have for him. Hold it there, allow it to grow and expand; reach out with it from your body to touch his. Allow your love to move inside him, gently, as far as he will allow it to. Notice where it stops. Notice how his body shifts, his breathing alters. Does it speed up or slow down? Does he sigh? When love touches deep inside, there is a sigh of acknowledgment, a deep sigh similar to when an infant nurses and has been taking in milk and love from the mother. The love you are giving and he is receiving is a specific kind of food, a kind that we all need. With each deep sigh, love goes in deeper feeding and nourishing his body and soul. There is a point when the deep part of him becomes satiated, and there is that deep, satisfied sigh and often a little quiver will accompany it as he relaxes into receiving your love.

Now, let your love wrap around him and hold it there gently. Nothing to force here, you're just allowing. Notice whatever comes to you without censoring. Notice whatever feelings you have. You may see parts of him you hadn't seen before, discover new things you love about him. You may find yourself falling in love again and deeper still, becoming entranced and dreamy. And you may see and know things about yourself you hadn't before now. You may have stood before your lover with no clothes on, but has he seen you naked? There are many ways to be naked before your loved one in the moments of revelation. The energies of our souls transmit meanings in the invisible force field that is created when heart meets heart.

Now move to more specific areas of his body. Look at his hands and touch one of them with your heart field. How does it feel? How does it look? Is it happy, sad, mad? Does it have significant male or female energy in it? Now do the same thing with his other hand. How does it feel? You may find that assumptions you had are not true and that possibly you have never really looked at his hands this way, with the gaze of your heart, before. Do the same thing with each of his feet. Hold each foot in your hands as you do this, feeling each one, loving each one. Yes, now, you hold his penis in your hand, send your heart field, your love, your caring there. How does it feel? How do you feel seeing him this way? How does his member respond to this kind of intimate touching?

As you do this over time, you will notice the energy in each part of his body changes in response to your love. Love infused with intimacy and heart changes everything it touches. Each part of him will become more alive, ensouled; the intelligence that is there will wake up and become part of your lovemaking and soon, a marvelous conversation begins between your bodies.

My thighs were the ugliest part of my body. I didn't like them and tried to change their shape over the years, and I did. But changing the shape of them outwardly never changed the feeling of them. They didn't feel like my thighs; I didn't recognize them. I was dissociated from them, so of course they didn't feel like mine. It was one of the first of many secrets I told my lover and was astonished to hear how incredibly erotic he thought they were. As he spent time loving them, adoring them, talking to them and being friends with them, they began to change, and my relationship with my own thighs changed. I began to appreciate them, to see them in a new light, to see everything wonderful about them I hadn't been willing to see. I noticed the shape of them, the strength of them, the texture and color of them.

When you give love to parts of his body, to his hands, for instance, love doesn't linger on the skin, it moves below the surface and goes in as deep as he will let it. Each time you spend a few moments loving them, holding them, love goes in a little deeper, below the skin into the intelligence of muscles and tendons altering holding patterns. It goes into the blood, to the heart, to all the organs, and the ego states, as well, eventually get fed with this love, and they begin to let go of holding patterns.

> *If you want to know God,*
> *Then turn your face to your friend,*
> *and don't look away.*
>
> RUMI

To feel the touch of Spirit on your body, the touch of another human heart touching your heart, you must go to your lover with all defenses put aside. Vulnerability allows access to feelings. Letting down your defenses is the hardest thing of all at times, for the part of us that enjoys our defenses and the space they create has tremendous tenacity. You may need to negotiate with this part of you that is afraid, for it is the fearful part that holds onto armoring. We learn to wear many masks and to develop personalities as we go through life to give us a sense of protection. Those masks and personalities are developed to protect the small Child inside us. But it is just that Child in us that needs to feel this touch, needs to be touched, be seen by another human soul and by the Spirit that moves through all things. It is the Child in us that remembers what it felt like to be immersed in, surrounded by, bathed in that energy field, the Great Mystery, the heartbeat of Earth, the original mother, before coming into the world in human form, and it is that feeling we search for all the days of our lives. It is that feeling, that touch, that we need, in part, to be whole. We need that feeling from our partner, our parents, our friends, for it is love without judgments, it is seeing without condemnation, and then we can begin to feel our presence in life is welcomed and needed.

ANCIENT HISTORY

The concept of the relationship as a vehicle for the sacred is thousands of years old. A bronze sculpture of Shiva's consort, circa 950–960 CE, is known for its blending of sacred sensuality, sexuality, and spirituality.[8] Elaborate statues such as these were commissioned by kings to depict and honor the gods and goddesses of sexuality and fertility. The most famous Indian statue is of Lord Shiva reaching out to touch the breast of his consort, Uma-Parvarti. Hindu sculpture can often be explicitly and unembarrassedly erotic. Physical grace and sexual prowess in kings and queens were regarded as vital and admirable attributes in a ruler. In Hindu tradition, outlined in the Rig Veda, the erotic *rasa,* or flavor was considered one of the nine *rasas* comprising the Hindu aesthetic system. The Rig Veda, an ancient Indian text of sacred hymns, begins with the creation of *kama,* sexual desire: In the beginning was desire, and desire was with God. In the Hindu scheme of things, the gratification of *kama* remains one of the three fundamental goals of human existence, along with *dharma*—duty or religion—and *artha,* the creation of wealth. The sacred poetry of the Vedas was primarily written by people overwhelmed by the beauty and power of nature, which they personified and deified as a pantheon of gods and goddesses. Nature was alive in a pantheistic and animistic worldview.

The explicitly erotic sculptures along with the long Indian literary tradition of erotic devotional poetry may at one level be read as metaphors for the longing of the soul for the divine and of the devotee for God. Yet such poems and sculptures are also clearly a frank expression of pleasure in life and love and sex.[9]

In the ecstatic poetry of Kabir, Mirabai, and Hafez, God appears frequently as a lover. It is seen in the writings of Rumi, the Persian poet, whose love affair with Shams demonstrates the sacred fabric of love and devotion, mysticism and eroticism. The Kama Sutra, India's sacred love text, describes the finer points of sexuality and love, the art of living and of sensual pleasures including food, perfume, lotions, incense, flowers, and fine attire, not simply acrobatic sexual positions.

Well known for his interest and explorations in sex and erotic literature, Sir Richard Burton (1821–1890) brought the Kama Sutra to the English-speaking world, eighty years before the sexual revolution of the 1960s. In response to the "Obscene Publications Act of 1857," he founded the Kama Shastra Society, devoted to publishing and circulating erotic and sexual literature that would be illegal to publish publicly. In *Pleasure Bound: Victorian Sex Rebels and the New Eroticism,* Deborah Lutz examines two groups of sex rebels devoted to challenging the morality of Victorian England. The Cannibal Club and the Aesthetes included prominent artists, poets, socialists, and clergy. Their activities were often met with ostracism, arrest, censorship, and jail time. Oscar Wilde spent two years of hard labor for being gay. The members were freethinkers and rebels challenging the rigid morality of the day. They championed unpopular ideas and stereotypes of sexuality and women's suffrage. Cole Riley wrote that "[t]hey saw how difficult it was for women to break out of the stifling laws and stereotypes of the time. They knew that a society could never be truly progressive if women do not equal legal and voting rights, and full rights over their own bodies, including birth control and abortion."[10]

> *Yes, I am a free lover. I have an inalienable, constitutional and natural right to love whom I may, to love as long or as short a period as I can; to change that love every day if I please and with that right neighbor you nor any law you can frame have any right to interfere. And I have the further right to demand a free and unrestricted exercise of that right, and it is your duty not only to accord it, but, as a community, to see that I am protected in it. I trust that I am fully understood, for I mean just that, and nothing less.*
>
> VICTORIA WOODHULL,
> "AND THE TRUTH SHALL MAKE YOU FREE"

8

The Language of Love

The Movement of Great Things

There is memory of ocean,
the swelling of waves,
the movement of great things,
just beneath the surface.
My conscious mind staggers,
a part sleeping begins to waken.
What is this great thing?
That has caught us up?

Beloved . . .
Shall we find out together?
Shall we travel to a land
where two-dimensionality does not rule?
Where all that we encounter gazes back at us?
Where directions for the journey
are written in the shape and textures of the land?
Where we see, as far as the eye can touch,
the soul of us opening outward?

Shall we take that step together?
Leave the comfort of the porch,
and strike cross country,
to find the place where the Teacher lives,
the place where the big and the little become one,
the place from which we came long ago,
the place we have heard calling since before we were born?

Shall we go out Beloved and take the path before us?
Shall we let the perfume of our love
fill all our three bodies?
Come, take my hand,
it has awaited the deep you to fill it,
a length of time too long for remembering.

Come Beloved, let us take this journey together.
My feet are hungry for the first step.

STEPHEN HARROD BUHNER,
THE TASTE OF WILD WATER

There is a language to love, and it involves more than words. It is a communication in which directed meanings are passed from one person into another. It flows through the heart field in which love is wrapped and then into the other; an exquisite dialogue that transcends our common language. When two people are in love, this is the linguistic medium they share.

Each part of us has a different story to tell. As we touch with the fingers of our hearts, we read the text of each other's lives. There are stories waiting to be received that live in hands, shoulders, eyes, feet, knees, breasts, and intonations of voice. Our stories are breathed in by the other, and we are then taken to places we have never known, places we have imagined and longed for. Many of our stories have been held secret, never shared before. When another person receives the stories, takes them deeply in, in a sense he lives them experientially. Over time, the threads of one person's life are woven into the fabric of another.

Each part of a person's body has its own distinct feeling and meaning. When you explore your lover's body, you explore the terrain of his life; you enter the geography of his deepest self. We spend time with and hold in wonder the meanings of the other.

It is the saddest thing in the world to have love to give, to feel the urge to love until you feel your heart nearly burst from it, and have no place to set it, no ground tilled to receive it. Or to have it only partially received or censored so that only a tiny portion of your giving is received. The most joyful thing is to have your love welcomed, recognized, and given a home, a resting place. A place it has longed to be for all eternity.

You can't have, or give, too much love.

> *A journey makes us vulnerable, takes us from our more secure environments and commits us to the unknown. Perhaps this is why the journey has so often been our basic metaphor for life itself. Our life journey is a precarious pilgrimage, a passage through landscapes of promise and peril, a crossing from the darkness of the womb to the shadows of death. We travel in the hope that the light will not fail to guide us, that the star will not be lost, that homecoming will be granted and love not withheld.*
>
> THOMAS MERTON

Our body, the lines in our face, and the look in our eyes hold the stories of who we are, how we became who we are as well as all the wounds and the wonder of us. Stories are the narratives of our soul's journey. They tell of the events, people, and places that touched us and how we were impacted by them. When the stories held in our body are received by another, there is a softening in the soul, an opening to feel the touch of another human heart. There is a release, then, of the burden of carrying stories alone. There is an ebb and flow in all this, a back and forth, a rising and settling, as each part of us opens to receive the other; a knowing of the other's interior world opens and love deepens. Someplace in the middle the two meet, and together they discover a new world. After awhile, who I am begins to move inside the other, and the other inside me; his story becomes mine and mine, his. And the lives we had before are changed.

The language of love has sound, shape, texture, movement. There are sighs, tears, a tensing and relaxing of the shoulders and breath. The person hearing the thing receives it in his heart field, and there it has a place to live.

When one finds her voice, her life takes on grace.

LADY IN THE WATER

LOVING WITHOUT RESERVATION

It's all too easy to be casual about a thing, a life, a concept. It's all too easy to fail to follow the golden thread all the way to the finish, to see it through to the end, as far as it will go, heeding the ebb and flow, rise and fall, obvious and subtle oracles. Out of fear is born the habit to hold something back. We never know when we might, once again, find ourselves with a long swim, alas, back to shore.

It takes a long time to be willing to love without reserve.

And thus, as intimacy feeds the soul of love, a new verse, a new story is written. We become something new, something joined, influenced by the other, changing from moment to moment. As we walk in the world with this new thing inside us, those who encounter us can experience this new song that is being written.

Love is the willingness and ability to be affected by another
human being and to allow that effect to make a difference
in what you do, say, become.

GENEEN ROTH, *WHEN FOOD IS LOVE*

James Hillman writes: "A heart's image lies within each person. It is what we truly reveal when we fall helplessly in love, for then we are opened to display who we most truly are, giving a glimpse of our soul's genius.

People say: 'He looks so different—he must be in love.' 'She's fallen in love; she's truly changed.' When love moves the heart, something else is perceived in the idolized object, which poetic language tries to capture."[1]

Falling in love causes the imagination to unfurl. As the imagination expands, we fall in love deeper, wilder, more passionately, hungrily. Love is of the spirit, drawing the soul toward images painted on the heart.

Such love is not unlike reading a good novel; you find yourself in the story, engaged with the characters. You become invested in their lives and their adventures. You find yourself thinking about them during your day, wondering what they are doing, how they are doing, what's happening next in their lives. You look forward to sitting down with them again to look into their eyes and receive the story of their lives and travels. You witness the transformation of the characters.

Love is like this. It is to become obsessed, wild, madly, chaotically, deeply in love. Each waking moment is filled with thoughts of the beloved. I smell him, feel the touch of him wrapped around me as I move through my day. As my beloved opens to show me more of himself, his stories find a place inside me to live. My caring and love for him grows. I want to call him every hour to hear his voice and to say how much I love him. I leave love notes on his pillow, taped to the mirror, or tucked in his travel bag. I think of him during the day and dream of him at night. When I'm sitting with a cup of my favorite morning drink, I recall our time together, the way he looks at me and sees me, the sound of his breathing, and the feel of him inside me.

I want to touch him, caress his face, rub his tired shoulders, and hold him as he lays his head on my shoulder and falls carelessly to sleep. I allow myself each moment to fall in love with him over and over again. I tell him all the ways I love him, all the details of noticing him and his innu-endoes. The various laughs he has: the nasal snorts of fifteen-year-old humor, the snicker, the chuckle, the chortle, and my favorite, the deep, full-out belly laugh. Each laugh has a different quality to it, a different ego state that lets it loose in the room. Each laugh has a meaning in it, the meaning of which part of him is in the room and engaging with me or whoever else is present.

I want to know everything about him, and so I watch as he stands at his closet, doors open. He ponders each thing that catches his eye, and he imagines trying on each piece of clothing to see if it matches how he's feeling that particular day. It's a joy to watch him stand in front of the full-length mirror, looking at himself, turning this way and then the other. He settles into the clothes as each part of him responds to what he's put on. Then, if they all agree on the garments, he's set in his wardrobe for the day. If not, back to the closet they go.

When he walks into a room with his personal/sexual power entering with him, a force to be reckoned with, he has the power to take down any walls of China within me. And I give him that power gladly. I fall in love over and over again with abandon. I tell him all these things, describing in as much detail as I can my noticing of how he carries himself, how he feels in his body, how much I love watching him put on his favorite clothes that are like good friends wrapped around him. I tell him not only the details of my noticing him, but the meanings of them and how they impact me. Watching him prepare food with Eros and exquisite detail, then watching how much he enjoys eating the food is to read chapters, verses of his passion, his gusto, his patience, his reverence for life and love of food and sensory experiences.

To learn the language of love requires that we, out of love, out of desire, pay attention. The subtleties of this language are easily missed, passed over, ignored. As with the details in anything we are doing, there must be interested consideration. The ecstatic journey of sacred sex begins long before the physical act. Attraction and desire awaken us. A part of my soul reaches out to touch his, and in mutual desire, his touches mine. The dance of getting to know a lover is chaotic, frightening, and exciting. Old pains and hurts rise to the surface, and we may doubt our choice to enter into a relationship again. Eros causes chaos in our previously ordered life. In the midst of chaos, we are forced to travel to our interior. Psyche, the goddess of soul, is excited at the possibility of new experiences, but we struggle between our fears and a new opportunity for romance, love, sex, and intimacy and the changes that may result.

I had been dating a man sporadically for three months vacillating between, "I want this," "I don't want this." Talking to each part of me on both sides of that fence, we all finally came to an agreement that yes, we want to explore this with him. Why not, after all? I was recently divorced after a sixteen-year relationship. He was tall, ruggedly handsome, strong, intelligent, interesting, very sexy, charismatic, fun. He had great lips. *And* he had his own boat on the Mississippi River. It would be an adventure if nothing else. We had a date planned, so I drove the hour and a half down river to his house. Excitement was building. I had packed an overnight bag and decided that this would be our first night of sleeping together and having sex. We hadn't talked about it until we were sitting on a park bench overlooking the river. He asked me if I would spend the night, if we could just sleep together.

Surprisingly, my fears came up again, but I went back to the agreement I had made with myself to explore this. "Yes, I think I'd like that very much." Of course, I thought "just sleep together" was code for "let's sleep together and have sex." Much to my intrigue, surprise, and a little disappointment (I needed to get laid), we actually . . . slept together. We hugged, kissed, caressed, told stories about our lives, and fell asleep in each other's arms. We had a sweet, intimate sharing and the movement toward a deeper relationship. I woke up feeling shy. He'd seen me naked and heard some of my life stories. Would he still want to have sex with me? He was leaving the next day for a month-long river trip. Desire built and hunger grew. I wanted this man.

When we were together again on the houseboat, passions were high, hunger nearly overcame us. Still, we didn't have sex. Damn. Until the next night. And it was sweet as honey dripping from the comb.

I didn't tell this story to advocate waiting. It's a personal choice how the dance of having sex for the first time goes and when. The sexless nights we spent together were windows into understanding who this man was. He was romantic, sensual, tender, and strong. It was important to him to build desire, to share something of ourselves, to set a foundation for whatever might follow. We slipped into a comfortability with each other. Our bodies fit together, our lips and tongues somehow already knew each other, knew exactly how to move and talk to each other the way lips and tongues do. We both enjoyed touching, kissing, snuggling, and cuddling immensely. I wanted him. I loved the way he looked at me and the smile that lit up his face when he saw me. I loved the feel of his hands on my body. I loved the smell of him. We began the relationship making love without the in-ing and out-ing and sweating and moaning. However, once we started in-ing and out-ing, we didn't stop. There were wonderfully few sexless nights after that.

I surely loved that man but I think we grew mutually frustrated with each other over time; he with how I always wanted more from him, the fights I started, the growing chasm between our value systems, and I with his unwillingness to go to deeper levels of intimacy. We were both strong and independent. He had a well-established career and I was just beginning to understand who I was and what I wanted my life and work to look like. Our lives overlapped infrequently and he understood me less as I began to make deep changes. The lack of deep intimacy in the relationship, my rudimentary relationship skills, and the changes I was making left me feeling unhappy and unsatisfied. I hate endings but I knew that I would never get what I wanted there and I began to feel a pull in another direction, away from that relationship.

I left the relationship less than gracefully. I was in the middle of my fourth decade and had begun to create a body of work that was mine. I could feel my time in the Midwest coming to an end, something new beginning. When I decided to let the relationship go, I resigned myself to not knowing if there would be another partner or other lovers, but I knew I would be devoted to building my work and teaching.

THE SMELL OF LOVE

Each one of us has our own unique smell, the smell that is our soul signature alone. Sexual attraction is much about smell. Gustav Jager, a German physician and hygienist was the first to formalize the concept of pheromones, which he named anthropines. He correctly identified them as lipophilic compounds that are associated with skin and follicles that determine the individual signature of human odors.[2]

Some deep part of us can smell the other even if it's unconscious; it's part of our unconscious attraction but often comes to conscious awareness during sexual intimacy. You can tell a great deal about a person if you learn to smell below the surface, to the core of a person. And you'll know if his smell is a good match for you, if it's seductive, intoxicating, erotic. It's important to the health of a relationship if you like your partner's smell and if you like him in general. The smell of a person changes as his internal world becomes more whole. A musty smell can indicate that there hasn't been much love in the deep part of him. Lack of intimacy can smell old and rancid. When love is there, feeding a person's soul and whole being, the smell is sweet and fresh as clover.

Almost as soon as I told the Universe that, lover or not, I would not stop doing my work, my new lover appeared in my life. As he and I grew over the months and years together, I watched him change, grow, and become more himself with my love, with part of my spirit living inside him. I could see him relaxing in the trust that had grown between us, a dependability of one upon the other. There is trust in our love, in our friendship, a knowing that the other will be here: we will be at each other's back and come to each other's aid; we will listen to each other's struggles, joys, dreams, and insights. The desire and hunger is still there, passion is still there, but without the urgency, without clinging in desperation for fear that it will end. Desire and passion need tending to; they need spices and seasonings as well as attention to subtle moods and needs, yours and his.

I often go to the watching place inside me to see myself from new perspectives, a perspective that changes as I change. I hardly recognize who I was even a few years ago. My posture is more erect. More often than not, I walk with confidence through the world. Parts of me have awakened— parts that were asleep and in danger of becoming bitter in my old life because they did not have a place to be alive in the world. They are living in the world now, learning to walk and talk, being educated, becoming part of a fully integrated human being.

I've learned how to love myself, how to fall in love with myself. Such self-love happens most easily when the love of another human being is let inside, is granted permission to pass all the defenses, the objections, and arguments against this act. When I allowed love to pass through all the gatekeepers and journey as rivulets into the deepest parts of myself, parts of me that had never been touched by love, then the journey of loving myself began.

I became my own advocate, knowing what my needs and wants are, saying them out loud as needed, and working to get them met either by myself or by someone else. I learned to do this straightforwardly without the drama of games or cons or sideways attempts. I learned to say no first by giving myself permission to say no. It takes patience and focus and in the beginning is challenging. The closer I came to resolution, to truly giving up game dynamics, the more the scared parts of me escalated, the more focus it took to let them know I was serious. I seriously wanted to be free of old scripts and dramas.

This is an uncomfortable time when love flows inside to the deepest parts of the self that have never been touched by love; the places inside that are bent and crooked. Love doesn't travel in a straight line. Like the tip of the ocean wave after it's crested and fallen and now meets the shore and the two create a whole new thing, never straight, and the water changes the beach, the rocks, the sand, and the muddy shore, and the shore changes how the water moves, its speed, its impact, and how it moves back away from the shore into the ocean again.

Doing this repeatedly, I let his love come into me, touch me, fill me, grow me, expand me, change me. His love fills all the spaces inside me. He lives inside me, in my heart, and is in my soul. All of him, every part of him, every story of him, each heartbreak and the original wound of his birth family are now part of me. Nothing of him is hidden or secret from me, and nothing of me is hidden or secret from him.

As the original wound in each of us is healed, made whole by the other's love, our psychological structure is altered. The defenses and games I played have been given up, seen for what they are, and rendered obsolete. I'm not willing to sacrifice myself to keep peace and, rarely, to make someone else happy, though there are times when it's important to put my needs aside temporarily to strengthen our relationship or to tend to something that is more urgent.

I reach for words to describe the depth and breadth of my love for him. I do the best I can with the words at hand. I search the lexicon grasping for others. A thousand words I say each night, and none come near to the depth and breadth of my love for him. There are no words big enough, strong enough, or whole enough to hold the meaning of my feelings for him, though I try. I say "I love you," words that I have and are the truth of my feelings, and yet, they are pale ashes compared to the kaleidoscope of colors that are in the feelings.

Attempting to fill three words, three syllables
With the depth of my feelings for you

Resembles mining the secrets of the ocean
Holding still the moon
Or painting rainbows in the sky
With crayons

FROM THE AUTHOR'S JOURNAL

I want the words that hold the meanings of how I feel. I want to make my feelings known to him, and when I least expect it, the language of love is made known to me. Here inside me, inside him, flowing between us like a sweet, gentle stream it has been all along. The bee was telling me where it was, what it was, and how it tasted. It is that invisible field that pulses from my heart to his and back again. How ignorant of me.

The language of love is the language of falling in love each day. To learn this language, you must allow yourself to feel, to be aware. Each time I look into his eyes, hear one of his many laughs, or see him walk into a room, I'm aware of many subtle and visible responses in me. My posture changes, I feel the petals of my heart unfold, I feel my soul smile inside. That is love talking.

Love is spoken when I do things that make him happy, those moments when I'm in service to his happiness and joy. His happiness is inextricably woven into mine. Love speaks through the little things I do, just by him taking joy in me. The part of me that came alive in our friendship is free to voice the running commentary she has on life's absurdities. She knows she can be herself, spontaneously without censorship.

Beauty is love. When beauty and love are more than skin deep, a luminous glow radiates from a deep well, sourced from the love they have for themselves; it comes from deep inside them. They're magnetic and attractive and upon seeing them, your eyes are transfixed, following them across the street. And this language is more than skin deep; it's preverbal, beyond the surface, and past fantasy. The language is real, rising up from the deep ocean of self; it travels across the surface of the body and is taken up in the breath of the spirit that moves through and enlivens all things.

Letting the love inside speak, giving myself over to it, to its textures, sights, sounds, and poetry.

This Simple Thing

I awaken slowly, reluctantly,

from a deep, and glorious sleep.

What is this thing that awakens me?

What is this invisible touch on my spirit?

Ah, it's you my love.

No need even to open my eyes

I feel what you are doing

Touching without fingers

I smile knowing you are here.

You've been watching me while I sleep

love

ecstatic I

in this simple thing.

FROM THE AUTHOR'S JOURNAL

LEARNING TO LET GO

When I met the man who wanted to take this intimate, sacred, ecstatic journey with me, I was forty-four chronologically and around three years old psychologically. I wasn't very grown-up, educated, or sophisticated in my interactions. I played a lot of games and had few life skills. I was emotionally shut down for the most part, and my fallback survival plan when things got too challenging was to emotionally run away by withdrawing. I fought the urge to withdraw, to shut down. I struggled with my demons and kept going until I reached the other side of it.

I knew a lot about sex and, to a degree, love. But I knew precious little, experientially, about going all the way with love and intimacy, about trusting another or of giving myself into his keeping, and less about how to nurture a healthy relationship. I only imagined how letting that much love in all the way could change me, for I had only seen a few hints of those changes in a few people who had begun to go there. I was about to learn the true meaning of vulnerability, that searing openness and exposure that is sourced from utter defenselessness. I was about to learn the true meaning of surrender. I was about to discover that my understanding of self-love was immature. Many times on the journey, I wanted to run away, to go back to my old life or create a new one that didn't involve having to face the best, and worst, parts of me. Feeling that vulnerable and tender was terrifying and painfully uncomfortable. I'd often rather chew tacks. It distorted my sense of self. Only in the midst of the journey could I see how my soul was distorted, fragmented, and a little crooked in places.

The prospect of letting go of myself completely, of trusting another so completely, someone who could truly see, who wanted to see every part of me, petrified me with fear and shook me at my core as if a great meteor smacked down in the middle of my idea of myself. Just because you want something doesn't exclude being afraid of it. It filled me with so much terror that I stopped having deep, full-body orgasms. I became emotionally and sexually frustrated and was forced to own how deeply I wanted to have this experience with this man who could love me all the way without holding anything back, who was patient and nonjudgmental, who encouraged me to have that sort of full-body shivering pleasure. To do this, I had to change at the core level of me and go through this deep fear to see what was on the other side, what was so terrifying.

Wilhelm Reich used the term *body armoring* to refer to self-protection, or at least a sense of protection and safety. But body armoring is not localized; it affects our musculature and our nervous system, our ability to think clearly as it constricts our entire physiology. When impulses or emotions are inhibited, the body responds by tensing muscles. "Inhibited libido," he said, "is tense muscles and relaxed libido is sexual charm."[3] Body armoring affects our ability to have open, meaningful, relaxed, and passionate sex. The fear paralyzed my groins and created a tension that was impossible to unlock until I worked with the fear and the parts of me, the Child of me, that was terrified. I had created a split between my mind and body; my body embodied the fear and rage I had around vulnerability, changing behavior patterns, being sexual in a sacred and intimate way rather than just having sex or fucking. Vulnerability unleashes a great outpouring of human potential.

I wanted intimate relating, but I didn't know there was a price to pay. And the price I paid was everything I was so I could become the person I was always meant to be. I changed inside and out. My favorite clothes no longer fit the person I was becoming. My favorite earrings didn't look right. My favorite hangouts changed, and friends dropped away as my voice, my values, and my beliefs were restructured. There is a cost to freedom. I left my birth family and refused to be part of their psychosis or pretend that I fit in.

The language of love is felt in the kiss on the forehead or top of the head. The endearing moments when your lover is asleep, and the part of him that is bonded with you wakes inside him just enough to reach over to hold you, to feel you close and touch his foot to yours, to know you are still there. Love is there in the darkest night when in the midst of a nightmare, he's there, holding you, telling you, "Everything's all right." Love silently speaks in the still, quiet, dreamy hours of the night.

When it comes to sex, making love, and intimacy, our culture is still in kindergarten compared to other cultures such as the Japanese and Chinese, who have entire societies devoted to teaching young men and women not only about sex but about the body and how to make love to another with reverence as an expression of the holy.

The language of those cultures to describe erotica is marvelous, romantic, and delicate, using words such as *jade dragon, white tigress, green dragon, jade stalk, palace gates, yoni,* and *lingam.* Compare this to Western language that describes sex and reinforces lovemaking as a heroic performance with the hard-cock approach ignoring delicate desires, imaginations, subtleties, and those all too rare and precious moments of ecstatic intimacy and mystery. Instead, we use the words *private parts, pussy, dick, ball sack,* and *cunt,* as if to somehow insulate us from intimacy and tenderness. Those words are suitable to bar talk, but not always suitable in intimate moments. Intimate talk, no matter the words, has a feeling tone to it. It feels like intimacy, or it feels like distance. It draws you in or it repels you; it honors you or it discounts you.

Without the erotic, sensual Earth to inspire our choices and our architecture, our language, our life, where would we reach for words to describe our experiences? If we weren't sexual beings, what would the Washington monument and space shuttles look like? We know a phallic symbol when we see one. We recognize sperm as a prototype for ships and weapons to invade foreign soil. Our skin cells are modeled after the skin cells of leaves and bark and animal hides; they die and shed and are replaced by new ones.

> *Virtually no one has enough accurate, judgment-free information about sex. We don't watch other people do it, we can't find many accurate representations of it in the media, and few of us talk honestly about it with each other. It's almost impossible to know the full range of sexual thoughts and behavior of the people around us— and, therefore, impossible to know how much we have in common.*
>
> MARTY KLEIN,
> *YOUR SEXUAL SECRETS*

THE LANGUAGE OF SENSUALITY

The word *sensuous* comes from the Latin *sentire,* "to feel," and the related word *sensus,* "to feel and perceive." Sensuous refers not only to the physical senses but to any means of feeling, as intellectual or aesthetic sensitivity and intuition, as in the sensuous pleasure of walking in the rain, the sight of soft snow falling in the moonlight, and the way the air smells fresh and clean after a spring rain or monsoon. Sensuous powerfully appeals to the senses in a sexual or quasi-sexual way. John Milton invented the word *sensuous* to have a synonym of *sensual,* minus the association with sex. He used the word in an often-quoted formulation of what poetry should be: simple, sensuous, and passionate.

Sensuality is a language of love and sex. It is a language of our body and of our nature. When something is sensual, we respond bodily and experience it through our senses. Skin is sensual when it is soft, smooth, and supple. Well-formed muscles are the sensual, erotic landscape of the human form. As skin and our bodies age, we begin to take on the look of stone and tree and landscape that has been shaped and worn by the elements. Georgia O'Keefe is well known for capturing the sensuality and eroticism of stone cathedrals and landscapes in her paintings. Best known of her collection is her flower series capturing the resemblance between the petals of flowers and the female vulva.

> *I had to create an equivalent for what I felt about what I was looking at—not copy it.*
>
> GEORGIA O'KEEFE

A warm summer breeze on our exposed skin and the way warm bathwaters wrap around our bodies are sensual and erotic experiences. The sway of a woman's hips, the breath escaping softly in a sigh, and the way food is prepared slowly with care and attention to details can all be sensual experiences. Anything that is sensual is erotic and satisfying to our physical body and senses. As we grew in the womb, we were infused in the warm, sensual fluid of prebirth waters. We have an innate understanding of the meaning of and a need for the sensual.

We all know what sexy is when we see it; we feel it when it walks into the room. We feel the impact of it, our heads turn in that direction; we feel pleasure, are intrigued, interested. Having been trained out of looking and seeing, we watch out the corner of our eyes, trying not to be noticed noticing. There is an energy that comes off a body when sexual energy is either part of who the person is or is part of who the person is trying to be, or what they are wanting to communicate. It's sexual energy, attractive, magnetic, irresistible energy. We can't help but turn our heads and be drawn into its orbit.

Sexuality has a language of its own; it speaks in the subtle movements of the eyes shifting and darting, the movement of a thigh, carriage of the body, long, supple movements involving posture and shape; the way a low-cut blouse exposes the mysterious valley between bosomy mountains, or a skirt slides up to show the inside of a thigh. Whether our look is sly or withdrawn or direct and substantial, if our hair is flowing or pulled tightly back, and the ways we hug and touch; spontaneous, passionate, full-body embraces or one arm barely touching a shoulder are speaking the languages of intimacy, sexuality, and invitations. Standing with one hip slightly forward, the set of shoulders, the tilt of the head, use of makeup around the eyes and mouth are sensual ways we present ourselves in our bodies and speak a voiceless communication about how we feel about our sexuality.

> *Sexual and creative: these are important words and concepts. You are a sexual being—all humans are. It is up to you to determine how free or how stifled you will be as a sexual being, but you are a sexual being. This sexuality is the core of your creative process, for it is the core of YOU. Sexuality is the deepest part of self-identity, for it is how you relate to SELF and how you relate to others.*
>
> ALAN SEALE,
> *INTUITIVE LIVING AS A SACRED PATH*

The language of love is a quality, an essence. It is not a form or technique. It's not learning to speak Spanish or Russian. It's a language that is multisensory, multilinguistic, not confined to the voice box and a few hand gestures—though the erotically placed and rhythmic hand gesture is linguistic.

Each of the languages love speaks has meaning. Snuggling and cuddling are filled with meaning. How our bodies and psyches respond to touch is meaning rich. Rigidity in his body or yours and where it's held tells you much about holding patterns and armoring. How he kisses, what position he likes most, and whether he likes to look at your vulva or not, gives you glimpses at his inner world and how he feels about sex and himself. One lover preferred entering me from behind while standing up. The intimacy of face to face was often more than his comfort level would tolerate.

Being aware of the language of love and sexuality increases our sensitivity to the pervasiveness of these communications happening around and in us. If we understand that we are sexual beings transmitting sexual messages we can shape them directly, become conversant in the dialects and raise them to sophisticated degrees of finesse, nuance, and subtleties. Sacred lovemaking is the divine alchemy of the numinous, physical, spiritual, sexual and soul. The language of love is that of beauty, sex, art of nudity, and earthy sensuality.

The language of love has many forms and expressions. Whether it is expressed through the spoken word, poetry, song, paintings, or the sacred gaze, the language of love is an essence, a meaning-filled communication. It always comes from and through the heart, so the form matters only in as much as it is your medium of expressing the essence in any moment. In sacred sex, the language of love is expressed through the heart, the joyful attention to details, heightened perceptions, and the physical embrace.

9

Sacred Sex

Do You Recognize Me Now?

Can you be completely one with me
And still come back to yourself?

Can you live in our surrender
and carry it back and forth
between the world of time
and the world where time does not exist?

Can you live on the undefended edge,
where the breezes of love blow
not just for a day or a month or a year, but for an eternity?

Can you be defined by that wave
into which our two waves merge?
Can you live in its trajectory
and die in its embrace?

Many men have asked you to dance,

but has anyone asked you to dance like this?

With or without bodies, it does not matter!
Will you be all that you are in its fullness
and let yourself spill over into me?
Will you harvest your tears with mine
and water the ground with them?

Will you bring me into the secret caves
of your doubts and your fears,
allowing the moonlight to guide us
through the snowy woods?

You have come to me from deep waters,
ascending from the center of the circle.

Now as I dance, moving around the circle
from one partner to the next,
I once again await the depth of your eyes
and the electricity of your hand.

But I am lucky that the dance ends
before we come face to face.
I know when that moment comes
I will be lost forever, and so will you!

You see, I am not just the one
who comes to you in the dance. Rumi says:
"Lovers don't finally meet somewhere.
They're in each other all along."

Do you recognize me now?

Rumi says: "Gone inner and outer,

no moon, no ground or sky."

Has anyone asked you to dance like this?

PAUL FERRINI,
DANCING WITH THE BELOVED

When I met him, I didn't know much. I knew just enough to feel a spiritual imperative to keep him in my life if even from a distance. We had in us the drive to reconnect, and like shy teenagers, our first meeting was awkward, an undercurrent of unknown passion made balance difficult. There was that powerful attraction, the way metal filings respond to a magnet. His smell, his movements, his cells were astoundingly familiar, and though I didn't understand at the moment, or for a long time, I recognized a kinship in him. There was a great urgency in me to get his attention, engage him in a conversation; some part of me needed to keep him within arm's reach, the manner or form did not matter.

The urge to reunite, an invisible compass pointing each in the direction of the other, came at just the right time to save each other's life. Ten years came and went before we became lovers. It felt as if we had waited our entire lives to do this dance of ecstatic, sacred love with each other. The first night we made love, I saw the place before time, before the two of us were born, the agreement we made to find one another. I understood the tension, the awkwardness, the discomfort, the attraction, the fear I'd felt all those years. I was suddenly catapulted out of the half-sleeping state I'd been in.

Rabbi Zalman Schachter-Shalomi, founder of the Spiritual Eldering Institute, had these reflections about sex.

I remember thinking of sexuality as that lousy trick that God played on us. How could God do such a terrible thing as to implant in us an urge that is so difficult to resist? This very same urge has been reinforced time and time again since we stopped being amoebas and turned into humans. Just think about how this was reinforced. I had two parents, four grandparents, eight great-grandparents. They all did it. Now see how it spreads out to countless beings who all did it. Now think of the children who will have children who will have children who will have children who will all do it. And all this fantastic amount of genetic information is concentrated in one flesh, as it were, of transmission. How else could it be but ecstatic? How else could it be when so much of the past has to transfer itself to so much of the future through such narrow orifices? It can't be but ecstatic.[1]

LOVING THROUGH SPACE AND TIME

When we became lovers, we were living in different states, he on the East Coast and me in the Midwest. We talked on the phone several times a week. He often began the conversation telling me something funny that had happened or that he'd read. Laughing together closed the distance, and we slipped into the growing comfort of our companionship. Hearing his laughter, the ache and longing of missing him squeezed around my heart. I so wanted to hold him in my arms.

A thing happens when you miss someone so desperately; the intensity of feeling and need becomes a solvent to all armoring; the shielding we've put up for protection is ineffective. With the armoring and shielding taken down, it becomes possible to surrender to what is there. Somatically, the body responds by letting go of tensions and relaxing the musculature. There is yielding to feeling, and you let yourself follow it, feel it all, everything that is there between the two, inside you, inside him, growing and expanding, filling the room you're sitting in, expanding to fill each room in the entire house, and it continues expanding to fill the neighborhood and the town and beyond. There is no end to its expansiveness.

Our phone conversations took us deeper and deeper into another reality, a place very much like my time sitting in zazen, though there were 1,100 miles, 23 hours of driving, or 8 hours of air travel between us. As we talked and gave ourselves over to feeling love for the other, we slipped between the cracks of reality and illusion into the numinous. Boundaries unraveled. Distance dissipated. Time and space transcended, and we were in each other's presence. Reality began to shift, and soon we could see the other strongly, clearly. Simultaneously, we each felt the other's presence near us, felt the rhythm of our breathing and passion growing between us.

We reached out with our love and touched the other's cheek. The sweet, fecund, anciently familiar scent of him filled my senses. Pictures began to appear before my eyes, and inspirations rose up in the gaps between words. "This is what we do when our soul leaves our bodies, when we are gone from the Earth plane, this is how it feels," I whispered. I felt his hands on my skin, his breath on my face, felt him penetrate me, slowly, deeply, as we breathed together, whispering declarations of desire, love, and longing. Years later, we still engage in sacred phone sex, e-mail sex, shower sex, keeping the livingness of our bond whole.

I believe that this is what we are meant to do, are born to do; dance ecstatically with the beloved in the throes of sacred sex, of giving oneself over to sacred traveling in other worlds, suspending time and space. This is the state we are yearning for, aching for, longing for. This is the feeling we are looking for in our relationships, that awe-fullness to experience something wholly other, completely outside ourselves and our normal experience, transported, transmuted, enraptured, and caught up in the sublime.

Sometimes the numinous catches hold of us spontaneously. Paying attention to it or not, the feeling gets us to pay attention, to sit up and take notice. Reality begins to shift like the movement of Earth's tectonic plates. Perceptions are altered during this shift; the room becomes luminous, filled with light. Colors shimmer; the edges of things that were a moment ago solid become blurred. You are in nonordinary reality, taken through yourself, outside yourself, into the realm of the gods where the gate is opened by the simple joy of the expansive heart, the feeling of the bond between the two of you: all that you are, all the other is, is in this moment where nothing else exists but the exquisite warmth from the fire of love, birthed from the depth of intimacy. In this moment joy rises up, your heart spilling over with so much love you can no longer contain it, and it has nowhere else to go but to spill out the corners of your eyes.

When you go to your lover, go with a sense of wonder and awe as if for the first time. Let your hunger for him, your love for him crack open the shell to reveal the soft, tender center of the heart. With the armoring fallen away, you gain access to the more subtle feelings. You are able to see and feel with your heart. From this place awakens the natural wonder of the child. The same wonder you had as a child long ago, exploring the world around you, splashing in mud puddles and intently watching insects, following their minute movements. Allow that natural curiosity and interest to overtake you as you look into your lover's eyes.

Remember your first times together if you must, to bring that freshness and newness, all that attracted you to him. Bring that to this place until you can marry the familiar and newness spontaneously. Let your eyes soften as your gaze falls on him. See who he is, this being sitting before you: see his goodness, his fears, his passions, his soul, and the child he once was. Become naive once again. The words *naive* and *naïveté* come from French *naïf,* "natural, inborn," which comes from Latin *nasci,* "to be born," and *natura,* "birth." They describe inborn characteristics. The same Latin word gives us our words *native* and *nation.* To be naïve is to be childlike, natural, and native, aboriginal in your own skin.

Seeing with your soul is what Rumi referred to as "gazing raptly." In most social situations and even during lovemaking, we rarely make eye contact, rarely see who we are in conversation with. We learn to not look, to cast our eyes away, shut down our hearts and are barely present with the other. Sacred sex means being fully present in body, feeling with skin and heart, attending with mind, and seeing with eyes. Will Johnson in describing this experience of depth seeing says, "Just stay connected through the gaze, keep surrendering to the current, and accept whatever's around the next bend. Where does this river run to? If anyone knows, there would be no way to tell you. The only way you can find out is to jump in yourself, surrender to its current, and trust its wisdom. Rumi and Shams must have surrendered completely, and the journey they took together is still rightly revered."[2]

❧ EXERCISE ❧
Depth Seeing

For this practice, eliminate as many distractions as possible, relax as deeply as you can. Holding the gaze and heart field are hindered if there is tension held anywhere in the body. Tension in the body will become a distraction, and your mind will want to focus there. Breathe into it and free your body of it with each exhalation.

Sit face-to-face across from your lover. Look directly into each other's eyes. When you begin, you may find you are naturally drawn to the left or right eye or both simultaneously. There are no rules here. What's important is that you relax into this, keep your eyes soft-focused. It's helpful here as well to have a sense of your peripheral vision. It's impossible to have pinpoint vision while your peripheral vision is enhanced. Keep in mind that your heart field is not unidirectional; it radiates 360 degrees around your body. No matter what sexual position you choose in any moment, you will both be wrapped in the field of the heart.

Allow your heart field to expand while you are gazing. Let it reach out and touch your lover, noticing when the two fields meet and how that feels. Hold this gaze as the fields of your heart touch and then pass into each other. You may feel a little "buzz" in the center of your chest as his heart field touches you. Keep breathing easily. With your gaze and the field between you, you'll begin to feel a magnetic pull bringing the two of you closer as your souls begin to merge. Shifts will begin to occur in your body and your awareness. Colors will become brighter, luminous, filling the room. You'll feel strange sensations in your limbs, your head, and every cell of your being as the life force begins to pulsate and radiate throughout. As if a great cloud has been penetrated, your vision will be clearer, your perceptions sharper.

Notice also how your lover's body looks and feels to you as well as everything that is happening inside and around your own skin. Let your seeing become your thinking. The moment your mind becomes active, you will lose the gaze. It's nothing to fret about; gently, not willfully, return to your gaze and heart-field awareness.

When our eyes meet in that soulful gaze, it is the feeling in the gaze, the feelings that result in the gaze, that distinguish it from merely looking. It may seem as if you've opened a great book of memories with all the attendant feelings and emotions. You're beginning to ride the wave of ecstatic union, where physical boundaries begin to fall away easily from you and from him. As the physical boundaries fall away, the two of you feel as if you have touched the source of all that is and you've entered the territory of the gods.

It is the place where day and night entwine as lovers, where wave after wave falls in upon itself, where the real of day slips past and the numinous presents itself. The longer you hold this state and the deeper into the bliss of ecstatic, soul-to-soul communion you go, the sooner you will no longer be riding the wave but will be the wave. The movement will sometimes be fluid, smooth, and calm; at other times a turbulence will rise up inside you. Calm or turbulent, it does not matter, you are going somewhere, to a land where colors have taste and smells have sound. In the soft, sweet gaze of your lover's outward eyes, you begin to feel drunk with love, drinking deep, deeper into his inward eyes, the place of his soul looking back at you.

There is a feeling in the room now, between and around the two of you; it's palpable. Feel it. Drink it in. Anchor it into the body memory. This is what is real, this feeling, this experience. It is beyond ordinary, day-to-day living. This feeling can be brought into all that you do. It is what an ensouled life feels like. An ensouled life is a real life.

To get comfortable with this kind of intimate seeing, practice it often for as long as you can. This can be done in any position and during any activity. You'll begin to know the territory and maintain your balance in the presence of whatever arises inside you the more you practice. You'll fall in love with this feeling of being in the gaze/heart field, wanting to do it with all those you love. With practice, you'll soon be moving in the world gazing at everyone you meet, if you wish.

❧ EXERCISE ❧
Sacred Sex

Take your lover by his hand and bed down with him. Keep your heart field wrapped around him as you lay naked body to naked body, eye to eye, breath to breath. Bring your lips to softly touch his as you gaze into his eyes, feel the ebb and flow, the in and out of his breath. Match your breathing, inhaling his exhales, exhaling as he inhales your sweet breathing. Breathe together like this as you hold each other's gaze and until you feel you have the rhythm of breathing together, sharing the atmosphere between the two of you. It's okay if you miss a breath, just return to it. Return to his eyes, his face, his heart, his breathing until you feel your two souls embrace. Be aware of that feeling of the numinous, of your two souls, as you slowly begin to be enchanted in the sacred space you've entered into. Hold it as long as you can, breathing naturally. In that rapturous gaze, you are enthralled, enchanted, absorbed. This is a feeling state and it is invisible. The experience within the gaze is the entwining of two souls. Holding the gaze as naturally as you breathe affords a shift in consciousness. Let it shift without restriction; follow where it leads. Looking with only the physical eyes is one dimensional. To gaze is to look with the eyes of the soul.

Hold that feeling of rapture in your heart, your energy field—that sophisticated organ of imaginal seeing we call the heart and your awareness as you begin sensuously to travel the landscape of his body with your hands and eyes, your lips and tongue. Take your time. Let your heart feel and see. Feel the textures and curves of each part of him. Let your hands travel around his body as if for the first time, getting to know each part. Explore with other parts of your body, the back of your hand, your forearm, and your feet. Notice that each part of his body has its own personality and that each is communicating with you, with your body and each part of your body. Notice what they are saying, communicating. Notice where he holds tension, which parts are holding back or are afraid, take extra time breathing love into those places, holding them in your heart and its extended field.

Keep in mind you are feeling and sensing your way. Don't fret if you can't hold his gaze at the same time. There is no dogma about what is right and wrong. When working and playing in the realm of the sacred, there are no rules; there is simply following the feeling that presents itself. Follow that, wherever you are drawn to look and gaze there. Follow whatever feelings arise, notice all that is happening. Notice that when you are in this state, your peripheral vision is greatly expanded.

Where do you feel you want to spend more time, lingering, savoring? Continue dropping deeper and deeper into the soul union, giving yourself over to this journey, this exploration, this ecstatic dance of sacred loving. Gaze deeply at each part of him. Engage yourself with the sweet fragrance of his body, of his sex. Become intoxicated with love and longing to have his soul, his smell, his love, him, inside you. Take his fingers in your mouth, his lips, his nipple, his penis. Each movement you make is slow and deliberately organic, following the energy of each moment, filled with the rapture of love and the depth of your union. Make love as if it's the last time you will ever make love. As your desire and excitation builds, slowly slide him inside you as you continue breathing and holding his eyes in your gaze. Hold him in your heart, sending your deep love for him through the invisible field of energy and your deep seeing. Feel everything, hear everything, smell everything. Become inebriated with feeling, swept up in the ocean of sensing. Feel your sex organs talking to each other, send your love for him from your heart, through your belly, down into your vagina, wrapping around his penis. Pay keen attention to his movements, his breathing, sounds, and smells; his responses are communications from his deep self through his body. Follow the waves of ecstatic love and passion, of sexual energy, as they travel throughout your body. Your vagina will begin to feel more ensouled, more sensitive, alive, and aware. It has its own intelligence as any part of your body does.

Permit whatever images, feelings, emotions to arise and fall away. Allow any sounds that rise out of your deep self, your body, your passion to be part of your lovemaking. As he moves inside you, talk to him with your hands, send your love through them, explore his body, light touch here, more pressure there. Let your fingers and the intelligence in them slide between your two bodies to touch the base of his penis, then his testicles, and that sweet soft crease between his leg and groin. Let them slip along the length of his penis inside you. With each movement notice what that part of his body is communicating to you. Try out different ways of moving with him as he moves inside you. Raise and lower your hips, move side to side, slow down, speed up as he thrusts, penetrating all your bodies. Allow your erotic, sensual, sexual self be completely, freely involved in sacred sex.

You may discover emotional wounds or physical scars you hadn't felt until now. Send your caring into those places, fall in love with each one. You'll touch parts of his body he doesn't really like. Take your time here. They especially need to be noticed, caressed, kissed, and loved. Keep breathing your love into them with your breath and heart. Really notice him in ways you have not in the past. If you find your mind beginning to chatter on, gently return your attention to breathing through your heart and to gazing.

In essence, you give yourself over completely to loving him, to being in service to the sacred communion of sex as holy devotion.

After lovemaking, continue holding this space you're in, hold him in your arms, gently kissing his forehead, pronouncing your love for him and how wonderful it is to be with him, how good he feels, all the while keeping your heart field wrapped around the two of you.

Practice often until having your heart field involved intimately in your life becomes as natural to you as breathing. You can have sacred sex and wildly passionate sex at the same time. Sacred sex isn't about holding anything back. That's what fucking is; it's holding back parts of ourselves, holding back love, and, especially, holding back feeling and intimacy. Sacred sex means holding nothing back in order to transform mechanical sex to sex as a divine, fluid, ecstatic experience of two bodies becoming one numinous, boundary-less body.

Sacred sex creates a bond between two people, as does sharing heart fields with anyone you are intimate with. To bond with someone is to bring a particular kind of power into the world. A bond is an exchange of soul food. As you bond with someone, a link is created. It must be worked with consciously, with intention and focus.

Whether or not you practice the gaze/heart field in a sexual relationship or with an intimate friend, you can have this experience, this soul-to-soul meeting with the energy that is birthed between the two. Let the energy take you deeper inside your own feeling body and into the psychic field of the other. You are moving away from "knowledge of" to what we call "knowledge with." The gods speak to us through sexual potency and the bond of intimacy, which in turn makes possible an awareness of the world of the gods.

NURTURING THE THIRD BODY

A numen is a local divinity or presiding spirit. When people commit to each other, there is a third entity that is created, that is birthed into existence from the bond of you. The third being created from the bond of the two is an indwelling force or quality that animates or guides the relationship. It is a spiritually alive being. Something that comes into being that is more than the sum of its parts, more than the two of you. Sex is more than the sum of its parts.[3] Just as Earth is more than the sum of its parts. Sacred sex is a ceremony, if you will. It is a communication with the invisibles inside us and the spirit of the relationship.

The third that is created is birthed through and because of the relationship. It is brought into being, into essence, as an invisible thing, the *anima* of the relationship. You can't see it, but you can feel it. And your feeling of it will allow you to work with it directly, to shape it, to tend it, nurture it, and feed it with the love between you and your awareness of its presence. Once you become aware of this third being, bring it into sexual touching, into sacred sex. It's a palpable presence, one that gets stronger the more you nourish it through the relationship.

The two people in the relationship hold this third being in the fore of their hearts and minds. All decisions must be deferred to the whole so the choices that are made ideally enhance the whole or at a minimum maintain the energy and never take energy away from it. Be certain that the soul of the relationship is taken care of and accounted for moment to moment. The third being lives not just in the bedroom; it is alive and becomes part of your day-to-day living. Even if the two of you are in separate households, or separated by miles, the third being that is born out of your bond is still a viable and integral part of the relationship.

A Third Body

A man and a woman sit near each other, and they do
    not long
at this moment to be older, or younger, nor born
in any other nation, or time, or place.
They are content to be where they are, talking or
    not-talking.
Their breaths together feed someone whom we do
    not know.
The man sees the way his fingers move;

he sees her hands close around a book she hands
    to him.
They obey a third body that they share in common.
They have made a promise to love that body.
Age may come, parting may come, death will come.
A man and a woman sit near each other;
as they breathe they feed someone we do not know,
someone we know of, whom we have never seen.

ROBERT BLY,
LOVING A WOMAN IN TWO WORLDS

A JOINING OF SOULS

Sacred sex calls us to participate directly in the immense and infinite boundary-less spiritual landscape. It calls us to participate in, within and to transform physical boundaries as we deconstruct, re-create, and recover our authentic being. Sacred sex is not a technique; it's a living communication or conversation, not a dead language of antiquity. It's a communion, a holy sharing of the sacred texts of our mind, body, and soul. In that communion, we are filled with awe, our spirit lifted and moved to stillness.

As trust in each other grows, as a deep friendship and bond sets anchor, an interesting thing begins to happen. A conversation between each part of me and each part of him begins. During lovemaking, I'm aware of a conversation going on between my vagina and his penis, as they have their own conscious personalities. I feel his love channeling through his organ to places deep inside me. My hands talk to his skin, his skin talks back, our feet chat to each other as they caress and explore the other. As various ego states present themselves through parts of our body and varying sexual positions, there are opportunities to have conversations with each of them.

Being reunited after an absence, the parts of me that have especially missed him are eager to be reacquainted. The hunger I feel for him is all consuming. I can't wait to touch him, to have my hands on him, to smell him and taste him. Each part of me reunites with each part of him.

At times I feel like a flip book with a picture that changes as you quickly flip the pages; one ego state after another rises up inside me to meet him and to be seen by him, rekindling and deepening our friendship.

Sacred sex is the closest we come to joining our souls with another human being. It is a primordial and biologically encoded urge to marry our spirits during lovemaking, to feel the boundaries of our bodies disappear; to not know where one body ends and another begins, to be inextricably bound spirit to spirit, soul to soul, body to body, as two strands of DNA spiraling in and around the other. There is an innate need, a hunger inside us to know God, to know the infinite and boundless Universe through our sensing body, through the field of our hearts, through the waters of sex and semen and sweat.

Bradford Keeney writes about how the Bushmen in Kenya experience their kinship with Nature and God.

> When Bushmen say they own something, it means not only that they own the feeling for it but also that the feeling has transmitted its essence, its complex nexus of relationships, into their very being. We become the other—whether a friend or a butterfly, redwood forest, giraffe, or seahorse—through our intensely felt union with it. . . . You have to make love with God. The rest of the world seems to have had a marriage ceremony with God, but their marriage hasn't been consecrated. . . . Feeling God is akin to having sex or making love with God. It is a transmission and a reception of the highest and most powerful love. . . . If God is love and we get close to this big love, then how could it not be as amazing as the most intimate experiences of sexuality? [4]

Sacred sex happens when we are home in our bodies, and we allow any feelings to arise without censoring and allow the dreamer and the imaginal facility of the heart to be present in our lovemaking. Those parts of us are uninhibited, untethered, and move easily between the worlds of the ordinary and the nonordinary. They are the parts that travel in the world of the written word, when a good novel is able to take us into that world of fiction, making us completely unaware of the physical world where we are sitting with a book in our hands.

The dreamer in us is able to transcend physical boundaries, go beyond physical touch to the invisible, numinous, touch of spirit on our soul: the sublime. When we experience the numinous, we experience something external to ourselves that is greater than ourselves. The sublime and the transcendent are counterparts to the numinous. The sublime and numinous cannot be analyzed or dissected; they cannot be explicated. These are not matters solely for the mind to ruminate on. These belong to the realm of feeling. Rudolf Otto proposes that "the sublime may stimulate the capacity to perceive the numinous."[5] There is a tendency for the sublime and numinous to pass over into each other.

The major transformative experience of sex is to reach the state of the *numinous,* to fall away from the bondage of thought and religious dogma into the open palms of God, of the ancestors waiting for your arrival into the *mysterium tremendum,* the wild ecstatic state of bliss where your thinking mind is quieted, given over to the power of the moment. The body and soul surrender to the rapture and to the gods that have come to play, flirt, kiss, suck, nibble, love, and tease your mind out of linear, dogmatic thinking, indoctrinization, and walled schooling. The mind stops thinking and makes room for witnessing. "Some say Human Beings are the ground where the gods reside." Joan Halifax in *The Fruitful Darkness,* says, "But I am sure that it is not in us but in the interworld between us and sacred space that the gods finally arise."[6]

> *Consider re-entry into the wild. Become a wild shaman, a wild pagan, a wild Christian, a wild Buddhist, a wild Jew, a wild agnostic, a wild artist, a wild performer, a wild whatever you want to call it because the name is less important than the experience of being wild in this natural though always uncommon way of giving priority to mystery over mastery.*
>
> BRADFORD KEENEY,
> *SHAKING MEDICINE*

> *Eros: love-desire connective energy through erotic passion we overcome our habitual egoic insularity and reach out into the core of other beings. Blazing Eros recognizes no barriers; it is the organic impulse toward wholeness.*

That wholeness is the holy, the sacred. The word holy is
etymologically related to "whole," both of which refer to a
condition of completeness or fullness.

GEORG FEUERSTEIN,
SACRED SEXUALITY

Holiness is present at every dawn and at every sunset . . .
Holiness is in the rain, the snow, every season for the person
who embraces his or her own seasons . . . holiness is in the
smile we wear and the tears we shed. Holiness is the smile
we appreciate on others and their tears that we care for.

BRUCE DAVIS

To begin with what is sacred, what is holy, I bring it down, Earth into the soil of my body. It is not only something outside me, or apart from me. It is not found only in temples, synagogues, or churches, and it does not start and stop, no ending or beginning. The kingdom of sacred divinity is inside me and inside you. It resides in the space between us where our divine spirits comingle, where our souls intertwine and the boundaries of our bodies diffuse.

Unexpected things happen in the rapture of sacred sex. He's inside you, and the two of you are breathing, looking into each other's eyes. You feel his love moving inside you, going deeper as he moves inside. You feel overwhelming love and trust, and the room takes on a luminous glow. Spirit arrives; the third being has come to be with the two of you.

A Third Body
Lovers give birth to a third body.
Its lungs have the capacity
to breathe for two,
although they breathe
something other than air.
Its heart has the strength
to keep two alive,

although it pumps something
other than blood.

This body is not made of flesh,
but of thought and feeling.
It is the labor of two hearts
and two minds
that have learned
to dance together.

Although it is created by two
who live in separate bodies,
those two
inhabit this body
they have made together
when those separate bodies die.

PAUL FERRINI,
DANCING WITH THE BELOVED

The place inside you where you have been hiding grief and sorrow and fears begins to open up with the touch of his love. The place inside you may be a room. It has a flexible door that responds to the touch of his love. It opens, and all that you have been holding back, keeping safe and secret, begins to flow out in a river of tears. From the watching place inside you, notice as the room is emptied of its contents, and you see each part you tucked away behind the door. All the while you are making love with your man inside you. And he is making love with you, breathing with you, holding you. He holds you and loves you while you do the sacred work of letting the sorrow and fear leave your body, your psyche, all the holding in you've been doing is released as the touch of his love, his penis inside you touches the ground of you, and a great torrent of release sweeps through the two of you. What has been emptied can now be filled with something new, something luminous, a wholeness is created in the wake of exiting pain.

EGO STATES AND SEXUAL POSITIONS

As you travel deeper into the sacred territory of your lovemaking, you may notice him taking on a younger ego state. Listen to his choice of words; notice his playfulness and innocence, the feelings and emotions rising up from deep inside. If he is willing to make love from this place, a younger ego state, he needs to feel you are there to receive him, feel your love and caring of him.

Changing sexual positions facilitates a change in ego states. And these different positions can alter, or alternate, the male/female energies inside us. For example, the male on top, face-to-face position puts the woman in the traditional place of being receptive, open, inviting, and receiving the male. Being on the bottom is a position of vulnerability, submissiveness, if you will, and it naturally allows for younger ego states to emerge. The man on top from behind can bring to the surface unresolved issues of powerlessness and the rape element. It can also satisfy a need to be domi-nated or overpowered, to feel the strength of him pushing on you while in a position that compromises your strength.

The position most likely to access and facilitate *his* feminine nature is, as you might have surmised, the female-on-top position. He is then not only symbolically and emotionally, but also for real, in the position of receptivity. If he is willing, he can move from symbolically recep-tive to authentically receptive. That is to say that he makes a conscious choice to be receptive, to open up to receiving your love and letting it fill him.

There were a few times I became keenly aware of, and quite surprised by, the male in me inside my body, the strength of that part and, at times, its forcefulness. I felt the male in me using my arms and hands to hold my lover strong and tight. It took some time for my partner to get used to so much male energy between the sheets, but he spent time talking to the man of me, so much so that it feels at home being with him and is not shy about influencing our lovemaking. When I feel more male energy in me, I still love having female sexual organs. When I'm on top making love, I tend to have more male energy, but it is not the rule. Often I am the older, mature woman of me. Rarely, in my experience, does that position facilitate a younger ego state.

What is really fascinating is that as the relationship develops in strength, trust, and friendship, as your bodies and sexual organs become friends, it's fascinating to notice that his penis feels like it's yours. There often comes the moment that you can't tell who has the vagina and who has the penis. They are, and the two of you are, deep in the ecstatic state of lovemaking. The more your bodies speak to each other, the more your movements are exquisite and flawless as a finely choreographed dance, the more ambiguous ownership of sexual organs.

Which ego state is present during fellatio? It may be quite a different one during the giving than the receiving. Ingestion of semen has a mystical and potent history. In many cultures, it is considered empowering to the woman and feeds her subtle bodies. In every culture, it has the potential to increase intimacy in the relationship. It also has the potential to extend lovemaking.

But, don't take my word for it. Find out for yourself; that's where the fun is. As you play and experiment with changing positions, notice how you feel when you are on top. Do you feel more or less masculine, more or less vulnerable or powerful? More deliberate in your moves? How does he feel to you when you are on top? Does he feel softer to you, more yielding, more feminine, open, and receptive even? When you are on the bottom, beneath him, how do you feel? Do you feel more or less vulnerable? Which one do you favor and is the most fun? Which one is more frightening, uncomfortable, and brings up the most "stuff"? Does he look younger, older, harder, softer, or more mature in one position than another?

There may be physical limitations that prescribe which positions are the most comfortable if, for example, you have a physical disability of some kind. Level of fatigue may dictate the choice of positions as well. If your energy levels are low, try facing each other on your side, front to front or front to back. The important thing is to keep your heart field present in each position.

Give each position your attentive noticing. Which ego states come out in which position? Follow that energy; let whoever wants to be present, be present. You're not in charge; you become, if you will, your own spiritual midwife, witnessing, holding, allowing younger parts of you to emerge, say what they want to say, ask questions they need answers to. Let your Child's wonder, curiosity, and enjoyment of sex rise to the surface. All the while, your heart fields are wrapped around each other, your spirits entwined as much or more than your physical bodies are, and engaged in soul-to-soul sharing. Return often to a state of vulnerability and naïveté (it does get less scary). Notice if any defenses begin to arise in you, any tensions in your physical body as well as emotional and psychological armoring that attempts to lock into place. Over time, you may notice that ego states shift position; they are not locked into one position. They are dynamic, evolving, and can move around as they become more integrated in who you are.

Act as if you're making love for the first time, and you're being present with every nuance, each movement, noticing everything and every detail in yourself. It's crucial to undefend moment by moment, opening more of yourself, more of your body and your deepest self, letting him enter every part of you. As his penis enters physically farther, his spirit, his soul essence, his love, his caring, his gaze are also penetrating the deepest oceans of you.

Notice each ego state that makes herself known. The farther he gets inside you, physically, emotionally, and spiritually, the greater the chance for deeply held ego states to emerge from being touched. See your lover through these eyes, the eyes of a young child who loves to look, to feel, and to see. The one who can see deep into your lover's interior world is intuitive and sensitive to what is happening.

As a fine woodworker knows the defining characteristics of each unique piece of wood he works with—the grain, color, smell, and texture—so too can you know the intimate and defining details of your lover inside and outside. The woodworker takes care to listen to the medium of his expression, waiting for the moment the thing reveals itself. It is no different with a human being; it is relationship and communication.

Don't be afraid to talk, to say how you feel, how much you enjoy the feel of him inside you. The more you talk, the less you'll stay hidden, and the deeper the sharing can go. Continue to be aware of the energy of your heart wrapping around him. Say out loud all the things you enjoy; your favorite positions, how his lips feel, how the two of you kiss. Explore each other's skin, levels of touch, the contours of your bodies. You're beginning the journey of knowing your lover, the geography of his body and the secret territory inside. Tell him all the things you enjoy about him—the way he touches your skin or the way he enters a room. Say out loud what you love about his body and his skin. Go into detail; find details in him that you love, that you adore, that you look forward to meeting each day. Murmur admirations as your fingers whisper slowly along the luscious, wonderful, erotic, curves of his body. Let your fingertips fluidly trace the movement of curvature where neck and shoulder meet and caress each other; continue along his arm to the curve of his hips as he lies on his side; linger in the valley, that sweet sway in the small of his back, drawing spirals with the tip of your finger. Follow the serpentine curves as your two bodies' entwine. How is he responding? Does he like his ears rubbed? Does he let loose a sigh when you touch certain parts of him? As you're tracing the lines of his body, you're also noticing how different areas of his skin have various textures. There are the soft parts of his body, his stomach, his ass, under his arms. Thicker, rougher skin is on his hands, his forearms, maybe his thighs. It's your caring, your love for him, your desire to know him intimately, to know the details of his inner and outer life, that slows you down to notice, to see. Adore each part of him. Fall in love with each one over and over, with abandon.

He will show you what shadows he casts that illuminate parts of his interior world. The behaviors he acts out, his habits, the choices he makes whisper at what is in the depths of his character. He may show you his thirst for intimacy and fear of it. Is he afraid of speaking in public? Is he uncomfortable being alone? Does he prefer to start his morning quietly and slowly, or does he wake ready to meet the day? What is his relationship with food? Does he love romance? Does he cry at movies? Is he comfortable with you crying at movies? What angers him consistently or spontaneously? What is his relationship with his family? Do you know what soothes him, inspires him, and excites him?

When you begin to see below the surface to places that were once hidden from view, when he begins to let your love travel inside to touch his deep child-self, an invisible thing is present there, between the two of you. That invisible thing is trust, unseen yet casting a shadow, a hint of its presence in the look of an eye, the touch of a hand, a secret shared. Sometimes fragile, sometimes strong as steel, trust is a foundational structure upon which the building of the relationship grows.

PART 3

Challenges You May Meet on the Road

10

The Dance of Trust

Trust yourself. Create the kind of self that you will be happy to live with all your life. Make the most of yourself by fanning the tiny, inner sparks of possibility into flames of achievement.

GOLDA MEIR

As you may have discovered by now, the process of getting clear, becoming aware, and knowing the deep parts of you as you practice sacred sex and intimacy can occasionally get a little rocky. You may feel off balance, disoriented, and you may even feel that you are shaken to your core. The thing is, when the boat rocks, you never know which way it is going to tip. Rigorous self-examination and trust in the process, yourself, and your partner are crucial. Then, it matters not which way the boat tips if trust is in the framework. Trust cannot exist without the possibility of betrayal, the two coexist on a continuum. Only those we trust at a primal level—ourselves, lovers, husbands, wives, sisters—have the power to betray us. To think it is possible to have any sort of relationship with absolute trust, containment, and security is to place yourself in a world that does not exist.

The degree of trust between people directly relates to the degree of intimacy they share. Trust and intimacy are dance partners, spiraling, embracing, and weaving the couple into a tighter matrix of relationship.

Inside the spiraling dance is the embryo of freedom; freedom to voice that which has been silenced, freedom to bend, to choose, to ask, to feel, to express. There is freedom from games, codependency and drama. And when you feel free to be spontaneous, your life becomes less a life filled with regrets, resentments, and searching and becomes more a life of expressing who you were born to be. Your life is authentic, and you are authentically being. All that you do is a reflection of you, and *you* are in all that you do.

The most immediate and deep healing I've experienced was with someone I completely trusted—someone who I knew could betray me because of that very trust, but who I chose to trust nonetheless—someone who saw all the broken and lost parts of me, as well as the intelligent, witty, intuitive, and charming parts. It was having all of me seen, acknowledged, and welcomed into the world, having my secrets received, that allowed parts of me to wake up, that enabled me to come home and begin healing and integrating.

BREAKING THE TRUST

Trust isn't a word or concept that normally comes up in everyday conversations. When it does, it has weight to it. Often, it's mentioned in the context of feelings of betrayal, broken trust, and broken promises or agreements. Trust is often taken for granted, meaning that it is not actively maintained. As we move into any new relationship, there is often a brief period of suspicion, doubt, and hesitation while the Child of you is checking out the other person. At some point, she'll make a decision that she is willing to extend trust to this person and explore the relationship.

Trust is always a decision. If you were to trace back incrementally how you got to the point of trusting someone, you would find a series of moments when you scrutinized the other person out of the corner of your eye, ran all the feelings you were having through your inner council, and got your Adult's information and the Parent's blessing. You would find the moment at which you made the decision based on intuition and feeling and whether or not the person's language was congruent with his behavior. Your Child is calibrating all these things whether you are aware of it or not.

There are few gray areas in matters of trust; either it is actively being cultivated or it is eroding; either there is trust or there is betrayal. You may find that you trust someone with your deepest self and be watching them at the same time.

Most often we don't consciously think about trust unless we feel someone has done something that causes us to distrust them. They have abused our trust or gone unconscious and let a mean or mad part of themselves say hurtful things out loud. It takes time to rebuild trust after it's been damaged. This is true whether the damage to trust is to the Child in us or the Child in the other person. We fracture or break the trust of the Child in ourself by not keeping our agreements with her, by abandoning her, or by undermining her trust in any number of small ways. We seldom consider the importance of building and maintaining trust in our own self to take care of our own security. James Hillman says, "What we long for is a situation where one is *protected from one's OWN treachery and ambivalence.*"[1] Trust should be treated as a real thing that needs tending for it to grow and strengthen the relationship. Getting to the place in a relationship where the two of you are able to relax into your bond, with trust as the adhesive, liberates both of you to be who you are with each other. Trust in yourself frees you to be spontaneous with a diverse palate of responses in your repertoire. Being in a relationship with someone whom you don't trust, or where trust has been damaged and not repaired, diverts energy away from intimacy.

When two people have a falling out, it usually starts with one person getting irritated about something. Say you are upset and decide to say something to your partner. But without the skills and experience of interior work and knowing yourself, a part of you, an unconscious part, takes over and says something unkind or damaging, even. Typically, your partner will respond with something equally hurtful, and then the two of you are off to the races. It's common in this scenario for old stuff to come out in the argument. You may bring out things you don't like about your partner, or all the other times they said something or did something hurtful. The reason this happens is that the part of you that spoke has been keeping a file on all the little irritations or slips of the tongue, broken agreements, or promises not fulfilled. In the Transactional Analysis model, it's called saving stamps.

That part of you—a paranoid part, most often the Predator or the unhappy Child—is keeping score, building an arsenal, and sharpening her blade. If a counterpart in him has been doing the same thing, the argument escalates, one of you leaves slamming the door, and all is quiet for a few hours. This is a version of what Eric Berne called uproar. You may be able to maintain distance while a cool breeze wafts between the two of you for a day or two, until it gets too uncomfortable, and one of you has to say *something*. Often it's just enough to break the ice that's been growing thicker: "I'm sorry we had a fight." "I'm sorry I yelled at you. I've been really stressed lately." Then you hug and go about your lives. Or, you have the most amazing, intense sex of your relationship. Often one of those or a combination is enough to return you to the status quo. A lot of us live our lives just that way.

Unfortunately, in this scenario, even though the two of you are able to cohabitate and return to "normal" life, there is a tremendous amount of accumulated debris between you. The part of you that was stressed—if in fact that is the truth, for we often lie or gloss things over to avoid the real problem—and lashed out has not gotten what she needs and has unresolved anger, rage, grief, or fear. The pressure has been released for the time being, but the underlying issue is, once again, being put under a lid. Russell Brand, the English comedian and disc jockey, said, "You know, these relationships we 'ave, everything sort of bubbles under the surface. No one ever says what they actually mean, do they? It's all a bit pappy and rubbish."

One Source of Bad Information

There's a boy in you about three
Years old who hasn't learned a thing for thirty
Thousand years. Sometimes it's a girl.

This child had to make up its mind
How to save you from death. He said things like:
"Stay home. Avoid elevators. Eat only elk."

You live with this child, but you don't know it.
You're in the office, yes, but live with this boy
At night. He's uninformed, but he does want

To save your life. And he has. Because of this boy
You survived a lot. He's got six big ideas.
Five don't work. Right now, he's repeating them to
you.

ROBERT BLY,
MORNING POEMS

‿ EXERCISE ‿
Following a Feeling to Its Source

Whenever you feel something pushing at you from inside, something trying ever so persistently to get your attention, don't ignore the feeling. Follow the feeling to its source inside you. Start by asking yourself, "What *is* that? What is going on?" Turn to face the feeling. If you had to give the feeling a name, what would it be? Mad, sad, glad, or scared? Depressed, grieving, terrified, or lonely? Ask your Child to come and sit with you; ask her to tell you what's going on. She will know. There will be a need she has and wants your help with it. If she's scared, she needs to feel not scared or at least she needs to know that the grown-up part of you will do everything it can to help her feel less scared. She may be sad, in which case you ask her, "What do you need to feel happy?"

If you've been working long hours, she may need physical strokes. If so, ask your partner if he would lie down with you and give you some strokes: stroke your forehead, rub your feet, rub your back, massage your head. Notice how you begin to relax; your breathing lets go in deep exhalations. If you've been holding a lot of emotion back to get through a difficult time, there may be an upwelling of uncontrolled emotion when the love coming through his touch reaches the Child inside you. You're being vulnerable and being held in the love of your partner, and your Child is being held by you, taken care of by you. It may feel so good to her, she may just want to weep a little. Let her; let the tears flow, or the laughter, or the joy rise up and the stress leave.

It's absolutely not necessary to wait until you know exactly what's going on for you. In fact, it's important in the beginning, until you gain facility with interior ego states, feelings, and emotions, and become intimate with yourself, to start saying out loud that you don't feel like yourself and it's distracting you from being present with your partner.

You may even say to your partner, for he has likely noticed that you're not feeling yourself, "I'm a little distracted right now. I feel funny, just not myself. Will you sit and talk with me so I can figure this out?" Or, "Will you sit and hold me?" It may come to light as you're describing how you're feeling that you've been afraid of the upcoming business trip he's about to take. Or you're disappointed about something. Or you're afraid about your finances. It could be anything, but you won't know if you don't look and feel. Trying to work it out inside yourself is possible, may be necessary, and is a valuable skill to have. However, if you are in an intimate relationship, enlisting your partner's help and support—a shoulder to lean on and a loving ear willing to listen—strengthens the relationship and takes the pressure off you. Unshielding yourself to create intimate moments can be a wonderful aphrodisiac.

MENDING THE TRUST

Once you have betrayed the trust of another, you must do interior work to analyze the dynamics of your behavior; what went unattended, what part was upset, what needs were not met? Then you must own your behavior and then do the necessary work to clean up the mess you've made in the relationship and make amends. It's important, if at all possible, assuming your partner is still talking to you, that he is involved in the repair; that he gets what he needs to feel better with you. It may take time to decide to trust someone again, to reestablish intimacy, but it can happen.

Trust can be repaired if the other person, and the Child inside him, sees that you are taking responsibility for your actions. Saying

"I'm sorry, I didn't mean to say that," might work for some people. It no longer works for me to say it or accept it. When I look at my transaction honestly, with a desire to truly know myself and be whole, I know some part of me meant to say, or do, that thing. It might be that I have been letting pressure build with no strategy in place to relieve it. Parts of me were getting really tired of not having a break; I went unconscious and quit thinking and paying attention. Replaying the event puts me in relation with the movements and communications. Only when I'm in relation to it will I have options from which to do something different.

This is where maintaining eye contact is essential. It's awkward and uncomfortable in the beginning. Scary, really. Maintaining eye contact while you make amends communicates your willingness to repair trust and intimacy. There will be a strong tendency to want to hide and feel ashamed for screwing up. It's important to not give in to the lure of indulging in feelings of shame but to proactively work to make the relationship whole again.

If your partner has hurt you, tell him what you need from him to feel better and begin to be friends again. Say everything out loud: "What you said or did really hurt me. I need to know why you did that so you will not do it, or any version of it, again." Sometimes a gift is needed to make up such as: "I want you to buy me a new futon," or "I want you to take me out for a really nice dinner." What you ask for should be equivalent to the damage done. It's important to have your Child involved in the request. What does she need? What would it take for her to feel counted again? Breaking trust, intentionally causing hurt in someone, is a discount to the Child and to the relationship. So reparations need to take both those things into account.

We all make mistakes and we have all been unkind at times. To heal the damage done from going unconscious, it helps to work at not feeling bad about it, to not wallow in the hurtful thing you did, not indulge yourself in carrying the bad feelings around. Take some time to talk to your Child so she doesn't walk around feeling bad. It doesn't change anything, and it expands the bad feelings between everyone involved for longer periods of time. Resolve it inside yourself as quickly as possible so movement toward intimacy can happen sooner. If necessary, put the bad feelings aside until later, work to heal the damage and the relationship first. That is primary in this scenario.

I had a habit of beating myself up for days after an incident of going unconscious and being unkind. I was a student of self-loathing; it was a familiar behavior. It took time to come to terms with what I had done, but mostly it took time to give up feeling like a piece of shit and reinforcing old scripts about my self-worth. It took a lot of work to come to terms with the predator in me, to integrate that part so she didn't act out. It took time for me to really get that I am capable of hurting someone emotionally. There is a need for rigorous self-examination, of listening to the voices inside, of watching your own movements and taking action to prevent any part of you that is upset from using your mouth. And then you must learn to self-correct in the moment. It's work, particularly in the beginning, and it gets easier. The more you do this work, the fewer mistakes you'll make and the less hurt you'll cause, and the more secure and confident you'll become in yourself.

> *You can be in a huge crowd, but if you don't feel like you*
> *can trust anybody*
> *or talk to anybody, you feel like you're really alone.*
>
> FIONA APPLE

> *Today I trust my instinct, I trust myself. Finally.*
>
> ISABELLE ADJANI

> *It is impossible to go through life without trust: that is to be*
> *imprisoned in the worst cell of all, oneself.*
>
> GRAHAM GREENE,
> *THE MINISTRY OF FEAR*

> *Someone to tell it to is one of the fundamental needs of*
> *human beings.*
>
> MILES FRANKLIN

INJUNCTIONS

An injunction is a writ or an agreement some part of you made to refrain from or forbid an act or speech. Injunctions around behaviors or stories are often made by a very young part of ourselves who made a declaration as the consequence of some painful experience. We have all made some vow, some agreement with ourselves. Injunctions range from never being vulnerable, never depending on anyone, never getting married, never trusting someone ever again, never sharing any intimate part of yourself or your story. Mine were to never trust or depend on anyone and to keep everything to myself. I had injunctions about how to behave in a relationship. I believed that the less that was said, the less opportunity there was for drama, misunderstandings, and miscommunications. The more I kept to myself, secret and private, the more likely the fragile little boat of the relationship and my life would withstand the storm.

I had injunctions about trusting men specifically and people in general. I had decided that whatever I was going to accomplish in my life, I would do it alone. I was the only one I could count on, who would show up and do all the work. A friend called it the Lone Ranger syndrome. It worked pretty well for a while, until I began to burn out. I was on the verge of complete exhaustion, with kidney pain, adrenal fatigue, and massive headaches. My hair was falling out by the handful, and my feet hurt all the time. I had to reexamine how I had structured my life before I became seriously ill. I began to really look at my birth family, our dynamics and unspoken rules about behavior, and consciously chose to do something different, to break the rules, including the ones I had made. As you can see, I've renegotiated those old family agreements. Saying forbidden things, breaking the rules, has terrified me but also liberated me.

Breaking injunctions, conscious and unconscious ones, changes the dynamic with yourself. Breaking an injunction about saying secrets out loud without talking it over with the parts of you that originally made the injunction may have serious consequences. Those parts of you can and will make a mess of things for you to get even and to get your attention. They don't like being left out of such life-changing decisions.

You may hear things like: "You shouldn't have said that. You're going to be sorry." "That'll come back to you." "What were you thinking?" "You moron!" The part of us that is scared gets activated and escalates the fear inside. Panic ensues. And you start bargaining with parts of yourself to calm the fear.

Hans Hofmann said, "The real challenge consists in being so true to oneself that sharing oneself nakedly with another person will be unselfconscious and honest, not marred by exaggerated expectations or apprehensions based on past disappointments or unfulfilled fantasies."[2]

SAY IT OUT LOUD

Everyone has secrets. Secrets are kept for essentially one reason: fear. Fear of abandonment, fear of being hurt, fear of being seen, fear of being too weird, fear of someone you care for being hurt are all powerful motivations to keep secrets. Secrets themselves can be a source of fear, fear of being found out. This does create a dilemma for anyone who wants to have intimacy and yet hasn't found a way to work with these fears. The human animal is a tribal species. We need other human beings for physical and emotional touch. We are not meant to do this dance of life alone. We may choose to retreat to the wilderness on a solitary quest to heal ourselves and, while out there alone, experience the spirits pushing on internal wounds and the crooked places inside, helping us to grow. But we cannot remain in the wildland alone. Without the touch and love of another human being, we would become physically and psychologically ill.

In a *A Blue Fire,* James Hillman expresses it this way:

How can we know ourselves by ourselves? We can be known to ourselves through another, but we cannot go it alone. This is the hero's way, perhaps appropriate during a heroic phase. The opus of the soul needs intimate connections, not only to individuate but simply to live. For this we need relationships of the profoundest kind through which we can realize ourselves, where self-revelation is possible, where interest in and love for soul is paramount, and where eros may move freely—whether it be in analysis, in marriage and family, or between lovers and friends.[3]

We all have a thing or two we want to keep close to our heart, something we may even take to the grave with us. If you have such a secret, it's important to find a way to have true resolution and forgiveness in yourself. Then make the conscious choice to keep the secret. The important thing is to choose from free will and not out of guilt or shame. Be attentive to the nature of the secret. Secrets have the potential to do damage to your deep self and to your relationship. Talk it over carefully with all the members of your inner council. The movie *Get Low,* with Robert Duvall, is a magnificent story of one man's redemption from a secret he carried for forty years, one that he wanted peace with before he died. It's well worth watching.

Secrets have a power of their own. Family secrets that have been kept for generations have a way of insinuating themselves into the psyche of current or future family members. Secrets such as the fact that your mother had an abortion before you were born, your aunt was hidden away in a psychiatric hospital, your great, great grandfather kept slaves, all have a way of slowly eating away at the fabric of family life as well as at the individual family members.

There is a distinct difference between keeping secrets, which is intentionally hiding information, and maintaining privacy. Privacy is "the right to maintain a nonrelational sphere of existence."[4] For example, when you keep sexual acts between you and your lover, husband, or partner away from the eyes of your neighbors, you are exercising your right to privacy.

Secrets can be used to create distance; for example, if you keep secret that you were beaten in a previous relationship, you might fear being physically vulnerable. If there was emotional abuse, you may be calculating how far you're willing to extend yourself emotionally. In these scenarios, you are holding back parts of yourself. If you secretly have judgments about your body, your sexual organs, an ugly part of your body, the inhibition you feel as a result will directly impact your sexual relations and your enjoyment of them as well as the energy you have available for enjoying life.

In relationships, keeping secrets about how you're feeling, what's working, what isn't working, what you need and want in the relationship and for yourself leads to loss of self-dignity, erodes intimacy, and creates loneliness. To have the depth of intimacy and sacred sex we've been exploring requires that we say things out loud. Speaking things out loud can be scary if you feel you are breaking personal beliefs, family, and cultural scripts about what is acceptable to say out loud and what is not.

Secrets *can* make you feel like a phony—inauthentic, isolated, angry—and increase anxiety. Being shut down from our feelings makes us feel disconnected and faraway. If you are secretly dissatisfied with how you and your lover have sex but feel too afraid to talk about it, resentment will start creeping into the relationship. Talking with your partner in a loving way about what each of you likes, doesn't care for, or would really love to have increases intimacy and sexual satisfaction. Sharing things that trouble you, scare you, or bring you joy and excitement increases trust and strengthens the bond.

Sharing secrets can build intimacy, but care still needs to be taken about what you tell your partner and how you tell him. Asking yourself the following questions can help you get clear about what to share and the motivations behind your decision to share it:

Is sharing this going to bring us closer or will it cause a rift between us?

Will saying this add to the life and wholeness of the relationship?

How can I say this thing without threatening our relationship?

Do I need to tell this for my own health and wholeness?

Will this secret push on his sensitivities?

Will this cause harm to my partner?

If you decide it's going to bring you closer, practice inside yourself saying it to your beloved or whoever it is you're going to tell it to. Imagine the impact you want it to have, the potential outcome, and how it might be received. Own the secret as yours without blaming or projecting.

SEXUAL SECRETS

The scripts we were given as children are often involved in the dynamics of secrets. They can be used to maintain the script—the beliefs we have about our bodies, ourselves, our sexuality and sex. For example, not telling your lover you have herpes or that you need added lubrication are shame secrets we have about our bodies. Marty Klein says, "Finally, using sexual secrets to fulfill childhood scripts is very costly . . . scripts emerge as the mind grapples with a single goal: preventing childhood pain. So scripts specifically ignore the needs of contemporary, adult situations."[5] When we hide our condition or our needs, we feel isolated, and it reinforces old beliefs that something is wrong with us and that something bad will happen if we reveal our secret. We keep secrets, we unconsciously think, to protect the child in us from harm. It actually creates the situation we are trying to avoid—feeling lonely, isolated, and unworthy. We can't protect the child from pain that happened in the past. Attempting to use secrets, sexual secrets, to protect the child gives us a false sense of power over our situation and relationships. It goes nowhere good. It degrades trust in the relationship and mistrust from the child to you since she's not getting her real needs met. Trust produces intimacy. Giving up old scripts produces freedom to choose.

Telling our sexual secrets and fantasies dictates that we give up ideas about what is proper and appropriate. That can be challenging since our society has many cultural rules about what is proper and appropriate behavior.

About every six months (usually after two glasses of wine), much to my partner's fascination, I loosen up my restrictions about telling parts of my past sexual experiences to him. Just when I thought I'd said everything, another few months would pass and we would be having fun—enjoying each other's company, bantering witticisms, telling stories, and sexually flirting—and I would spontaneously tell him about more of my experiences. When I first began doing this, it was fun in the moment, but the next day, afraid I had said too much, I would shyly go to him and ask if he still liked me and did he still want to be with me. I had to ask so the uncertainty would not become a caustic eating at my conscience.

Many of us have sexual fantasies that trigger shame and guilt inside us. This often has roots in religion, when children are led to believe that God magically hears *everything,* even our most secret and private thoughts. Having sexual fantasies is normal though there are many messages in the media and from religion that tell us otherwise. It's all right to have fantasies about actors since they are unavailable and can be objectified. But having a sexual thought about your neighbor, that's a little too close to home. Fantasies and thoughts are not bad, having them does not make you a bad person; however, acting out fantasies can be damaging to our relationships, our families, our lives.

Talking about sexual fantasies can actually bring people closer; they are intimate thoughts that can enhance a relationship and deepen trust. Noticing that someone looks attractive, sexy, or seductive doesn't mean you're going to run off with him. It means you're not dead. Making comments about it all to your lover or partner is a sign of trust and comfortability. You can make it playful and fun. Go back and forth: "Well, what about that woman. Do you find her sexy? What do you find attractive?" I know this has potential for escalating into something you don't want. So, be clear in yourself before engaging your mouth. Playful is the best approach; the more playful, the more fun it will be. If you are unable to be playful, it's best to wait until you are filled with love and feel self-possessed; that is, confident and not threatened by outside forces. If you and your lover are able to do this, it can turn into a kind of flirtation between the two of you.

TRUST, INTIMACY, AND SACRED SEX

It's actually quite a lot of fun when you are able to have a relationship with all the parts of you, to have facility with ego states and their needs, wants, and desires, and to know how each one expresses herself. Even more fun when you can cathect—put energy into or activate—any ego state or state of mind at will. Saying things out loud is a pathway to building trust and engages the other person. Share your thoughts, hopes, dreams, and insights with him. Getting to know each other this way, showing yourself to another person, communicates that you want to have a deeper relationship, that you trust enough to share your deepest self with him. Talking out loud is a way of thinking out loud. When you talk with your awareness in your heart, it opens up the imaginal realm to seeing things you hadn't previously.

During sacred sex, as you are arousing each other—talking about what feels good, sharing your love and feeling your hunger and desire building—maintain eye contact, especially when the temptation to close your eyes is greatest. Keeping your eyes open opens wounds, brings them to the surface to be seen and received by the other person. There can be tremendous emotional releasing. It's important, in fact, that you allow everything you are feeling to be felt.

Maintaining eye contact increases trust, healing, and bonding. You can see the other person, see his love of you, see that he is trustworthy.

With your eyes open, gazing into your lover's eyes, it's easier to stay present with your partner and with your feelings and body. Notice everything that comes up and stay with it; let it move through you. Let shame, discomfort, and fears have their place, their time for healing. Allow your child to be fully present here.

Closing your eyes takes you inside yourself, and it can be used to shut down the feelings that are arising when things get too uncomfortable. Honor everything that is happening, attend to every detail. Once you have facility with the territory of the sacred in lovemaking, it gets easier to stay present with what's going on between the two of you, what's happening inside you, what's happening inside him, where you travel inside him, the communications between your bodies.

As you continue to work with the different parts of you, you'll become more experienced, sophisticated, and adept in your responses to your child's need and wants. You'll also be more flexible in responding to old wounds, memories, and issues of trust and shame that will inevitably come to the surface at some, or several, points along the way. As well, you'll become more elegant in your communication skills, analysis, and responses with your partner as you become more whole in yourself, and over time, you will have a greater repertoire of verbal and behavioral options.

You may doubt what your Child is saying, your perceptions and sensing. It's always that way in the beginning. It's tenuous as the relationship begins and you're sorting out who's who inside. Trust yourself; you'll discover you know more than you think you do. You will find your way. Keep going. Ask questions and feel the responses in your body. Your ability to calibrate and attune to the nuances and subtleties will evolve into a system of sophisticated conversations and insights the more you work with ego states, feeling, and perceiving.

Once you trust yourself, then you will know how to live.
                                        JOHANN WOLFGANG VON GOETHE,

                                                                    FAUST

11

Healing Shame

I never learned hate at home, or shame. I had to go to school for that.

DICK GREGORY

Recognizing shame is easy; you feel the impact of it immediately. Your flushed cheeks may demonstrate outwardly your feelings, and the last thing you want at this uncomfortable moment is to be betrayed by your own physiology. Shame nags and gnaws at you, erodes your dignity, and inserts questions and doubts about your character. Feelings of being a bad person or an inadequate human being or having done something wrong permeate your thoughts and drain energy away from you. You'll spend hours, days, years trying to understand what happened and, mostly, how to unhook yourself from that miserable feeling inside you. The more complete your intimacy is with yourself and the more whole you are in yourself, the quicker you will find resolution to the matter and be able to derail shame before it becomes a runaway train carrying your dignity with it.

As you begin work to heal shame, an interesting thing happens as it does with any issue you are bringing to conscious awareness to resolve. Inevitably, because the Universe has a sick sense of humor and impeccable timing, people and events will magically plop themselves in front of you for the sole purpose of bringing up the issues you've decided you're ready to be done with. These people and events have an uncanny ability to shoot a stinging arrow smack in the middle of your shame button. It is one of the most irksome phenomena of healing psychological wounds.

WORKING THROUGH SHAME

My primary shame was around my sexuality, sex, and my body and feelings of inadequacy, of taking up too much space, and of not wanting to be a burden. Of course, there came into my life a woman who knew exactly how to shame me just as I was beginning to taste freedom from it. Everything I had shame about was pushed on in a single transaction. The particulars of what happened aren't important. What is important is the meaning in her transaction with me, which informed me that I didn't have a right to have needs, to be sexual, to ask for what I wanted, or to be happy. What it felt like to my Child was that I didn't have a right to be alive and to be who I am.

It was impossible to keep my balance, so after the shock of it wore off, I fell apart. I wanted to hide, run away, escape, and shrink into oblivion. I withdrew and nearly went catatonic, unable to move or breathe. I believed that if I breathed or moved I'd be seen, and once seen, something terrible would happen again. I shut down and was unable to think or analyze. My feelings became a tangled mess like those balls of fishing line left caught in a snag of branches.

It's difficult work to get out of that space. But it is possible. I untangled the transaction in reverse, one inch of line at a time, until I saw where and how it all began. Only then could I see that it wasn't my fault; I had done nothing to provoke it. "It's my fault" is the first place I would normally go. The woman who had hurt me had probably been scared or upset. But that didn't matter to me; what mattered was that she had done and said those deeply hurtful things. I told my Child that people are just mean sometimes and that we hadn't done anything wrong. I told her that I and others were immensely glad that she is alive.

I learned to go through this laborious process every time I experienced shame. I would feel it, go into shock and shut down almost entirely, then come back to myself, analyze the transaction, unhook it, and get mad.

When will my shame fall away?
When will I accept being mocked
and let my robe of dignity burn up?
When the wandering pony inside
comes calm to my hand.

Lalla

Shame has a physical response in the body and is a crisis of the soul. It's similar to embarrassment, but shame insinuates there is something abhorrently wrong with your moral compass. Simple embarrassment passes; you've committed a social faux pas, a breach of etiquette. Interestingly, it's usage in medical context is to indicate physiological distress as in respiratory embarrassment. And in Portuguese it comes from *embaracar* meaning "a noose" or "rope." Indeed, embarrassment and shame do feel like a noose, choking the life out of us, stealing our dignity and our energy. We feel humiliated, mortified, disgusted with ourselves, unworthy, disempowered, degraded. These are ugly, debilitating feelings to have in any moment, worse to carry them as a way of life. We lose our sense of self, and access to our strength is severely limited when those feelings are present.

Shame sticks like black tar. It causes significant physiological responses in the body. Your face gets red and feels warm as the blood vessels dilate, the sensation sliding up your face to the top of your head. Breathing gets shallow and moves up into your chest, with accompanied heaviness and tensing in the shoulders and limbs as if a tremendous weight has descended on you. It seems impossible to look straight ahead; your head drops and you stare at the floor. Moving becomes nearly impossible. Your only wish is to vaporize or die. Nausea may accompany the symptoms as your stomach tenses up. Your head feels like it's being squeezed in a vice grip. You become keenly aware that the only sound you hear is that of your heartbeat thrumming in your ears. Shame isolates you in the depth of deep loneliness. The urge to cover yourself, to hide, run, or disappear, is paramount. Rodin's sculpture *Eve after the Fall,* where Eve is depicted as lowering her head and covering herself in shame, is thought to be the origin of the word *shame,* meaning "to cover."

Girls blush, sometimes, because they are alive, half wishing they were dead to save the shame. The sudden blush devours them, neck and brow; they have drawn too near the fire of life, like gnats, and flare up bodily, wings and all. What then? Who's sorry for gnat or girl?

ELIZABETH BARRETT BROWNING

Shame is that horrible feeling that I have no control over my life; that someone else has control over how I feel and behave, and I am a mere puppet flailing in response. To save myself from shame, I unlocked each belief about myself that I encountered in the midst of shame. With time, self-loving diligence, and a little rage to keep me focused, I could see the roots of shame and where they were anchored inside. "Oh, that feels like the time my uncle grabbed my breasts and wanted to have sex with me." Most of my shame around sex and sexuality I internalized from my family's discomfort with it and their belief that sex should be a secret. And because I had a strong sexuality, they seemed to feel that there was something demented about me, something inherently and morally wrong with me. Family secrets are a common source of shame. Not talking about your aunt being in a mental institution brings up the shame you feel about being different, or the internalized belief that being in an institution is shameful. Just because something is not talked about does not mean it doesn't exist. It is as present as the elephant in the room that everyone ignores.

Looking back to year eleven, if I had felt that I could tell my mom about the hired hand, I imagine I would have made different life choices. I would have felt more empowered in my life to do so. The event wouldn't have had any power in my life.

At sixteen, I was raped. Telling my parents about it was the most hideous thing I remember having to do as a young girl. Their response was outrage at the man. Fortunately, they didn't blame me. The way they chose to support me was to notify the sheriff. What I really needed was to be held and nurtured and to feel their love. I wanted to be asked what I needed. My family was skill-less in the nurturing department. I hated knowing they knew that I had sex, forced sex, yes, but sex it was. I felt ashamed, weak, stupid, incompetent, and utterly fucking alone. After the sheriff left, the whole subject seemed to be erased. It was never talked about again. It was gone, deleted, vaporized, as if it never happened. I wondered if I was overreacting and began to question if it even really happened. The lack of humanity and intimacy from my parents when I needed it most warped some part of my psyche, and I always felt a little crazier after that, a little more feral.

Their response seared scars into the depths of me. As a survival mechanism, the sixteen-year-old I was at the time became my primary ego state. She was the tough cowboy (not cowgirl) and biker (not biker chick) and full of rage. She is still a major part of my personality, an active part of me, though she is more balanced, more whole in herself and integrated. She is the one who can smell bullshit before it walks in the door. She protected me for a long time and is still a significant part of me, but now she is integrated with all the other parts of me, and they are all friends.

She has her own wardrobe, you see: harness or cowboy boots, several black leather jackets including a vintage biker jacket, two pairs of Levis and two pairs of Gap blue jeans (each with a different attitude), and dark sunglasses. And she hand rolls her own cigarettes. She's most comfortable in bars and saloons where the wood is darkened from years gone by when you could still smoke cigarettes in pubs. The lights are soft, low, and kind. The men and women there have a kind of wild hunger in their eyes, nostrils flaring; they've come looking for something. The gods who love this kind of scene are there always. Eros is sitting on one beam in the ceiling and Dionysus on another, and Psyche is hanging out on a bar stool, waiting for someone to sit down and start chatting.

I don't have regrets about any of the things from my childhood. Nor do I carry hate or rage toward any of my family; sadness has taken its place. I'm certain I wouldn't be who I am without them or those childhood experiences. I have grieved for the young girl of me, for the rape, the sodomy, and for the fact that I was so utterly alone.

Shame has its functions. People who have experienced shame have a sense of humility. They have an understanding of suffering, humiliation, and their own humanity. It can also teach us about ourselves, our limitations, our weaknesses, the limits to our competence and autonomy. It can show us where we've let ourselves down and can strongly motivate us to act. Also, it teaches us to have a sense of humor about ourselves. It's a fast way to break the shame cycle.

I hadn't thought about shame for some time when something interesting happened. It was a nonevent, really. A person just walked through the room, didn't even make contact with me. It happened to be someone for whom I have a tremendous amount of respect. I was having a beer with the guys a few days before I was to take part in a ceremony. Part of preparing for that particular ceremony is to eliminate alcohol among other things. I had participated in this ceremony several times over the last year, was familiar with it and how to prepare for it. It was still five days out, but here I was, having a beer. When I saw this person (the facilitator of the ceremony), I felt ashamed, like I had done something wrong. Later that night as I was lying in bed trying to sleep, I kept looking at this feeling and the images it brought up; then analyzing it. Why would I feel that? He didn't even see me, as far as I knew. And the preparations for the ceremony are "suggestions" (yes, that's justifying my behavior and it's true). I called up my inner council to ask why I was feeling so ashamed. The answer was there immediately: "You feel this way because you strive for and have a perfection complex. You don't want to fuck up or lose your integrity. Primarily, the root of it is that you want to be the good girl. And, you didn't do anything wrong." Ah, that was it indeed, for it rang a clear, resonate tone. I talked to the young part of me that strived diligently in my family to be the golden child, the peacekeeper, and the perfect daughter. It was the little girl of me that felt shame at breaking or stretching the "rules." I let her know that nothing bad would happen, that I understood what she was feeling, that I was sorry I hadn't talked it over with her and for putting her in that situation. I asked if she would like to give up that old script. There was an immediate and vigorous nod and a clear, "Yes, I want to." She didn't have to "try to be good" any longer. She could relax and be herself and let her natural goodness flow unimpeded, unforced. She could give up being good for others for the sake of being good.

Shame numbs us to our sexual feelings. We feel we are not good enough or have no right to enjoy sex. On the other hand, we may feel we have to "put out" in order to be loved, or we overcompensate sexually in order to not feel. We may have internalized the message that "good girls" don't have sex, or if they do have sex, they don't enjoy it, and when we do, we feel a deep conflict and shame about it.

THE SHAME OF SEX

Shame is tightly wound into our sexuality, our feelings about sex, and our sexual organs. Shame seems to have a built-in navigation system that heads directly to our sexual organs—the vagina, uterus, penis, testicles. These are organs that, when engaged, make us feel alive, so it's not unusual for shame to bring up "right to be alive" issues side by side with "right to be or feel sexual" issues. We become ashamed of having breasts or a dick, ashamed of being alive, and we want to apologize for being a man or a woman. We apologize for our life. It's not an accident that shame issues are intimately attached to illness and diseases of the reproductive systems in men and women.

When I got the diagnosis of cervical dysplasia, every atom in the room vaporized. The only thing in my line of vision was each sexual relationship, encounter, rape, indiscretion, seduction, and heartbreak (the ones I received and the ones I caused). I felt dirty, betrayed, ashamed. I didn't need to be a rocket scientist to see that my sexuality, my feelings about it, and my sexual history were all, directly and plainly, laid out on the delta of my diseased cervix.

Brené Brown researched shame through hundreds of interviews and came up with this definition of shame: "the intensely painful feeling or experience of believing we are flawed and therefore unworthy of acceptance and belonging."[1] When we feel shame, we feel a deep disconnect, a separation from the experience of being alive, wanted, needed, acknowledged. We feel we don't belong, that something is wrong with us, and that "wrongness" casts us out.

Shame breaks the contact between people and is sometimes employed to disrupt intimacy when it gets too uncomfortable. Or we project it onto other people, it's hard not to when all we see is seen through the lens of shame. People sometimes use it to mask their own sense of unworthiness and unhappiness. It's a cruel game to play. As Nietzsche said, "What do you regard as most humane? To spare someone shame."[2]

What I have done that has worked for me is everything that I describe in this book. You can't prevent people from being unkind. You can heal old shame. There will be occasions when you feel shamed or are ashamed, either as a response to something you've done or said in an unconscious moment or from someone else. Recognizing shame can stop you from sliding down into the abyss of self-loathing. These are times when self-love, self-compassion, and self-awareness are crucial. To recover your authentic self from the wounds of shame, begin with what's real. The real is what we are always seeking in our lives. The real is what is true in any moment. It is also that which holds up over time.

This is not an academic or intellectual exercise. We're going for what's real, and to get the pieces of, to get a sense of the real, before anything else we must feel and think at the same time. Feeling is our body's innate intelligence; it is our internal GPS, our Grounding Positional System. Without it, we are left to our judgments, fears, and old scripts. We are easily influenced and slide (or are jolted in some cases) from our center by outside forces. Truth begins with and inside the body.

✍ EXERCISE ✍
Identifying Shame

The following statements help reveal internal beliefs. As you say each one, notice how you feel. Does it feel true for you?

I deserve what the person did/said.

I'm not worthy.

I'm a piece of shit.

I don't belong anywhere.

I deserve to be abandoned.

I am unwanted.

I am unlovable.

I am ugly.

I am dirty.

I am not important.

I am a burden to others.

I don't deserve to live.

I don't have a right to be alive.

Being born was a mistake.

I am not smart enough, not thin enough, not strong enough, not cute enough, not funny enough, not fun enough, not [fill in the blank] enough.

Notice how you feel with each statement. What comes up inside you? Do you feel angry, justified, arrogant? Do you shut down and deny the statements?

These are defenses against shame, so we don't have to feel shame's real effect on us. We create defenses to survive the impact. We may resolve to be perfect, so it doesn't ever happen again; we get enraged to divert attention from our flaws; we withdraw to separate ourselves from others and intimate interactions.

These are all archaic belief systems that have poisoned how we are, who we are, and how we behave. The wounds they cause are deep. We've believed them for so long we have contempt for ourselves. The choices we've made with those beliefs inside have been contaminated. Shame scripts go to the core identity of being a human being. Like computer software programs, they can be rewritten. And it does take time to learn to be a software programmer. Have patience with yourself, be kind and nurturing. Do things that feel good. Shame is part of the cult of secrecy. Talking about it out loud to another person breaks open the secret, diffusing the power of shame. Ask for support and regularly get physical and emotional strokes. When you hear these scripts inside you, it's important to *hear* them and what the part of you that is saying them needs from you to feel better. Create new, supportive, and life-affirming scripts. Accept your humanity. Being born is not shameful.

When we begin to heal shame, whether it came from our family of origin, from relationships, or ourselves, grief will be part of the healing. Grief is a natural response to the losses we experience in life. There is grieving the loss of childhood that never was. We grieve the love and affection from parents that weren't there. We grieve for the pain we caused others. We grieve for how we abandoned ourselves and created a false self. We grieve that we've lived so long without truly knowing ourselves. We may grieve that we haven't grieved. This is especially true for men who are told some form of "it's not manly to cry or to show grief or sadness."

Here is where working with your Child, which is essentially reparenting yourself, is deeply healing. Ask her if she would come and talk with you. Hold her in your lap, close to you. Say to her all the things you needed to hear at her age: "I love you." "I want you in my life." "I need you in my life." Tell her that you're sorry she has carried so much shame and sadness. Tell her that the two of you can talk about things, take walks and explore the world together. Tell her that you are proud of her, how cool, smart, and fun she is. Ask her if she has anything she wants to say, if there is anything she really wants to do. As you have this conversation, really be present, in your heart, so the feeling in the words goes to the deep parts of you, which is where *she* is.

To reparent ourselves is to override the damaging scripts and messages we took in when we were children. In this process we can give ourselves new words, new messages, new ways of thinking, and feeling. We give ourselves permission to be alive. Being alive is having feelings, needs, and wants. In this process, we write ourselves anew.

I had decided to take a job as a nude model for the life-drawing class at the university. This decision stirred up every belief I had about myself. The four months before the job began were spent in deep conversations with every part of me, including my body. I was terrified. Every unkind and critical view I had of myself and my body came up. Each day, I would stand naked in front of the mirror and look at what the students would be seeing. It was painful and frightening. I talked endlessly with my Child who was afraid something bad would happen, who was terrified of being naked in front of others. It was one of those life-altering decisions, the kind that you don't fully understand as you make it. Yet you do know that someday its meaning will become clear. I was crying with fear as I left my house the first night.

The professor hadn't arrived yet, so I sat on the beat-up old couch across from his office. Holding my Child and talking to her, a peculiar thing occurred; I felt a shift begin to happen. I felt bigger, stronger, and more capable, and a sense of deep peace seeped into me. I was proud of myself. Still, I was a little shaky as I walked into the studio awhile later. As I stood in front of the class and let my robe fall away; I was keenly aware that fear and shame were falling to the ground with it.

Along with reparenting, we are also giving ourselves new behaviors. The words alone won't change much. The old beliefs are anchored in how we hold our body, how fluidly or awkwardly we move. They are held in our breathing patterns, the way we hold our hands, curve our shoulders, and move our hips when we walk. The sum of all past moments is held in *totalidad* in our current physical body. Though the moments are past, the body remembers the patterns and follows their dictates. Keleman says, "It's been my experience, as others', that those who are not held enough have a fear of falling and hold themselves stiffly away from earth. Those who feel shame for their sexuality and dislike for their bodily responses never really hold their ground with others. They are always proving themselves or shrinking. They are weak-kneed."[3] Until I had intimacy and deep love, I had a paralyzing fear of heights. I couldn't even drive the mountain roads without nearly seizing up. Interestingly, when I felt less than powerful and wobbly, my left knee slipped out of joint easily and painfully. Both of these experiences have been transmuted through the practice of sacred sex.

As you do the internal work with all the parts of you, I strongly encourage you to get deep tissue bodywork to release the holding patterns. Weekly massages, Rolfing, tai chi, and Feldenkrais work can all facilitate repatterning and letting go of how your body has held beliefs. Watch someone whose walk and movements you particularly enjoy. Follow them without being noticed and begin to take on their walk and body movements, copying them as closely as you can. Notice how you feel with this new movement. When you are out for a walk or stroll, try altering your stride, the movement of your hips, the swing of your arms, the length of your stride until you find something you want to incorporate. Changes will occur in your body as you work with your ego states, as well as with the following exercises.

The following exercise will take you deeper inside your own body, deepening your relationship with your own piece of Earth, giving you a sense of place inside your own feet. We explored earlier how each part of the body has its own intelligence. Different parts of our body can hold tremendous amounts of emotional, psychological, and spiritual, cuts, scrapes, and bruises, as well as physical stories, injuries, wounds, and pains. Parts of our body can also be sources of tremendous power, wisdom, and strength.

Each of us has a part of our body we would rather not have touched or noticed. Every one of us has a part of our body that we wish were different or completely gone. Most of us have a part of our body that we hate. We walk around hoping no one will notice. We wish we wouldn't notice or have to look at those parts, or that some magic cream will make it all pretty. A friend used to call me *mujer de mas cremas,* woman of many creams. Creams are superficial. Beauty comes from within, when, at last, love fills all the unloved places.

ஓ MEDITATION ஜ
Loving the Body

Sit in a comfortable, quiet place where you won't be disturbed for a few moments. Take some deep, relaxing breaths. Now, see before you the ugliest part of your body. How does that part of your body feel? Is it mad, sad, scared, glad? Ask that part of you if it has anything it needs to say to you. Do you feel shame in or toward that part of your body? Does that part need anything from you? What would it take for that part to be happy? Is there anything you want to say to it? How do you feel seeing a part of your body that has repulsed you and has been discounted for so long?

When you're ready, thank that part for coming to be with you and talk with you.

Spend time each day working with this part of your body until it begins to feel happy, and you can feel it integrating into your body. Treat this part just as you have your ego states—as intelligent, alive, aware. It has needed something from you. For you to be healthy, this part needs to be tended, loved, held, and appreciated. Our bodies work hard for us; they are the vehicles through which we enjoy and experience sacred sex, the touch of a loved one, the embrace of a child, earth, sand, grass under our feet, and the sun on our skin. Journaling about this relationship can take you deeper into the meanings, insights, and understandings of that part of your body. Your body is the temple of your soul.

TOUCHING WITH LOVE AND ATTENTION

When you touch your lover in that loving way, you may have noticed how he, and different parts of his body, respond to being touched. If you touch on a place he's not comfortable with, he may tense up, pull away, or hold his breath. You may do something similar if he touches, or comments on, a part of you that you don't want to be seen.

He may volunteer a comment on it, or not. The important thing is to not force the subject but keep the communication open. You could say what you're skittish about, what you love, and what you're shy about. What parts of your body are really sensitive to being touched, sensitive in the sense of "it makes me really uncomfortable to have my tummy rubbed." Actually, it frightened me in the beginning. Abdomens are so soft and vulnerable. Since the first tentative touching, I've come to place his hand when I need to be touched there or when I feel like I want to work more with my fear around it. I place his hand on my lower abdomen (that's so not a sexy word); I breathe deeply, breathing in his touch, all the time talking to the part of me that is afraid. In the beginning, I didn't go too far past the moment of serious discomfort, just enough. Now I can let his hands go there uninterrupted. I'm aware of the love with which he touches me there, how much he loves that part of my body as he communicates all this through his hand and heart, talking to my belly. It's a conversation that flows between his hand and my belly and between each part of our bodies.

This next exercise will experientially give you an idea of how people hold stories, beliefs, and values in their bodies.

❧ EXERCISE ❧
Depth Reading on a Stranger

Find a full-body clothed photograph of someone. You can use one from a newspaper or magazine. Choose one that shows the whole person, head to toe. I discourage you from using a photograph of a relative or close friend. In the beginning, it's too challenging to separate out your own feelings for this person and what you are perceiving. So, at least for the first few times, choose a photograph of someone unknown to you.

Hold the photograph in front of you. When you look at the photograph, you won't see the whole person all at once. Your eyes are going to be drawn to one place, then another, then another. When we look at something, we see it in a series of snapshots. Where were your eyes drawn to first? Stay there for a moment. How does that part of the person feel to you? Write down everything that comes to you. Ask your Child to tell you things about that part.

Feel that part with your heart field, how does it feel? What's the second part you were drawn to? How does that part feel? Do this with each part you are drawn to, asking your Child to tell about it, then your heart field. Were you drawn to the top or bottom of the body or to particular body parts, like the hands? Are there any parts of the body that seem "invisible"?

Next, take a sheet of paper and hold it vertically over the photograph so that part of the paper is covering half the person. Notice everything about this half. What is the hand doing? How does the eye look and feel? What kind of "energy" is coming off that side of the person? How does the foot feel? Write down everything. Move the paper so it's vertically covering the other half of the photograph. How does this half feel? What are you drawn to? Does this eye look the same or different from the other one? The foot? Is the energy on this side the same or different from the first side? How does this person feel about their sexuality? Are you uncomfortable asking this question? How do you feel looking at this person as a sexual being?

Repeat the exercise as you move the paper so it's covering the bottom half of the person, horizontally. Go through noticing and asking questions. Then cover the top half and again ask yourself how various parts feel.

Remove the paper and look at the person in the picture again. Do you see anything different or new that you didn't the first time? How do you feel seeing these things?

Get a full-body, clothed, head-to-toe photograph of yourself. Keep the picture facedown. Take some deep breaths. Now, turn the picture over and hold it in front of you. What is the first thing you notice? What stands out, gets your attention? How does this part feel? What are you drawn to next? How does that part feel? Is it mad, sad, scared, happy? Really see yourself in your body. How do you feel seeing yourself? Look at your eyes. How do they feel? Can you tell who, of you, is looking out of them?

Often people have splits in their bodies, discernible demarcations where parts are unintegrated and disconnected from the whole person. Can you see where yours are? It can be revealing to cover half your body photograph vertically with a piece of paper, noticing how one side looks. Notice everything: the look in your eye, how you're holding your hand, the direction of your leg and foot, if there is any energy coming off that side of your body, How does it feel? Then move the paper to cover the other side. How does that side look? Are there differences? Is one side more alive than the other? It's not unusual for one side to have more masculine energy than the other, leaning forward ready to move with fist clenched or pulled back trying to be unseen and diminutive. You may have to move the paper back and forth a couple of times to really notice your eyes. Are they the same on each side? Are there different feelings coming from each one? Before integration it's not unusual for a different ego state to be looking out of each eye.

Now move the paper horizontally covering the top half of your body in the photograph. What do you notice? How does that part feel? Are you stable in your feet, grounded, or about to be airborne? Cover the bottom half and repeat the process, really noticing and seeing what is or isn't there. From your photograph, can you tell how you feel about your own sexuality? How do you feel seeing yourself this way?

SEEING BELOW THE SURFACE

This will give more insight into your body dynamics, physiology, and holding patterns. It can be both instructive and disconcerting but doing the exercise with a desire to know yourself, and for the love of yourself, will help ease the tension around it. Give yourself permission to really see. With practice, you can begin to see below the surface to the truth of what lies there waiting to be revealed.

> *The knowledge of nature as it is—not as we imagine it to be—constitutes true philosophy. He who merely sees the external appearance of things is not a philosopher. The*

true philosopher sees the reality, not merely the outward appearance.

PARACELSUS

Taking a few moments every day to work with different parts of your body will, over time, deepen your relationship with yourself. You'll feel more integrated, more alive, as parts of you, inside and out, begin to be part of your life, part of you.

The more you are integrated in body and soul, the more resilient and flexible you will be in dealing with shame—whether old or new, self-shaming or from the outside. As you work with trust and shame and healing from the inside, you'll discover an openness of spirit, a healing of the soul, and have new ways of responding to the challenges of becoming a human being in diverse cultural, social, and interpersonal relationships.

12
Freeing Ourselves from Sexual Tyranny

If a woman hasn't got a tiny streak of harlot in her, she's a dry stick as a rule.

D. H. LAWRENCE,

THE POSTHUMOUS PAPERS OF D. H. LAWRENCE

I present this chapter for calm, reasoned study of pornography and prostituion—topics that are sticky, discomforting, and hairy ones to navigate. The mere mention of the word *pornography* stimulates an array of responses from various quarters. Finding ways to address these topics without shutting down the discourse forced me to get clear inside myself about it. I'm not flat about it. I have strong opinions about pornography and prostitution, which directly relate to free speech, expression, and the right to choose. These are not the same opinions I held twenty years ago, which is one reason I've included these topics.

For five decades now I have labored as an apprentice human being. As the apprenticeship enters its the fifth decade, I can still see the remains of a few contaminated beliefs, which, in the continuation of my self-training, I am working to detoxify.

There are costs to this dance, and regrettably, I fear my son and my lovers paid a good share of the price of me becoming who I am, but primarily of who I wasn't. The issue of pornography, *my* issue with pornography, came slowly to the surface when my son reached adolescence. My husband found copies of *Playboy* and *Penthouse* magazines in his room and reacted by blowing a gasket. I timidly concurred, agreeing that these magazines demeaned women and were somehow going to turn him into a pervert.

Even then, something about my husband's reaction and my compliance with it felt very wrong. Something about our insistence that he not have them in the house was terribly misplaced. For a young boy reaching adolescence, having *Penthouse* and *Playboy* in his room is a rite of passage of sorts, and there is nothing wrong with him having them. How else would he find that his interests and curiosity are normal? Moreover, every boy and girl deserves to have their own room, their personal space that is just theirs, away from parental tyranny. The way we handled it was poor at best. The worst is that it may have caused shame around his natural curiosity and emerging hormones and sexuality. That is especially regrettable given that my husband had nude photos of me in his dresser drawer at the time. It could have been an opportunity to talk about sex, sexuality, intimacy, and relationships. I never took the time to ask him what he thought of looking at nude women or photos of other people having sex. How did he feel about it? Did he enjoy it? We could have talked about why finding the magazines was so upsetting to my husband. About how he was trying to recover from Catholicism and his own contaminated baggage around sexuality. I didn't take the time to point out to my son that these were actors and though, yes, some people enjoy bondage, being submissive, being overpowered, not everyone does, and certainly not everyone looks the way porn actors do nude. They get paid very well to keep those hard bodies in shape for being photographed.

Pornography and prostitution are social quagmires where passions erupt from both sides of the slippery spectrum of controversy. While passions rise over the topics, understanding of them gains little foothold. The debates over pornography are embedded in moral and political ideologies, and as long as the debate stays under those blankets, misunderstandings of the nature, meanings, and functions of pornography flourish. As long as the debate remains in the hands of the church, that bastion of morality, and politicians who wrongly assume that morality can be regulated, it will be difficult to see the possibility that pornography and prostitution may actually have redeeming social functions and value. But as we lose sight of what our individual and social values are, the topic of pornography becomes ever more confusing. How do we begin to sort through these issues when our social value system is corrupt—with banks, Wall Street, corporations, and the government engaging in deceit as policy—and any recourse through the Constitution is undermined?

Sex has been difficult to talk about, not in the least because our culture is not clear about it. We have conflicting messages coming to us from a variety of sources. Our own feelings about sex and our sexuality are often convoluted and contaminated with toxic messages. Sex is challenging to talk about because it is moist and leaves a wet spot. And as Eric Berne says: "In fact, it is more than wet, it is slippery. Anyone who ignores that is going to feel a little sticky talking about it."[1]

I have not always been a proponent of pornography or prostitution, though prostitution held a special allure for me when, at sixteen, I considered it as a profession that might be able to get me away from my home. It took an entire twenty-seven seconds for me to dismiss it, as I was too damned scared of life to get myself past the Iowa border. Nonetheless, it required a certain level of devotion to clarity and freedom to sort through my beliefs, thoughts, fears, and assumptions, as well as the debates and opinions around those subjects, and create my own beliefs and values.

SACRED SEX AND THE WORLD'S OLDEST PROFESSION

My efforts to find writings on sexuality, ecopsychology, nature writings, Deep Ecology writings, sacred sex, tantric sex, and sexual history that made connections between Earth, Nature, and human sexuality were nearly futile. Those connections are seldom made though there were a few noteworthy exceptions. Interestingly, it was a woman who chose prostitution as a way of life and made a very good living at it who made the clearest connection. In her book *A Woman Whose Calling Is Men,* the pseudonymous Aphrodite Phoenix writes about the divine side of prostitution.

Behind every situation that feels earthy and sensually connected, good to oneself and others, and naturally health-bestowing, atonement with Goddess can be fathomed as the underlying spiritual cause. I believe that all prostitutes who experience an increase in feminine power are women who, consciously or not, partake of psychic nourishment from what Sue Monk Kidd calls "Feminine Divine." It's the reason we insist that the work doesn't harm us, and that there's more to the work than just raking in money from meaningless, anonymous sex. In our work we're experiencing a spiritual feminism.[2]

Prostitution has been present in nearly every culture and age of the human race. In some cultures, prostitution was viewed as a valuable and healthy part of the culture and economy, such as in ancient Greece where it was a cult of beauty and profit. In some countries it was a royal enterprise, a principal source of revenue for the state, and women and boy prostitutes were trained in the finer points of their profession. Prostitution was common among the Yuma Indians of California and the Colorado tribes. In China, Japan, and Thailand, prostitution is a common form of barter. Even married women participate, sharing the proceeds with their husbands.

Scenes depicting sex on undulating beds and mattresses as well as seated positions were found etched on wine-drinking buckets, or *situlae,* from the Iron Age in Europe. Archaeological evidence suggests that prostitution existed in ancient Rome, as seen in brothel tokens, called *spintriae.*[3] Each token, slightly smaller than a U.S. quarter, depicts a sex scene on one side and a roman numeral, I through XVI, on the other. It's been suggested that the number on the coin related to the cost of the sex scene on the obverse side. Coin specialist Aleksander Bursche of the University of Warsaw undertook his own study and surveyed modern-day prostitutes about the coins, inquiring which acts they charge more for. They told him that positions that afforded deeper penetration, such as sex from behind, caused more vaginal soreness and thus they cost more. Geoffrey Fishburn at the University of New South Wales argued against this theory, noting that the same sex scene appears on coins of differing numerical values and identical scenes show up in Pompeian murals.[4] Another argument suggests that the coins were merely poker chips. Regardless, it does raise titillating questions and suggests the openness of sex, as well as a sexual repertoire, in ancient Rome. Or perhaps, coins, goblets, and murals depicting sex scenes were an homage to the power and eroticism of sex, the beauty and art of naked human bodies entwined in sacred sexual acts. They may even be the earliest versions of pornography.

> *Obscenity only comes in when the mind despises and fears*
> *the body, and the body hates and resists the mind.*
>
> D. H. LAWRENCE,
> "A PROPOS OF *LADY CHATTERLEY'S LOVER*"

The word *pornography* has a long, convoluted, and interesting history. It comes from the Greek *porne,* meaning "to sell," and *graphos,* "to write." The sex workers in ancient Greece were referred to as the *porne,* which included both women of importance and boys. They were required to wear elaborate clothing and pay taxes. And in the ancient Middle East, prostitutes were the first to have contact with men returning from battle in order to help them assimilate back into society and recover from the shock of war. In seventeenth-century Japan, the *oiran* were courtesans and considered "women of pleasure." The highest ranks of courtesan were available only to the wealthy. They were often practiced in fine art, dance, music, and calligraphy, as well as the art of sexual fulfillment, and were well educated.

The Egyptians had sacred prostitution as did the Persians, who learned the trade from Libya. In Israel both male and females practiced prostitution. The cult of Venus or Mylitta (the Assyrian name for Venus and counterpart to Ishtar, in Greece her name was Aphrodite) in Babylonia passed into Cyprus and Phoenicia. In Cyprus, temples sacred to Astarte, the goddess of fertility, love, and reproduction, dotted the landscape. She had a strong presence until the cult of Yahweh emerged among the Hebrews. The Hebrews knew Astarte as the goddess of the Sidonians and continued to worship her at temples in Mizpah built alongside those of Yahweh, which angered him greatly. Worship of the ancient goddesses formed the basis of many cultures and civilizations who oriented life around them with ritual sex, seasonal goddess celebrations, and elaborate rituals honoring the deities. "The advent of Christianity and its relatively puritanical views on sex all but killed off the sex cult, but during the world's polytheistic zenith it was one of the firmest pillars of society."[5] In Armenia, Venus, was worshipped under the name Anaïtas. Young women lived in Anaïtas's temple and offered amorous services to foreigners. The women left all their earnings on the altar as an offering to the love goddess in hopes of securing a husband.

Innana, the Sumerian goddess of sexual love, fertility, and warfare, can be dated to the city of Uruk, known as the "city of courtesan," circa 4000 to 3100 BCE. Innana was celebrated and honored at sacred sites and temples along the Euphrates and Tigris Rivers. Eanna, meaning "house of heaven," is the name of the temple in Uruk dedicated to Inanna, where sacred prostitution was a common practice. Innana, considered an aspect of the Great Mother, was a fierce warrior; she was often depicted on the back of a lion. And she is the center of pleasure, "the one who makes women and men turn to one another in the night."[6] Innana gave the gift of blood to women, the healing blood that flows at the new or dark moon that cleanses the body and prepares the womb for the next cycle of the moon's influence on a woman's cycle.

After the fall of organized prostitution during the Roman Empire, many prostitutes became slaves until the movement to abolish slavery swept the land, and prostitution was reinstated as a legitimate business during the Middle Ages. Though the medieval Roman Catholic Church viewed sexual relations outside marriage as sinful, prostitution was seen as a tolerable alternative to the greater evils of masturbation, rape, and sodomy; however, the church often urged prostitutes to reform their wicked ways.

Courtiers played an essential part in Renaissance Europe. Royal marriages were made primarily to preserve the bloodline; love and passion was not part of the equation. So it was common for members of the royalty to seek sexual companionship from other people at the court, hence the origin of the terms *to court* and *courtesan*.

One of the oldest documents having to do with prostitution was written in 1266 in Venice. The Maggior Consiglio, or Greater Council, decreed the night watch to expel every "woman of evil life" from the houses of citizens. After the women were forced out of public houses, they took their business to private houses, or houses of prostitution, which initially were off limits to the night watch's watchful eyes But then a second council decree gave the night watch the power to expel evil women and men from private domiciles and fine them: They were now being forced out of business from their own homes. After a time, wisdom prevailed; the authorities conceded the futility of outlawing prostitution, and the Maggior Consiglio decreed (they liked to decree in the day) that a place in Venice should be found to house the prostitutes.

> Whereas, by reason of the multitude of people constantly coming and going, it behooves our State to see to providing some place in Venice proper for the habitation of sinful women:
>
> It is hereby commanded to the Captains of the City Wards to examine diligently all places on the Rialto which might be suited for such a purpose, and after due examination, to make report to us in writing, namely, concerning the most suitable place and the conditions under which the women in question may be kept there, with which report let them come before the Council of Forty and make their findings known.[7]

Prostitution will always have a place in human society. St. Augustine, demonstrating his understanding and knowledge of mankind observed: "Do away with the prostitute in the human scheme and you will upset everything through an incursion of lust; put them in the matron's place, and you will bring injury and dishonor upon the latter."[8]

THE BEGINNINGS OF SEXUAL LIBERATION

Wilheim Reich coined the phrase *sexual revolution,* though its roots may be found in the eighteenth century during the Enlightenment, and later the term *free love* came into being during the same century. An early proponent at that time was Mary Wollstonecraft. Wollstonecraft argued that women should not give up freedom and sexuality. She thus made a personal choice to not marry her partner. Later free love proponents included Mary Gove Nichols and Hannah R. Brown, as well as male advocates of the movement such as William Francis Barry, in the mid-to-late 1800s and Gloria Steinem in the twentieth century.

The early feminists spoke out and wrote against marriage and were radical in their thinking of the time and had a profound impact on sexual relations of their eras. In 1798, the radical Swedenborgians August Nordenskiöld and C. B. Wadström published the *Plan for a Free Community* in which they proposed the establishment of a society of sexual liberty, where slavery was abolished and the European and Negro lived together in harmony. In the treatise, marriage is criticized as a form of political repression. The challenge to traditional morality and religion brought about by the Age of Enlightenment and the emancipatory politics of the French Revolution created an environment where such ideas could flourish.

Charles Fourier, in France in the early nineteenth century, coined the word *feminism* and said that the suppression of passions is not only destructive to the individual but to society as a whole. He argued that all sexual expressions should be enjoyed as long as people are not abused and that "affirming one's difference" can actually enhance social integration.

Though considered scandalous at the time, out-of-wedlock children and sexual liaisons seemed acceptable behavior for admired artists, who were following the dictates of their own wills rather than those of social convention. In this way, these artists were in step with their era's liberal philosophers of the cult of passion, such as Fourier, and their actual or eventual openness can be understood to be a prelude to the freer ways of the twentieth century.

Josiah Warren and the experimental societies viewed sexual freedom as a clear, direct expression of an individual's self-ownership. Free love particularly stressed women's rights since marriage laws and measures that discouraged birth control discriminated against women. Discrimination against women continues to this day. Sarah Seltzer, writing for *AlterNet,* reported on the House's passage of H.R.358, the notorious antiabortion and "Let Women Die" bill.[9] According to Seltzer, a major proponent of the bill was the Council of Catholic Bishops, who heavy-handedly and successfully lobbied for some of the worst measures in the bill, taking rights away from women—while the bishops were in the midst of fighting charges of child sex abuse. Meanwhile, in June 2010, in Phoenix, Arizona, a woman, eleven weeks pregnant with her fifth child, was admitted to St. Joseph's Hospital and Medical Center. She had a right-sided heart failure and was told by her physicians that if she continued the pregnancy she would die. The woman agreed to an abortion. Unfortunately, she was in a Catholic hospital, which forbids abortions. The doctrine of the Catholic Church would have let both mother and child die. Physicians turned to Sr. Margaret McBride, the administrator at the hospital, who gave her approval for an abortion that would save the life in front of them, the mother. By making that decision, she was automatically excommunicated by Bishop Thomas J. Olmsted of the Phoenix Diocese.

In speaking to the sixth International Pre- and Perinatal Psychology Association of North America, Jeannine Parvati Baker, midwife and founder of Hygieia College, spoke movingly about how the dominant culture insulates people from their own vitality.

> From the current "war on drugs" to the obstetrical theater, to the church and temple, people are seeking safety from the raw power of life. Yet birth is as safe as life gets. The ways we scare ourselves from being wild woman, mother, midwife and healer are rooted in fears by the dominant culture. To revision God from being only Father, or Father and Son, or even Divine Parents can help us become free to be fully inspired lovers, connected to our power to be our own healers.[10]

Recognizing that sexuality is spirituality and that ecstasy is a divine right will begin to move us back into a harmonious relationship with the other gender, with our sexuality as a life force, and with the body and ground of our own being. This is the first healing we are called to do.

If there is anything to be ashamed of, and I use the term cautiously, it is in denying our sexuality and feelings and that Earth is alive and intelligent. It is in not doing something to alter the rate and velocity of our march to self-destruction. It is in not holding our governments, schools, religions, and ourselves accountable for the choices made and the behaviors that come of them.

Reverence for our lovers, partners, and children can translate to reverence for Earth, for the nonhuman, numinous dimension of wilderness, of Nature. If the separation that is extant among human relations can be made whole and intimate, then our relationship with the community of Earth can be. Regaining our sense of awe and wonder and our ability to fall in love over and over again from sunrise to sunset will begin to bring the sacred back to our daily lives. Experiences that draw us up and out of our egocentric lives into the larger reality, the community of all beings, must become integrated into our daily lives. Integrating sex into our lives, unapologetically, will inevitably integrate our personal power, our creativity, our voices and bodies for deep and lasting changes in our lives and in our society.

> *When I speak of the erotic, I speak of it as an assertion of the life force of women; of that creative energy empowered, the knowledge and use of which we are now reclaiming in our language, our history, our dancing, our loving, our work, our lives.*
>
> AUDRE LORDE

We have been taught, programmed if you will, to distrust our eroticism, our sexual power, our allure. Some of us have accepted part and parcel the archaic myth of the fall of man by woman. By accepting the programming and the stories, we have committed a crime against our basic human nature, our bodies and psyches as sexual. The old arguments are beginning to crumble as women speak out and begin to take back and own their rightful place in the arena of sexual freedom. There is hope and a rumbling in the subconscious of women slowly awakening.

> *When sleeping women wake, mountains move.*
>
> CHINESE PROVERB

THE POLITICS OF SEXUALITY: AN ANCIENT ARENA FOR CONFLICT

> *To discuss the nature and meaning of obscenity is almost as difficult as to talk about God. Until I began delving into the literature which has grown up about the subject I never realized what a morass I was wading into.*
>
> HENRY MILLER,
> *HENRY MILLER ON WRITING*

The politics of sexuality is the most ancient arena for human conflict, on par with the domain of religion as a source of conflict, large and small, but then, the two have been bedfellows for thousands of years. It also in large part causes intrapersonal conflict, that is, conflict inside the self. Many, many people watch porn, look at porn magazines, even as they lie to themselves, their partners, coworkers, or priests about it or in some way hide the fact. Many people talk about the subject of pornography, but even talking *about* pornography is an intimate, self-revealing act and is wrought with fear, anxiety, and suspicion.

> *And no, I do not believe it is blasphemous to compare oppression of sexuality to oppressions of race and ethnicity: Freedom is indivisible or it is nothing at all besides sloganeering and temporary, short-sighted, and short-lived advancement for a few. Freedom is indivisible, and either we are working for freedom or you are working for the sake of your self-interests and I am working for mine.*
>
> JUNE JORDON,
> "A NEW POLITICS OF SEXUALITY"

The politics of sexuality, more than any other oppression, is the exploitation of sexuality for power. In fact, religion has been the vehicle driving the oppression and politics of sexuality. It could be a religion in its own right, the religion of the sexual oppressors or the religion of the sexually oppressed. I do not believe that any one man or woman has the right to tell me what I can or cannot do or what I shall like or dislike or attempt to dictate my behavior regarding my sexuality and how I express it. I do not believe I am blasphemous in saying that pornography has a valid and legitimate place in the scheme of human sexuality. I will go further and say that pornography plays a vital role in relieving the pressure of religious and politically sanctioned morality.

In *Ensouling Language*, Stephen Harrod Buhner writes, "Sex must be *integrated* into Western cultures as an active and accepted part of what it means to be human for its repression is inherently connected to the ecological and cultural problems we face."[11] Integration—to merge, to infuse, to bring together—means no part can be left out. When sexual expression in the form of pornography is left out of something as basic and essential as our sexuality and as inherent to our human beingness, there is a hole left in its place. A hole is there in the place where sexual expression should be, and where holes are, degradation of the wholeness of human beings takes place.

> *I kind of like occasional acts of public lewdness. A little bit of real obscenity and indecency actually makes me feel more secure. I get nervous always being on the extreme by myself. Public acts of sex or penis fondling all add to the "wow, I'm not in Kansas anymore" feeling.*
>
> Dale Pendell,
>
> *Inspired Madness*

Part of the problem and legalities around pornography is that it is difficult to define what is objectionable, what goes too far. D. H. Lawrence was right when he said, "nobody knows what the word obscene means." [12] In 1964, Supreme Court Justice Potter Stewart admitted that he couldn't define what material is obscene: "But I know it when I see it." In America, all pornography is legal except that which is deemed "obscene." The legal definition of obscenity in the United States is that it "must be shown that the average person, applying contemporary community standards and viewing the material as a whole, would find (1) that the work appeals to predominately 'prurient' interest; (2) that it depicts or describes sexual conduct in a patently offensive way; and (3) that it lacks serious literary, artistic, political or scientific value." [13]

As you can see, there are problems with that definition. Contemporary community standards are changing. Obscenity is subjective, that is, its meaning lies in what we bring to it—how we view it and what we think of it. I'm more offended by rudeness, unconscious behavior, and sex without intimacy. What I find truly obscene is an endless war based on lies and misinformation. Our foreign policies, U.S. banking system, public schooling, Catholic priests sexually abusing children, people losing their homes and jobs, and children starving—these things are obscene, vulgar, indecent, cruel, and morally reprehensible.

I don't find pornography offensive or obscene; I do find fuck films distasteful perhaps, extreme maybe, raunchy sometimes. I do find pornography and nude photos titillating, interesting, exciting, yes. Always it gives me permission to live outside the box. "But in legal parlance, obscenity is a category of speech—speech about sex—that falls outside the protection of the First Amendment. Or so, at least, the Supreme Court has said; many legal scholars find no basis in history or logic for this 'obscenity exception' to the First Amendment."[14]

> *No argument for the suppression of obscene literature has ever been offered which by unavoidable implications will not justify, and which has not already justified, every other limitation that has ever been put upon mental freedom.*
>
> THEODORE SHROEDER,
> *CHALLENGE TO SEX CENSORS*

> *As we move toward sexual maturity, hyped-up sexual excitation becomes secondary, and the quality of our feelings determine sexual identity. That's the difference between adolescent and adult sexuality. What we see around us is a great deal of fantasy stimulation to make us feel excited. We have manipulated ourselves into accepting stimulation rather than feeling. We've done this by sacrificing our bodies as the sources of our feelings of aliveness, and becoming addicted to the brain and nerves as the pleasure center.*
>
> *Or, conversely, if your heart and your honest body can be controlled by the state, or controlled by community taboo, are you not then, and in that case, no more than a slave ruled by outside force?*
>
> JUNE JORDAN,
> "A NEW POLITICS OF SEXUALITY"

Sex writer Violet Blue has organized a new movement, Our Porn, Ourselves, whose goal is to bring sex back to its rightful place, to ourselves. To that end, the organizers wrote a manifesto setting themselves apart from right-wing or old-guard feminists who maintain the dominant culture's rules of behavior regarding sexual repression, freedom of speech, self-expression, and the pursuit of sexual health and liberation. Blue writes, "We women are tired of people trying to control our sexuality by telling us what we should or shouldn't like sexually (porn) based on what someone else thinks is best for us. It's like keeping women in a perpetual state of being children about sex. And women who say they are feminists make it worse by discounting all the women who find porn to be an empowering sex toy. Or if not, to at least give us the benefit of the doubt that we can make that decision for ourselves, thank you very much."[15]

Our Porn, Ourselves Manifesto:
Pro-Porn Principles

WE who declare that organizations such as Feminists Against Pornography do not speak for us.

WE who want the world to know that organizations such as Feminists Against Pornography do not represent feminists as a group.

WE who believe that every woman has the right and power to enjoy her sexuality as she decides.

WE who believe that to tell a woman how she may or may not enjoy her sexuality in any way is to deny that woman of her rights over her sexuality.

WE who state that any woman who attempts to control the way another woman enjoys, explores or expresses her sexuality is in fact creating a world that is harmful for all women.

WE who state that we are women, and we like pornography.

WE who state that as women, we are not harmed or threatened by the creation or viewing of pornography, and we wholly support the rights of gender to view, create, and enjoy pornography without judgment.

WE who want a world in which pornography is simply a sex toy enjoyed by all genders and sexual orientations, where women and men view porn within their own self-defined healthy sexuality, without being considered sick, twisted, wrong or morally ill, and that men who enjoy pornography are no more likely to beat their wives, rape women or become pedophiles than anyone else in society.

WE hereby declare ourselves as adult women capable of making our own choices about our bodies and enjoyment of explicit visual stimulation for our sexual health and well-being.

WE hereby demand that our voices be heard.[16]

On July 22, 2010, Facebook removed the Our Porn, Ourselves Facebook campaign page, according to Our Porn, Ourselves official website. The organization Pornography Harms claimed victory and thanked Facebook for removing "a very inappropriate pro-porn page with links to pornography that our children had easy access to."[17]

Pornography plays a vital function in the sexual health of human beings. It has been one of the most important places of discourse on sex and sexuality. Pornography shamelessly exposes that which has been kept secret and hidden. It gives our unnamed desires an arena. Pornography exposes us to sex that turns us on, turns us off, intrigues, satisfies, helps expand our ideas of what we like, what we don't like, what we might like if we had an opportunity to try it, and it increases the likelihood and frequency of orgasms, with ourselves or others—a vital function of vitally functioning people. And, who would think of killing or fighting while looking at naked breasts or cocks?

Through Facebook and other Internet tools, we have the ability to have community discussions around any topic of our choosing. It may be that Internet porn sites will be the arena where community standards regarding porn are set, not by legislators or bishops.

About every forty to fifty years, or two generations, there has been a sexual revolution. July 19 and 20, 1848, Lucretia Mott and Elizabeth Cady Stanton organized the first public gathering in the United States to address the rights of women. They were joined by Susan B. Anthony and Frederick Douglass, a former slave. It was the Seneca Falls Convention located in Seneca Falls, N.Y. There they drafted the Seneca Falls Declaration of Sentiments calling for women's right to vote, to own property, and to have equal access to education and employment.

The late nineteenth century birthed a trifecta of women's organizations: the Suffragists who worked for the right of women to vote; The Social Feminists who birthed the Women's Trade Union League, the General Federation of Women's Clubs, the National Council of Jewish Women, and the National Council of Colored Women; and the Radical Feminists who argued that for social and economic equality between men and women. This latter group produced Alice Paul, who introduced the first Equal Rights Amendment in 1910.

Elizabeth Cady Stanton developed the "Bloomer Costume," a proactive alternative to the restrictive Victorian dress of the day. The "free-lovers" of the nineteen century advocated that sex had functions outside of procreation and encouraged the relaxation of external controls in order to experience more personally responsible sexual expression and experimentation.

The 1920s ushered in the radio, talkies, women's suffrage, and those wild women, the flappers who came to represent the independent woman of the twenties. The Nineteenth Amendment was ratified granting women the right to vote. As attitudes toward women changed and birth control became available, a sexual revolution followed.

The years following World War II found people less likely to defer to external authority on behavior and morality than they did in the previous fifteen years of depression and war. The decades of the 1940s and 1950s saw the rate of single mothers more than double,[18] Alfred Kinsey researching and reporting on *Sexuality and the Human Male* in 1948, Elvis Presley gyrating on the television screen, the appearance of Hugh Hefner's inaugural issue of *Playboy* magazine in 1953, and Lucy and Ricky Ricardo sleeping in separate beds on *I Love Lucy*. In the sixties, the first films depicting nudity and sexual intercourse were *Midnight Cowboy* and *Romeo and Juliette*. Woodstock, love-ins and social activism rose alongside rock and roll, the Vietnam War protests, and the Civil Rights movement.

The twenty-first century is showing another sexual revolution as the new feminists are writing erotica and producing pornographic films. Sexting, home erotica, and porno films are available to anyone with a camera and Internet access as YouTube has made self-broadcasting possible. The World Wide Web makes available nearly any form of erotica, pornography, nude photos right in the comfort of your own home. Meanwhile,

Occupy Wall Street is the largest, most organized, peaceful protest in our country's history as social revolutions are fueled by the energy of sexual revolutions: Eros and Psyche.

PORNOGRAPHY: HARMFUL OR CRUCIAL?

In the United States alone, a pornographic video is produced every thirty-nine minutes; 11,000 adult movies are released per year—more than twenty times mainstream movie releases. In 2006, the sum of international revenues from pornographic videos, sexual novelties, magazines, "dance" clubs, pay-per-view television, and the Internet was approximately $97 billion.[19] That figure is more than the combined annual revenues of the NFL, NBA, and Major League Baseball. In the United States, revenues for pornography are larger than the revenues of Microsoft, Google, Amazon, eBay, Yahoo!, Apple, Netflix, and EarthLink combined. It's rather mind-boggling to consider that $3,075,64 is being spent on pornography internationally every second. The United States produces more Internet porn than anybody else on the planet.

Recent studies point to porn-induced sexual dysfunction.* *Psychology Today* reported on a growing problem with porn-induced sexual dysfunction.[20] Sexual desire and erections respond to dopamine signals. Dopamine is the reward chemical in the hypothalamus and the central nervous system. Hundreds of young men are reporting erectile dysfunction due to overstimulation from viewing Internet porn. There are enough studies now to show that, indeed, continual stimulation of dopamine from masturbating to Internet porn *can* cause erectile dysfunction due to desensitization and rewiring of the brain. It is reversible when stimulation from porn is removed.

These studies suggest porn addiction is the cause. It may be involved, but the more I read on the subject, the more red flags are raised. For one thing, if you do anything repeatedly, including working at a repetitive office or factory job, desensitization can occur. If I eat the same meal every day, my taste buds get desensitized and the food no longer looks appetizing or tastes good to me; I get no enjoyment out of it. Porn addiction, or any addiction, is a *symptom*,

---

*Note that there are also contrary studies that refute these findings.

not the cause. If we focus on overuse of Internet pornography, we do a severe disservice to young men. There may be women having similar problems with overstimulation from or habituation to Internet porn (are women having porn-induced clitoral erectile dysfunction?), but men are the most studied since, without an erection, the possibility of great sex with an intimate partner is severely limited, which causes a cascade of other problems, including anxiety, shame, self-esteem issues, relationship difficulties, and functionality.

Are the arguments that porn increases pedophiliac tendencies and makes men want to rape and therefore increases the risk of child abuse and rape legitimate? Aside from any studies done on these issues, think about it reasonably for yourself. Would a person with a healthy moral compass about right and wrong behavior be even remotely interested in viewing films that depict children in sexual acts? Assuming you could even get them to sit still for it. No, people who engage in pedophilia are pedophiles to begin with.

As Theodore Shroeder states in his work, *Challenge to Sex Censors,* "obscenity exists only in the minds that discover it and charge others with it."[21] If we were to reflect objectively on the subject matter we would find the law of nature; that is everyone performs the very acts they attribute to others.

Porn films are films and as such are incapable of forcing anyone to do anything he or she doesn't want to do or of being a leading cause of divorce. The leading cause of divorce is the *decision* to divorce. Pornography is a pressure valve, releasing social and cultural oppression. Studies have repeatedly shown that pornography actually decreases the incidence of rape and aggressive sexual acts. There are more incidences of rape and violence against women in countries where there is no porn than there are in countries where pornography is available. And there are statistics that reveal, without mention of pornography being an instigator, that: "one out of eight women will be raped while in college and 84% of women who were raped knew the assailant."[22] A story in the *Huffington Post* reported, "Rape within the US military has become so widespread that it is estimated that a female soldier in Iraq is more likely to be attacked by a fellow soldier than killed by enemy fire."[23] Rape in the military is not gender specific, it crosses lines. "According to the Veterans Affairs Office 37% of the sexual trauma cases reported last year (2010) were men."[24]

The questions not being asked are: Why so much "porn addiction" in the first place? And why so much emphasis on it? Why such high statistics of rape in the military? What is missing in our lives? Where is the meaning to life? What do we need to have fulfilling lives? If our life is empty, we may turn to anything to feel better momentarily. Porn is not the problem. The problems we face and apply Band-Aid treatments to are much, much deeper. Perhaps we need to look at the deeper issues of a lack of intimacy, the economic debacle, endless war permeating all of our psyches, rampant lack of hope and opportunities, and the mess we are creating for the next generations. Perhaps porn use is the morphine of the masses so we don't have to feel how bad our lives are. Pornography has always been around in some version. It will always be here.

SEXUAL PLEASURE IS OUR BIRTHRIGHT

Isn't it curious that the clitoris is designed solely for pleasure? It has nothing to do with reproducing the species. It's a sign from God, a direct communication that we are meant to have and enjoy sex outside of procreation. A woman's vagina has its own cycle of sexual response, lubricating about every fifteen minutes during the sleep cycle. Another signpost saying, "Have sex, a lot of sex, often." Studies have shown that as a man ages, or becomes depressed or bored in his relationship, his testosterone levels drop. Studies also show that just talking to a woman he finds attractive and sexy will increase a man's testosterone levels by 12 percent. The most obvious and familiar male sexual response is the erection. There are other clues males generate that indicate sexual interest and arousal such as the steady but not penetrating look in his eyes, the way he holds his body, and the movement of some invisible thing that leaves him and travels to the woman.

Pornography is not shameful, nor is watching porn, though there are many people and institutions that would prefer we thought it so. They work very hard to make it shameful and to make those of us who enjoy it feel shameful. Shaming does work temporarily as a behavioral modification tool, but the cost is detrimental to the shamed.

Pornography educates us about bodies, showing us there are many kinds of bodies and that sex organs are not all the same. Like fingerprints, every human body is different and unique. There are numerous shapes and sizes and colors of labia majora and minora, penises, clitorises, breasts, areolas, and asses. In some, the labia majora are predominant; in others, they are nearly nonexistent and the labia minora are the most distinguishable features of the vulva. The subtle shading and colorations that occur between the clitoris and the sacrum are fascinating and beautiful. Pubic hair comes curly, straight, kinky, long, short, red, black, blonde, brown, groomed, trimmed, and shaved.

Adults often use pornography with their partners for sexual stimulation—to break up monotony or to increase intimacy. For many people, watching other people have sex is, well, sexy and a turn on. People who view porn tend to choose porn that is within their comfort zone, or they may go beyond what is familiar to them and use it to explore, to answer questions they might have about what other people do, and, then, perhaps, to experiment. They want to watch someone else do what they have only thought about trying out before doing it in the privacy of their own bedrooms.

Isabella Rossellini took the porn world to new heights with her short *Green Porno* films, which she made for the Sundance Channel. She has combined the elements of short stories, animals, and sex. "Not everyone is interested in animals, but everyone is interested in sex." The *Green Porno* short (one-minute long) films depict animals, sea creatures, and insects reproducing, yes, having sex. "They are quite scandalous," says Rossellini. "They make love in funny ways. Some of them are hermaphrodites, some change sex during their lifetime—things that if we would do it as human beings, we would be arrested. But they do it naturally."[25] These fantastic clips can introduce children to sex and reproduction in the animal world. They're short, frank, funny, and refreshingly candid. The costumes and props are all made of paper, so it's like watching a live puppet show.

The problem for some people is the disconnect they experience between what their body is telling them and what their internal programming is telling them—that it's wrong and perverse to view porn. We have the same feelings about pornography that we have about anything that is too revealing, embarrassing, obscene, private, and explicit as well as exciting, interesting, and life affirming. Porn allows us to go to our imaginative extremes. Author Dale Pendell says, "There *should* be extremes that are in bad taste. Extremes by definition are in bad taste. You have to allow that. That's what tolerance is. And tolerance is the basis of any kind of free society. And the only hope for people who want to live without Big Brother."[26]

Listen to your body; it knows what feels good. There is nothing inherently wrong with pornography or watching it. Well, except when you let it interfere with your job, and you miss busting a $550 million Ponzi scheme. Investigations revealed that during one week in 2008, a supervisor at the Securities and Exchange Commission attempted 196 times to view porn on his office computer.[27]

READING THE INVISIBLE INTO VISIBILITY

Personally, I don't really like a lot of the porn that's available. It's poorly filmed and acted. Fortunately, that is changing as more women get involved in the industry. More art porn is available, more erotica, which is what I prefer over hard-core porn, though I do occasionally wander outside my porn comfort zone.

Looking at artful, nude photographs of men and women is something I enjoy from time to time. I love looking at the human form and find that looking at nude photos of women, or two women entwined, or a man and a woman entwined, or two men wrapped around each other is erotic, stimulating, and pleasurable. Porn has helped me be more accepting and understanding of myself and my differences and similarities to other women. I feel sexier looking at photos of nudes. The more intimacy I have with myself and others, the more permission and freedom I give myself to express my sexual desires and needs, as well as my sexuality, the more fulfilled I am. Not only am I more fulfilled, I feel more powerful, stronger, and focused and am able to effect change from that place. Personal power and sexuality are inextricably connected.

My lover and I enjoy occasionally looking at photos of nude women posing in provocative positions. Sometimes it's just men, sometimes men and women. We do "readings" on the models. We do readings on nearly everything, so this is no different. If there is a page of thumbnail photos, we let our gaze scan the page and pick the one that gets our attention, that stands out the most. Frequently, the same one gets both our attentions.

We then click on that thumbnail for a closer look. In the photo some part of her body will get our attention, and we'll say out loud everything we see. Our eyes become soft focused, allowing us to see how she feels about that part of her body. Typically, the part of her body she really loves, the part she gives the most attention to, puts more energy into, will be more noticeable to the onlooker's gaze.

Most people are adept at hiding, making invisible, essentially, the parts they don't like. You can notice this as you sit waiting in airports or doctors' offices; one person will get your attention over the others, then, as you continue looking, some part of his body will get your attention over other parts. Looking deeper still, you'll begin to see how he feels about that part of his body, and then how that part of his body feels. If you put your gaze on the part that is hidden, you'll see just how that person feels about this part of his body.

Looking at nudes is a good practice for doing readings (developing intuition). You'll be able to see which people really enjoy their bodies, which parts of their bodies are more alive than others. My lover and I talk about what we like, what's appealing, what isn't, and how we can bring it into our relationship. We talk about my posing for him, or dressing up or down, which can lead to playful foreplay and wonderfully passionate, intimate lovemaking as our desire rises.

Consider looking at nude photos of men and women online—there's so much available in the privacy of our own homes now. You'll get a sense of how magnificently, marvelously, variously the human body is crafted in men and women. And, if you allow your seeing, your gaze, to look at the models, you can easily see if they enjoy their bodies and what parts of their bodies they really like and inhabit.

You'll discern more for yourself about what is attractive to you beyond superficial looks, what inside of them is attractive that is coming to the surface. Consider it research if you must, or just enjoy the show. If you are able to get comfortable looking at naked bodies, you'll become a healthier sexual being. Talking to children, or anyone, about sex will be easier as a natural extension of it.

If we had a more pluralistic sexuality in our culture, deeper intimacy and connections with lovers, partners, family, friends, and Earth, and more freedoms, would this not translate to reducing the denial of sexuality, sex, and the freedom to express it? A pluralistic sexual environment would lead to fewer power struggles as equality became more the norm.

Having pornography in the relationship is problematical when one of you feels a need to keep it secret from the other. Secrets and shame are thugs lurking, hand in hand, in the shadows, where they like it best. Feeling as if your lover isn't present while making love right after he watched a porn film isn't pornography's fault. There is a flaw in the relationship, which may be an unwillingness to be intimate or vulnerable. Also, a lot of people really don't know how or what it means to be truly present while making love. There may be an inability to consciously ask for what one needs in a relationship.

The problem is not pornography. Or pornographers. Or addictions. Or drugs. The source of the problem lies in our inner beings. We are terrified of ourselves, of intimacy, of our power. We are terrified of seeing the truth or speaking our truth. We are afraid of saying no and even of saying yes. Afraid of unveiling ourselves. The crimes against essential human dignity stop with me. The sin of lying to our children, of deceiving them and ourselves must become something else. Placing the blame on something outside ourselves will not change our behavior or circumstances or how we feel. Each of us has our own private ways of dealing with or avoiding the pain of our lives, the pain we see in the world, the pain of growing old. If watching porn helps, don't deny us that as we find ways to be alive in the midst of the heartbreaks and pain.

13
Healing the Human Soul

I became a visitor to some wounded part of myself.

CHARLES BOWDEN,
BLUES FOR CANNIBALS

The longest and most exciting journey is the journey inwards.

KONSTANTINE STANISLAVSKY

Having intimacy in our life necessitates that we be selfish. The word and concept of *selfish* has gotten a lot of bad press; anyone who is selfish, acts selfish, or takes care of themselves is seen as greedy, negative, or bad. When I talk about being selfish, I'm talking about putting your needs and wants first. When you do that, you are being intimate with yourself, which enables you to be intimate with others. It brings you into alignment with, and accountable to, yourself. This is one of the hardest things to do if we have been raised to put the needs of others before our own. It is also often used to pretend to be intimate. Taking care of others, putting their needs before your own, is a way to withdraw, to take yourself out, of true intimate relating. Taking care of others, worrying about their happiness, tending to their needs is a façade of responsibility preventing you from *being* with others.

Pretending we're something we're not precludes us from being real. Taking care of someone can sustain a relationship, but it does not feed it. Intimacy nourishes, deepens, and changes relationships and each participant.

There are times when we want to and need to put our needs on hold. If a friend has become ill or is having a difficult time, you can be of service in the true sense. When it becomes a way of life that interferes with your being present, real, and intimate, it is a problem.

It took me a long time to understand this and the importance of it, longer still to exorcise the belief and habit of putting myself in second or third place. Once I did, the sense of freedom I experienced propelled me to experimenting with this until it became a way of life, an expression of my intimate self. From that place, I could see how being second or third was unkind to me. It reinforced childhood injunctions about not being seen or taking up too much space.

Gandhi was once asked by a friend if his reason for living in a village and serving the people there was purely humanitarian. Gandhi replied, "I am here to serve no one else but myself; to find my own self-realization through the service of these people."[1] Gandhi's liberation was India's liberation. His insistence that "personal change and the ability to bring about social change are linked," is one of his legacies.[2] To know, to feel, to experience myself in the presence and contrast of others is empowering, sometimes joyful, sometimes extremely challenging.

There is genius in each one of us. Every person is born with a soul, and that soul has an urge, a drive to do something, to be something, to create, to labor, to teach, to become itself, to express itself, to awaken our innate gifts and talents from dormancy. It's not so much the form of what you do that matters; what matters is that you do it in response to the movement of the soul. And that in that movement toward soul fulfillment, you do it well, with finesse, with *el mundo* of you. Genius is simply to become an expert at being yourself, mastering the subject of your soul. It is not the same thing as being intelligent or having a high IQ; it is a specific *kind* of intelligence. Genius is natural talent, creative power, heightened intuition, excellence, and imagination. The genius in each of us embodies all those things, and it demands that we let the genie out of the bottle; let it impose itself onto the world, let its power into the room and through your life. When we are able to do this, we bring Eros and Psyche, sexual energy, love, our hearts, our imaginations, our understanding of spirituality and the numinous into all that we do; to become masters of the soul's journey, to become geniuses in sexual and intimate arenas, to become geniuses of our interior worlds. To bring the genius of your heart's perceptions into the world is a legacy to leave those who will come after. Living by the genius of the heart allows your soul to grow. When we are able to do this, we stop looking for meanings and begin to give meaning to our life in relation to the forms or vehicles the soul needs. That's a really nice legacy to leave, especially where soul and genius are concerned. Our legacy is the imprint of our soul on the world.

The form through which these things are expressed changes according to the needs of the soul; the form itself is part of the expression. It is not the actual expression itself, but the essence of the person that matters. For example, artists use various mediums to express their soul's urge to create and inside the medium—the form—is expression—the act. Out of that action comes the essence or meaning. It's important to have flexibility with the form to facilitate higher development of the soul. Soul needs the form to be dynamic and fluid in response to its own growth.

When I teach, consult with clients, work with plants, spend time in the wilderness, hold my granddaughters, or make sacred love I experience some of the happiest and most ecstatic and joy-filled moments in my life. These are areas where my genius lies, where it is given expression. I'm in service to what is fulfilling to me, challenges me, and moves me toward being all I imagine I can be. Being in service to my soul means to take in soul food, to nourish and sustain my soul so that, in turn, my soul can sustain and nourish this body to which it gives form. As well, I tend to the caretaking of my body, that temple to my soul. When I teach or talk to the ancestors or make pilgrimage to the sacred waters of the hot springs, or when I am able to help a client my soul is fed. These things fill a need in me that would be unmet if I let my fear make decisions for me—fears of teaching, of writing, of fucking up. Especially if I am afraid going into a teaching weekend, it gives me pause to self-examine, to work in interior time becoming the master of my destiny, and to remember why I'm doing it—why I *must* do it. I calibrate the level of fear and level of joy I have as I approach something to the level of importance it holds for my soul.

I have a well-developed, irritating and exasperating habit of putting myself in situations that look uncannily like a box from which there is only one way out—one I have not discovered until I am in the box—and where the old ways out no longer work. Moreover, the old ways are not supposed to work. I have to go through the distress of finding new solutions to new paradoxes, reinventing myself continuously. It forces me to make choices from a grown-up place and a place of vulnerability, maturity, and freedom from reactionary behavior. It is in those difficult moments that character is defined; it is the difference between seeing a thing through to the end and abandoning oneself. This is what Michael Meade calls "the right kind of trouble."[3] The right kind of trouble is deeply troubling to the soul: it can manifest as a period of heightened irritability, restlessness, and perturbation or can even bring on full-blown depression or a psychotic break. These are signals that the soul is disturbed with the status quo, that there is a great need to go to the depths of yourself to find your way through the difficulty.

We all have our unique ways to innovate and grow. The best choices are those that are made from free choice, free will. Choices made from fear, from old habits, or from "should" are doomed to failure and regret. Freedom comes from the prices paid and the time put in to rewrite yourself over and over again, moment to micromoment. It's hard work; the rewards are immeasurable. It is the work that defines and distinguishes between Homo sapiens, the species to which we belong, and more fully developed human beings who have a complete range of emotional, spiritual, feeling responses—who have become the "I" that is I from living and being truly alive.

If one more person chooses to become undefended, to become more whole, the circle of life becomes more healed. Hope has new life, extending out like concentric rings reaching distant shores.

It is only since healing the original wounds of my family that I can look back and say I know that I have been blessed. I have a fierce determination and a voracious hunger that drives me on to seek out, find the root of, and harvest my own truth. I want to be free.

I knew freedom was possible, is possible still. Though I had excuses and apologies for my behavior, for my searching, for my dissatisfaction, eventually I gave them up. They served me not. Holding on to them depressed my motive force, weighing heavy on my soul. They were coping skills that kept me stuck in old patterns. Giving them up enabled me to take responsibility and ownership of my choices and behaviors. Letting them go meant giving up being a victim and taking up being empowered.

It took time to be confident in myself. Even after going through torturous decision-making processes, I would second-guess myself. I believed that if I made the wrong choice something horrible would happen. But more than that, I had no certainty, no self-possession, no sense of where I ended and someone else began; other people's needs were convoluted and tangled up in my own. From years of doing this work, I've retrained myself, watched how my body changed shape in response. I dropped "baby fat" when I was in my early forties. I've fallen in love with myself, become self-assured, possessed of self. My boundaries are more clear as well as my "seeing." I've given myself permission to feel everything, to live a life of the senses and of sensuousness, to live outside the conventions of the city and to join Dionysus in the wild woodlands and hillsides.

SEEING WHO YOU ARE

It's valuable to be able to see the impact you have on people in your life and in the world. Try stepping just outside yourself, as if hovering just above your head witnessing your movements through the world. Take note of how you've influenced people. Really see what their life would be like without you in it; see the void your absence would create. Come to know that you matter. *You matter.* The substance of you, the physical, spiritual, psychological aspects of you, is significant. If you feel less than significant, what would it take for you to feel consequential, substantial, influential, noteworthy? Be of consequence. Be outstanding. Be a force to be reckoned with, or will you live an unlived life?

Well-behaved women seldom make history.

LAUREL THATCHER ULRICH,
WELL-BEHAVED WOMEN SELDOM MAKE HISTORY

You are the authority of your life, the author who gets to pen a new story, a personal myth. Becoming the authority of your life necessitates you taking personal responsibility. You must show up for yourself and be accountable to yourself. Writing a life requires drafts, edits, rewrites. It begins with imagining what you want, remembering who you've always wanted to be, and making choices that support and move you in that direction, toward that person you know in your deepest self you are meant to be. That person has been inside you all these years, getting you to notice at times, waiting for you to say, "Okay, it's time. Let's do this dance. I'm ready, already."

There is a difference between being a writer and an author. Writing is writing, and being a writer is being a writer. As author, you are the original creator of a piece of work; you have given it existence and authority. Authorship determines, points to, and carries responsibility for what is created.

Feel the difference. "I'm writing my life." How does it feel? Where do you feel it? Now, try this: "I'm authoring my life." How does that feel? It has more weight, more gravity, more authority. "I'm writing my life" feels more heady, almost as if it's coming out of the eyes. The second one is felt closer to the heart and womb, where creativity is birthed from the fires of passion and imagination.

Reaching a state of grace is maturity of soul, courage of heart, and strength of character. Having a sense of humor and self-forgiveness and self-compassion, and being attentive to your intimate self will get you through difficult circumstances. Courage is needed for the obvious, to see inside yourself things you've been afraid to see. Loving yourself takes fierce devotion and courage, for many of us were not raised to love ourselves, to understand what that means and be curious about how self-love feels inside us. The willingness to be changed by the work, to follow it through to the end of your life—that is grace.

It is not tensile strength that is called for, but strength that is already there inside you waiting to be tapped and used. When I pray about strength, I don't ask for more strength. I ask to use the strength that is already there, inside me, and I ask for help in shaping the strength to fit the shape of the thing I'm working with. It calls for reliance on your self, self-analysis, self-correction, and an indomitable will to make yourself your primary relationship.

There must be a commitment to give up lying in all its forms; lying to yourself through the games you play and the justifications and excuses that support their continuation. We are ingenious at manufacturing excuses and justifications, but they are forms of self-imprisonment. It is beneficial if you possess a desire to get to the truth of things, to aim a searing hot arrow at pretense, burning away the masks, the self-delusions that cover the truth. The truth that comes from seeing and perceiving directly.

My definition of lying was expanded, much to my horror, by a plant who blatantly called me a liar. I was shocked to hear it and asked in reply, "Just what do you mean by that? I'm one of the most honorable people I know." She was not humored and responded with, "In many ways you are; however, you lie by omission. You lie by keeping your needs a secret. You lie by not speaking out. You lie by adapting to circumstances. And in so doing, you betray yourself. Therefore, you are a liar."

Ouch. That was painful to hear, but she was right. Oh, the ways we delude ourselves. I saw myself in each one of those statements, and I felt what a cruelty it was to myself, to me. Lying sucks the energy out of relationships and undermines agreements to be intimate. It's a hustle to present yourself as something you're not. People just don't look favorably upon being hustled. I thought about each lie, felt into each one, and set about to correct them. This is a good place to talk about devotion since it is easily derailed when we engage in self-deception. *Devotion* is a word that often conjures up images of religious fervor since it is often used in religious contexts.

There is a common misunderstanding about devotion and commitment. We think once we have committed to something or someone, everything is taken care of. Devotion and commitment begin first with deciding you want that person to be part of your life; you decide to be devoted and committed to him. You then confirm your commitment each day. Commitment is not something to be taken for granted; you must put energy into it to keep it spiritually alive. Deciding every day to be devoted to self-awareness and self-reflection engages all of you and keeps what you are doing in front of you. Devotedly doing the work is holding context for yourself. To hold context is to put energy into something; you think about, ponder, contemplate, pray if you pray, dream, and imagine the thing you are holding context for. You hold a macrocontext of the work overall and a microcontext for specific problems, issues, behaviors, and motivations you want to understand and resolve.

I knew I was beginning to heal when I found myself being spontaneous. Spontaneously, I was suddenly making fun of my own behaviors and joking about my family: "My sister's breasts are so huge they are registered as weapons of mass destruction." Being able to laugh at the absurdities of life and circumstances allows you to enjoy your own company. Explore yourself and your family from the perspective of a healed, whole person. Ask members of your inner council to join you in this. They see things you haven't. If there is an issue or person in your family that is particularly irritating, bring them to your inner council. You can bring anything to your council, by the way.

> *You grow up the day you have your first real laugh—at yourself.*
>
> ETHEL BARRYMORE

Understanding that you are human, and understanding what it means to be human, lays open the threshold of forgiving yourself for your human frailties, which is to have compassion for all your mistakes, the hurtful words that you uttered, the ways you failed your children. Allow yourself to be educated by life and by your mistakes. What happened before you became conscious is in the past. The past as it was has no place and no power now or in the future except in how it shaped you, mentored you, and allowed you to become who you are now. It doesn't have to order your life or condemn you to be who you were when you started out. You get to be different, and you can't get there without forgiving yourself. In forgiveness, we are no longer affected by our past.

This work heals the past. In time, the stories of our lives become memories, echoes, an imprint on the retina of the heart. They no longer have power over us. The scripts our families gave us can no longer influence us. The new life has no tolerance for old behaviors or indulging ourselves in what happened so long ago. The stories and the wounds that we carried are no matter. It's not the wound that matters; it's what happens afterward. And now is afterward.

Being the initiator of your life is a feeling thing. What feels good? What makes you happy? What will it take for "I will" to become "I am"? Imagine yourself on your deathbed and looking back on your life. What does it look like? What does it feel like? Do you hear a voice inside yourself saying "I could have"? What is the thing you could have done and didn't? Where did you stop yourself? What stopped you? Was it fear? Does it feel good to see these things? Are you willing to let fear and hesitation dictate your life? Are you ready to be the leading lady of your own life?

What will it take for you to feel good about who you became, the work you did, the legacy you left? As you look back on your footprints, do you like the imprint you left in your path? What choices must you make now to feel good when the end comes—and come it does to each one of us.

> *Is it not time to throw off the shroud? Is it not time to speak out, to cry out, to fly, to test wings, to fall, and to laugh with joy over the divine bruises?*
>
> GERRY SPENCE,
> *GIVE ME LIBERTY*

You can walk around unconscious (read, coma), or you can choose to be conscious, aware, awake, alive. You are getting closer to death, to biodegrading, to becoming compost and worm food, even as you read the words on this page. So why not go for it? Create your own myth; become the heroine of your own story. Choosing a life of awareness means giving up the option of going unconscious.

At some point you'll know you've crossed an invisible line that makes taking up archaic behaviors impossible. You'll know this has happened if you imagine yourself, who you are now, in the old life. When the new you is imagined in the old life, there is a feeling to it, an uneasiness, a disconnect, a misfit. It's sort of a prickly, queasy feeling in the pit of your stomach; your breathing gets shallow or you may even stop breathing. These feelings are communications from the new you.

Then there is grieving. You grieve for the childhood you never had, for the life you've left, and for those whom you've left, or who have left you, who have helped you along the way. There is grief for the unkind-nesses toward yourself, your body, your lover, your children, your parents. You grieve for the things you needed to hear as a young girl and the love you needed to feel but didn't. Grieve until you are wrung out and empty of grief, and you will find yourself on the other side of it. You'll know when you're there; it has a feeling to it. Say a silent thank you, I love you. And, good-bye.

Become the epicenter of your universe. You are the initiator. Initiate. Find your passion, your hunger, and follow it from moment to moment. Ask someone who loves you and who you trust to tell you how he sees you, what he sees and knows to be your strengths and gifts. Simultaneously feeling and thinking your way through this will take you far in crafting a life that brings you joy, fulfillment, and satisfaction.

Try on various scenarios in your imagination. Fill in as many details as you possibly can. Ask for help in whatever spiritual tradition that suits you, or create your own spiritual tradition and ceremony. Go to the mountain or the ocean and drink in the power that is there by the buck-etful. Watch the birds; listen to them sing up the sun each morning. That is ceremony. It can be simple or elaborate.

Ask the ancestors of your land, of your heritage for help. In Africa, they say they talk to the ancestors because they are closest to them, clos-est to Earth. God is very busy, they say, but the ancestors, they are here to help. They remember us. They want to help, so sit down at their feet, or do a walk about, or a medicine walk, and have a conversation with them. Give them details. As Sun Bear, the Ojibway holy man said, "If you ask for crumbs, you'll get a crumby life." This is your *life* we're talking about, your happiness, your joy, your soul's journey.

The ancestors want to help you. It's their adventure too, you know. They need you to live your life so they can experience what living is like through you. Until I began in devotion, to follow the Earth-centered path, I had a foolish idea that God and the spirits were above Earth, hovering or hanging out in some ethereal, shimmering, invisible-to-my-eye, holier-than-thou, untouchable-by-human hands heavenly realm, a cloud perhaps. I asked myself, Why would they hang out there when there are trees and waterfalls and the smell of cottonwood buds and lav-ender and a lover's perfume and sex all here on Earth? If I was God or a spirit, this is where I would be spending all my time, invisible or not. This is the place where things are happening. There are many things happening in the realm of the invisibles that I am interested in, but as far as sensate, kinesthetic, erotic, and sensual experiences go, Earth is the place. I fall in love with being here every day as I fall in love with my lover, deeper and fuller.

It brings our ancestors joy to see us having our dreams fulfilled. They need us to move spontaneously and freely through time and space. They love the sound of laughter and the lightning that flashes out your eyes when you are expressing the truth of who you are in the world.

In many cultures there are ceremonies that last for days, sometimes weeks, ceremonies with a never-ending fire and long dances with drumming and singing. Often a person dancing is taken over by a spirit; the spirits come to have the ecstatic, sexual experience once again, of blending soul and spirit and body. They come to the human world to help us, and they come to the human world to be helped, to play, to feel. And they come to share the journey and the wisdom of the ages.

Why is creating your own life important in intimate relationships? Intimacy begins with you. Intimate relationships are best fostered in an environment where both people are self-assured and self-possessed. Each person in the relationship must have a sense of their work in the world, something they take joy in, something that is their creation and a manifestation of their dreams. As a partnership, there must be some joint adventure, a shared dream and shared goals that you hold in your hearts and give energy to, things that strengthen the bond you share.

Self-awareness is the architect of authenticity.

Making unilateral decisions in a partnership, about the partnership, is a recipe for disaster. It is discounting the other and the spirit of the relationship. If you are in a partnership, engage your partner in the process. You must understand how important this is. Say what you have been thinking about, and ask for feedback. Hear, with all of you, what is being said. Ask for clarification if you don't understand something, don't let it lie there and ferment into assumptions and misunderstandings. Saying things out loud is a way of thinking and feeling out loud. And it's a way to fight for the life of the relationship. Not saying things out loud leads to secrets and these kinds of secrets are deadly to your soul and to the relationship. As you talk, you are often able to see more details or get excited about your possibilities, and it sparks the imaginative fires of the other. Speak up when something isn't working for you. Needs cannot get met if you don't know, or won't say, what they are.

Depending on your partner to make you happy, to be the source of your self-esteem, is most certainly a formula for disaster. His presence in your life, his happiness, and the joy and adventures you share together are all sources of and additions to your happiness. His joys and successes infect you, as yours do him. They cannot help but influence you; the two of you are bonded in body, soul, and spirit by the invisible connections between and around you. But he is an addition to you, not your source; you are the most important thing in your life.

> *If another person is the most important thing in your life, then you're in trouble and they're in trouble because they become responsible for your suffering and your successes. But if consciousness is the most important thing in our lives and relationship is means toward that end . . . ah! Then we are approaching paradise. We are approaching the possibility of actually becoming a human being before we die.*
>
> STEPHEN LEVINE,
> *EMBRACING THE BELOVED*

Maturity is taking personal responsibility in crafting a new life. Growing up, being a grown-up, has immeasurable rewards. There are few experiences that compare to having a sense of yourself moving in the world, capable, clear, and certain. There will be times when you feel wimpy, scared, and uncertain. Being a grown-up is being aware of all these feelings as each one comes up, and then tending to them. It means listening to the small part of you that is feeling these things. Take care to listen to what she's feeling; what she needs you to do. You won't know what to do for her if you are unwilling to listen. To listen is to be changed by what you hear.

You may need to ask your lover to rub your feet or your neck or to just hold you when you're not feeling like yourself. Maybe you need to say, "I feel wimpy, will you tell me all the things you like about me?" Yes, it's hard; it feels weird, uncomfortable, unnatural, and completely foreign. We have not been raised this way; we have not been given permission or encouragement to have feelings, to say them out loud in the world. And in our culture, all those uncomfortable things are in place to discourage exploration of that territory. The last thing our culture and our governments want is for us to be walking around feeling good, following our feelings, and noticing that life in these times does not feel good.

Let the Child of you do the asking. She is the one who needs to hear these things. Pay attention to the responses and let them trickle down deep inside you to touch her. With practice, you will be able to feel love moving inside you. You'll feel the changes it makes in your physiology. These changes come in response to love filling you up, lifting your spirit and enlivening you. This looks good on paper and in theory, but when it becomes as natural as breathing, it is glorious. After some time, after the deep parts of you have been fed love and know now that nothing bad will happen by being alive, by taking up space, by getting their needs met, your need to ask for support will diminish and become circumstantial. Emotional incontinence is temporary; you will build new skills, new muscles, and become familiar with the territory.

In the beginning, it is tiresome; you'll want to stop many times. You're breaking from old behaviors; secret agreements you made with yourself when you were very young are being changed and renegotiated. Part of you will be frightened when you break from family scripts and long-held values. I encourage you to hold that part of yourself, reassure her that you are watching, that you will let nothing bad happen.

SELF-NURTURING

Consult with yourself daily, throughout the day. If you feel overwhelmed, take time out or away. This depth work takes a lot of focus and uses energy, and at times you will feel depleted, wrung out, and you'll get irritated and pissed off at everything as you become exhausted. Stress on yourself and the relationship, upsets, and misunderstandings can be prevented by attending to how you are feeling and what you need and finding ways to renew yourself, to fill up your dwindling reserves of energy.

Consider giving yourself a no-value day—a day when you do nothing that counts toward anything but taking care of yourself. One day might look like this: Don't dress in street clothes; wear your robe and lounge pants all day long. Linger in bed for as long as you can or want to. Read for a bit, or sip tea in bed. Though, honestly, as romantic as that sounds and looks in the movies, in reality it can be awkward and clumsy. Nonetheless, you have to try it at least twice. Linger in bed extra long, bask in the afterglow of great, predawn lovemaking with your beloved or yourself. Read your favorite sci-fi or mystery novel for a few hours. Lie in bed until you choose the one thing that will next make you happy. It could be cooking your favorite breakfast or brunch or lunch. What would make your palate and stomach and the Child in you really happy? Maybe it's taking yourself out for a meal in a cozy, nurturing café. After the meal, maybe back to bed to read more of your sci-fi or mystery novel.

Be sensitive to situational renewal time. If I've been working with people a lot after a teaching weekend, I need time alone or to be held in silence and feel my beloved wrap his love and arms around me. Other times, I need to go alone to the hot springs or on a hike and talk to the ancestors, sit on stone and be filled up with wild landscapes. Maybe I need to gaze at Tree or Stone or River, and feel their gaze on me. If I've been writing all day and straining my eyes and brain, what I need is a glass of fine wine or a shot of tequila (with lime, of course, and no salt, please) and something between my ears besides what I've been writing about, so a good movie is in order. If I feel nostalgic and melancholy, then definitely a romance is in order. If it's been a difficult day, I may want an action, adventure, or karate flick where the bad guys get their asses kicked real good. What I need depends on what I'm feeling.

Ask your lover to take a day off with you. Let the Child in each of you choose something that would be really fun to do together. Plan several days over the next month. And stick to them.

As you are getting used to the idea, maybe even excited about authoring your life, I give you an exercise that will help you see things about yourself and take you into the territory of your values, beliefs, and deep feelings. Before beginning this exercise, consider making an agreement with yourself to not censor anything, to not hold anything back. You may take a few days or weeks to work on this, for as you move throughout your life in the midst of this assignment, you will find more things to add to each part of it. This exercise is designed to help you get to know yourself better, to see things on paper that maybe you hadn't thought of before. Writing also exercises your faculties of analysis and insight, and helps you to go deeper.

ᨀ EXERCISE ᨀ
Exploring Who You Are

Love

What do you love about sex?

What do you love about yourself?

What do you love about your body?

What do you love about your lover?

What do you love about your life?

Hate

What do you hate about sex?

What do you hate about yourself?

What do you hate about your body?

Is there anything you hate about your lover?

What do you hate about your life?

Authoring

If you could have any life you wanted, what would it look like?

What will it take for you to have that?

What steps do you need to take to get there?

Intimacy

How do you define intimacy?

How does intimacy feel to you?

Does creating intimacy frighten you?

Do you know why?

Are you intimate with yourself?

Do you want more intimacy in your life?

With your partner?

How will you create that?

I encourage you to use the word *hate* rather than substituting it with *I don't like*. They are not the same thing, you see. Hate has a particular feel to it; it provides energy to work with, and in lists such as these it lets you know which areas of your life stand out as needing to be changed, altered, redirected, and made whole. "I don't like" doesn't offer nearly the same energy, impact, or fuel for change. If you want to make real changes, deep changes, lasting changes in your life, "I don't like" isn't going to get you there. You need the passion that hate possesses. If you find yourself avoiding the word *hate*, you might add it to your list: Why I hate using the word *hate*.*

I feel ready to follow even the most trivial hunch.

WILLIAM STAFFORD

ECOSEXUALITY

It is impossible to be whole human beings, fully, consciously, functional human beings, as long as we are disconnected from our sexuality and as long as we deny that our sexuality is implicitly bound up with Earth's sexuality. As long as we continue refusing to see Earth and all her inhabitants and residents as sexual, the disconnect and impoverishment of spirit will continue.

All of life is sexual; human sex organs have evolved from the prototypes of plants and animals as evolution occurred. Peter Tompkins and Christopher Bird note that "plants have female organs in the form of vulva, vagina, uterus and ovaries, serving precisely the same functions as they do in woman, as well as distinct male organs in the form of penis, glans, and testes, designed to sprinkle the air with billions of spermatozoa, were facts quickly covered by the eighteenth-century establishment with the almost impenetrable veil of Latin nomenclature, which stigmatized the labiate vulva, and mis-styled the vagina; the former being called 'stigma,' the latter 'style.' Penis and glans were equally disfigured into 'filament' and 'anther.'"[4]

Then there are the bees who instinctively know where the pollen is and its quality and quantity. They take that information back to the hive,

---

*This exercise is a modified version of the love/hate/admire list found on page 65 of *Ensouling Language* by Stephen Harrod Buhner.

and with the shaking of their rear ends, they communicate all that information. Bees are prodigious and libidinous; they shake their sexual energy all over the place, and when we eat honey or bee pollen or royal jelly, we're eating sexual energy. They communicate by dancing. The male bees, called drones, carry "the wisdom of the hive" and keep it in harmony by swarming and "chanting." They also wait for females to fly by.

They fight until there is one who is able to mate with the female. They have sex in flight, then the penis breaks off and the male bee dies. There are advantages to being human.

Ducks have an interesting method of copulation. Forced sex is common, but the female duck has an elaborate system of vaginas that tricks the penis into one of several false sheaths. Only when the drake she chooses enters her vagina with his corkscrew penis will she allow her eggs to be fertilized. The human cervix has a complementary function. It is able to discern which sperm would be a good match; Hippocrates believed that a woman could regulate the acceptance or rejection of sperm. The cervix is able to "upsuck" or expel semen.[5] Midwives have been studying female sexuality and the reproductive patterns of women for 100,000 years. Midwives today carry gathered knowledge of ancient cultures of women who have intimate knowledge of their bodies, know when they are ovulating, and can say when conception occurred. Few women in the West are so in touch with their body's rhythms and cycles to be able to say when much of anything is happening.

Breast feeding prevents ovulation and suppresses a woman's menstrual cycle. Suckling infants stimulate the breast, increasing hormonal opiates that suppress the production of hormones involved in ovulation. I wonder if men who choose to nurse infants and children have a corresponding hormonal response; that is, does male lactation from breastfeeding suppress sperm-producing hormones?

We've become a culture separated from our own body of Earth, turning to cultural solutions for everything from birth control to stimulation, relaxation, sleep, and wakefulness. Plant-based birth control and knowledge of one's body has been found in the archaeological records dating as far back as 630 BCE. In the Greek city of Cyrene on Africa's northern tip, women used the plant silphium or laserwort (wild fennel). It became a prized plant for the freedom it provided to enjoy sex without the worry of pregnancy. The plant's importance is evident on a Cyrenian coin, that depicts a regal-looking woman sitting in a chair. One hand is touching the plant and the other is pointing to her genitals.[6] From the fifth century BCE in Greece, lemon halves were applied to the cervix as a spermicide. Plants as a source of bio-available hormones whose uses have stopped and started menstruation and alleviated premenstrual and menopausal symptoms were first taken seriously by the scientific community in 1933 when Boleslaw Skarynski found trihydroxyoestrin in willow, a substance that resembles estrogen. Hormone-containing plants have been used as abortifacients, aphrodisiacs, and contraceptives.

The use of plants as contraceptives is new information to humans. Animals have been using plants for all manner of healing and controlling population since they appeared on the scene (plants were here first). Plants as contraceptives have been used by animals since they evolved side-by-side on Earth's grand stage. A certain species of red clover, *Trifolium subterraneum,* is rich in an isoflavone that disrupts reproduction. Over three hundred plant species have been found to contain levels of phytoestrogens (plant compounds that mimic the female reproductive hormone, estrogen). Phytoestrogens are capable of turning reproduction on or off, depending on the timing of their ingestion. In birds and animals, they tend to decrease fertility. All animal reproduction is dependent on plant chemistry.[7]

Tompkins and Bird note that, in Teutonic mythology, "Baldur, god of light, had secretly gazed upon the naked form of the flower princess Nanna as she bathed in a stream. When her natural loveliness was enhanced by the energy over which Baldur ruled, his heart, said the legend, was pierced, and the marriage of Light and Flowers became a foregone conclusion."[8]

Gustav Theodor Fechner postulated the concept that believing whether plants have a soul or not changes one's whole insight into nature. If humanity admitted to an omnipresent, all-knowing god who bestowed animation on all things, then nothing in the world could be excluded from this munificence, neither plant nor stone nor crystal nor wave. Why would universal spirit, he asked, sit less firmly in nature than in human beings and not be as much in command of nature's power as it is of human bodies? "That it is a dark and cold world we sit in if we will not open the inward eyes of the spirit to the inward flame of nature."[9]

Then there is George Washington Carver, of slave descent, who became an agricultural chemist, later known as the Black Leonardo. Through his unorthodox methods, he was able to turn the peanut, useful only as hog food, into peanut butter and he used peanut oil to heal the atrophied muscles of polio patients. "Nature is the greatest teacher and I learn from her best when others are asleep. In the still dark hours before sunrise God tells me of the plans I am to fulfill. The secrets are in the plants. To elicit them you have to love them enough," he said.[10]

Not long before Carver's death, a visitor to his laboratory saw him reach out his long sensitive fingers to a little flower on his workbench. "When I touch that flower," he said rapturously, "I am touching infinity. It existed long before there were human beings on this earth and will continue to exist for millions of years to come. Through the flower, I talk to the Infinite, which is only a silent force. This is not a physical contact. It is not in the earthquake, wind or fire. It is in the invisible world. It is that still small voice that calls up the fairies."[11]

The December 11, 1995, online issue of *High Country News* reported the deaths of 342 migrating snow geese. Their last stop was a lake that filled in after the Berkeley open-pit copper mine in Butte, Montana, quit operations and closed the mine. The edge of the lake was lined with rocks heavy in pyrite, and when the water hit the rocks, it turned into sulfuric acid. In turn, the sulfuric acid leached metals from the ore, causing the lake water to be filled with arsenic, cadmium, copper, gold, zinc, and silver. When the geese drank the water, they were poisoned to death.

It has since been discovered that a curious, dark, goopy substance identified as live yeast appeared near the edge of the lake. Testing of the yeast found that it actually absorbed the metals in the lake, which is high in sulfuric acid. And not a mere 5 or 10 percent of heavy metals but as much as 85 to 90 percent. Further testing discovered that this particular yeast is found only in the rectal swabs of . . . snow geese.[12]

As I write this, there has been a frightening and as yet mysterious and unknown phenomenon: massive deaths of birds and fish have been reported around the world. Thousands of birds have dropped spontaneously en masse from the sky. Explanations that range from Orwellian conspiracy theories, end-of-world times, prophesies come true, solar flares, and government testing in the ionosphere are rampant. I don't have an answer. What I know is that we have no time to put off making changes, real changes, from deep inside each of us. Real changes cannot begin any other place—the kind of changes that move personal mountains and tap the reservoir of human potential buried beneath centuries of oppression, repression, line drawing, and all manner of violence to the human spirit and soul and to the soul of Earth.

> *Why not go out on a limb? That's where the fruit is.*
>
> WILL ROGERS

It is impossible to live in the world and not be in relationship to everything in and around you, to everyone and everything you come in contact with. It may be in balance or out of balance, but a relationship you do have. You can get a sense of this if you are able to drop labels for a few moments. For example, if you don't say, "I have an eating disorder," then what do you have? You have a relationship with eating; you have a relationship with food. You have a relationship with your body and with hunger. The next question is: What is the relationship with my body? Without using the words *good* and *bad,* try to describe the relationship and how it is. That takes you into the waters of your psyche to plumb the meaning of the relationship and how it affects your movement and your happiness. Try this on: "I have a relationship with food and my body that has been out of balance for some time. I use food so I don't have to feel or think. I've mistreated my body by overeating or undereating. I've acted like an enemy of my soul and body. I want to change those relationships."

If we suspend the use of labels such as *Muslim* and *homosexual,* then what are we left with? What is your relationship to men who love men? Would you know what a Muslim is if we didn't have a word for Muslim? What would your relationship be to someone from Pakistan or Afghanistan? To your brother who sleeps with another man? Relationships are not static; they are living and dynamic, mutable within circumstances and as values and beliefs change. You have a relationship with your children, and the relationship changes as they grow and become independent. You have a relationship with yourself, but do you know yourself, what that relationship is?

> *When your priority becomes consciousness, even more than relationship, then conscious relationship is possible.*
>
> STEPHEN LEVINE

Final Words

Nosce te ipsum. Know thyself.

TEMPLE OF APOLLO, DELPHI

Deconditioning also involves risk and suffering. But it is transformative, freeing the self from helplessness and fear. It unleashes the fifth freedom, the right to an autonomous consciousness. That makes deconditioning about as individual and personal act as is possible. Maybe the only genuine individual act.

JOE BAGEANT,
"AMERICA: Y UR PEEPS B SO DUM?"

Until we do the deep work of healing our individual psychoses, owning our sexuality, and calling on Eros and Dionysus, Aphrodite and Artemis, the ancestors, and our own inner guidance systems to create a change, all the words and lip service in the world are not going to change one iota of it. If it could, it would have happened far sooner than the time we find ourselves in. As Dale Pendell says in the *Los Angeles Times*:

284

It's not that if you make a place for Dionysian energy, that kind of wild and unpredictable God, that everything will go ok. It won't. That's not true at all. But the cost of trying to suppress it is even worse. Then you end up sacrificing your own children. In the United States today we have more people in prison than any other country on a per capita basis. The majority of these are drug crimes. It's a war against ourselves. It's a war against our children. It was a problem for the Greeks but at least they came to realize you had to admit a certain amount of chaos. You can't try to live risk free. If you try to live completely risk free you're going to destroy what you had. What's a really secure environment? San Quentin is pretty secure.[1]

It is characteristic of human nature to reach for, search for something outside ourselves, to transcend our experience and make some sense of it. Be cautious of becoming overindulgent and insistent upon giving up personal power and deferring to the great Oz (Oz was, as we know, a timid little man—it could have been a woman—behind the machine, not unlike a lot of us), the Christian God, or governments. Frank Herbert in his classic novel *Dune* showed us the tragedy of the "messiah delusion." There is no messiah, no savior waiting in the wings for just the right moment of despair to crack open and slip in to rescue us. No one will come down from the heavens and rescue us from the path of illusion and irresponsibility we've insisted on treading. There is no rapture coming. The Hopi have been telling us for thousands of years, "We are the ones we've been waiting for."

Charles Bowden poignantly asks us to examine what the real dilemma is.

Imagine the problem is not physical, imagine that the problem has never been physical. It is not biodiversity, it is not the ozone layer, it is not the greenhouse effect, the whales, the old growth forests, the loss of jobs, the crack in the ghetto, the abortions, the tongue in the mouth, the diseases stalking everywhere as love goes on, unconcerned. Imagine the problem is not some syndrome of our society. Not something that can be solved by some commission or laws or redistribution of what we call wealth. Imagine that it goes deeper; right to the core of what we call our civilization. And that nothing outside of ourselves can effect real change; that our civilizations, our governments, are sick. And that we are mentally ill and spiritually dead. And that all our issues and crises are symptoms of this deeper sickness. Imagine the problem is not physical, and no amount of driving, no amount of road will help deal with the problem. Imagine that the problem is not that we are powerless, or that we are victims, but that we have lost the fire and belief, and courage to act. We hear whispers of the future but we slap our hands against our ears. We catch glimpses but we turn our faces swiftly aside. The whistle is always blowing. There is no denying what is before my eyes. We all know the future; we only must say it and face it. There will be no first hundred days for this future; there will be no five year plans, there will be no program. Imagine the problem is that we cannot imagine a future where we possess less but are more. Imagine the problem is a future that terrifies us because we lose our machines, but gain our feet and pounding hearts.[2]

Imagine a world, our private world, where we refuse to lie and a world where rudeness is not common behavior. Imagine a world where each of us takes responsibility for our own lives and well-being. Buckminster Fuller articulated it best when he said, "All of humanity is in peril of extinction if each one of us does not dare, now and henceforth, always to tell only the truth, and all the truth, and to do so promptly—right now."[3]

Human beings are flesh-and-blood biological animals, and though we have access to the invisibles to work with, to pray to, to ask for help, they cannot do the work for us; it's not their responsibility to fix the mess we've gotten ourselves into. They come to aid us, to help us find our way, to regain our balance, to open doors and opportunities. It's up to us, then, to do the work.

There are pockets of people beginning to create change, willing to be innovative and creative and to say, "Fuck it, it stops here. I take personal responsibility."

> *You've got to jump off cliffs all the time and build your*
> *wings on the way down.*
>
> RAY BRADBURY

Take your life in your own hands and what happens? A terrible thing: no one to blame.

ERICA JONG

We need a growing body of people who are willing to make conscious choices and to stand up and speak truth to power, who are willing to own their personal power and sexuality and heal the wound between human beings and Earth. We need people who are willing to get their hands dirty doing the work, willing to stand outside mainstream thought and dogma, and especially, willing to go into the murky waters of their own psyches and heal from inside their own skins. We know so much but do so little. As Buckminster Fuller said, "We are called to be architects of the future, not its victims."[4] So we begin by deconstructing, dismantling what has not worked in our lives, in our interior world.

J. Krishnamurti said, "When you are really learning you are learning throughout your life and there is no one special teacher to learn from. Then everything teaches you—a dead leaf, a bird in flight, a smell, a tear, the rich and the poor, those who are crying, the smile of a woman, the haughtiness of a man. You learn from everything, therefore there is no guide, no philosopher, no guru. Life itself is your teacher, and you are in a state of constant learning."[5]

In every new movement that begins, its conception is traceable back to an idea. Ideas are at the heart of any new movement. The idea is not always clearly defined, but it is there, an ember, a spark; first in the imaginal then spoken and written. It's always waiting to be given form, made manifest, through the actions and in the lives of men and women.

Incorporating sacred sex more fully into our lives and living as the sexual beings that we are provides us with the challenge and opportunity to be a wholly integrated human being. Despite edicts to focus on the family, divorce and remarriage are common occurrences. Though not officially sanctioned, people are experimenting with alternatives to the nuclear family and traditional marriages—having open marriages, living with extended families. There are movements to incorporate pornography and Earth sexuality into our relationships. The question is no longer whether or not to explore something different; it is how honest, creative, innovative, and clear-sighted are we willing to be. We can no longer afford to ignore the sexual crisis and the need to be openhearted and open-minded in our understanding of sexual dynamics.

It would appear that each of us is evolving into a more responsible human being who can make choices from a place of deep wholeness. A human being who can make plans according to her own needs and desires and not fit into someone else's plan for her.

In the end, it may be our distrusting, fearful, inhumane relationships with one another and with Earth, with Nature, that will be the fall of the human species. To keep civilization going, we must invent new values about human beings and sexuality, bringing the wildness of Earth, inviting Eros and Dionysus, Aphrodite and Artemis into all that we do.

I revisited my family story rewriting it while in the arms of my beloved. That story is old and it no longer fits who I've become. I traveled the lands of gods and goddesses of antiquity (they're all still around, you know). I met some of the new ones coming up from the still-fertile, if latent, soil of our sexuality—that ruled by Eros and Psyche. I traced the roots of our repressed sexuality through religious and political oppression, through sexual revolutions, to the brilliance and courage of Lenny Bruce, James Hillman, Eric Berne, Marty Klein, George Carlin, Mary Roach, Aphrodite Phoenix, Laura Agustin, Erica Jong, Stanley Keleman, Henry Miller, D. H. Lawrence, and Anaïs Nin, to name a few.

The extremism, fanaticism, repressive attitudes, constipated beliefs, and hypocritical absurdities we insist we hold onto with tooth and claw continue to be bizarre and frustrating. I will be relieved when I see people leaving the church and linking back to Gaia's temples—those formed of green and flesh.

> *The people should not be afraid of their government;*
> *government should be afraid of their people.*
>
> *V FOR VENDETTA*

ANOTHER NEW SEXUAL REVOLUTION

James Baldwin said Shakespeare's "bawdiness" mattered to him once he realized that bawdiness signified "respect for the body." Bawdiness will be part of the new sexual, political, and ecological revolution. This is the new sexual revolution; a revolution of authentic voices. A revolution of earthy lustiness, boldness, out-of-the-closet complete ownership of sexual, sensual energy infusing everything we touch and breathe upon. The kind of revolution that pulls us out of the secret holding in and takes us out to Earth to self-baptism in the wild waters, mud between our toes and red clay under our fingernails. This will be a revolution that redefines *pretty* and *sexy* and one where beauty comes out of the body from self-love and adoration; the beauty that is created when we abandon ourselves to falling in love—with men, with women, with children, with nonhuman beings— and when that love permeates all that we do.

This revolution will link us back to our feeling, sensing bodies, our ground of being, and free us to say what is true and real. And it will fill the dry, calcified cracks separating humans and Earth with the slippery healing balm of sexual, sensual energies. It will call on the gods and goddesses of the old ways, those of the new ways, and the spirit beings of the places we call home to be part of healing the wild bond between humans and Earth.

The new revolution brings mythic elements out of the dreamworld and back to the interworld where humans and gods comingle. It will heal the biodegradation of *anima mundi* and the soul of each of us that has been happening since we humans took ourselves out from the wild glades. It will of necessity begin inside each of us. When you are able to say, "Enough is quite enough," and "What I've been doing hasn't worked out so well," then you have options available to you. Seek not happiness; it is surely a derailment. Rather, seek what makes your heart thrum and vibrate, what makes you come alive. Happiness comes when we engage in our soul's work. This is the arena in which healing of the Earth begins and takes hold.

Until one is committed, there is hesitancy, the chance to draw back, always ineffectiveness. Concerning all acts of initiation (and creation), there is one elementary truth . . . that the moment one definitely commits, then Providence moves too. All sorts of things occur to help one that would never otherwise have occurred. . . . Whatever you can do

or dream you can do, begin it. Boldness has genius, power
and magic in it. Begin now.

JOHANN WOLFGANG VON GOETHE

Live inside your own feet and partake of the adventure of your own soul. Follow the essence of things, the feelings inside, and the form will take shape organically. Have sacred sex, lots of sex, wild sex, passionate sex. Feel deeply and with abandon. Owning your personal power, your sexual power, and doing the work of personal healing through intimacy helps everyone. It does not happen until you free yourself and are then able to make choices as a free woman. As Erica Jong says in her novel *Sappho's Leap,* "Choice is the luxury of the free."[6]

Nothing we do happens in a vacuum. All that we do radiates out to the larger society. You are not finished falling down. Growth is the act of returning to your feet and dusting yourself off, gently. It is taking the next step, the unknown step, the one that opens the heart to the remarkable mystery of life, of being. Sooner or later, your life will be over. Two millennia ago Rabbi Hillel said; "If I don't do it—who will do it? And if I don't do it right now—when will I?"[7]

In closing—finally—I quote Eric Berne who continues to help clarify and inspire:

The somber picture . . . in which human life is mainly a process of filling in time until the arrival of death, or Santa Claus, with very little choice, if any, of what kind of business one is going to transact during the long wait, is a commonplace but not the final answer. For certain fortunate people there is something which transcends all classifications of behavior, and that is awareness; something which rises above the programming of the past, and that is spontaneity; and something that is more rewarding than games, and that is intimacy. But all three of these may be frightening and even perilous to the unprepared. Perhaps they are better off as they are, seeking their solutions in popular techniques of social action, such as "togetherness." This may mean that there is no hope for the human race, but there is hope for individual members of it.[8]

Talking to Children and Teens about Sex

It is easier to build strong children than to repair broken men.

FREDERICK DOUGLASS

In a time of universal deceit, telling the truth is a revolutionary act.

GEORGE ORWELL

Saguaros are almost never found in the open. Underhill . . . quoted some Papago words that indicate they may have had the nurse plant concept before it was suggested by Anglo botanists. The Papago belief was "saguaros have trouble getting started in life. They are so big. Like a fat child, they get sick. But paloverde grows fast like a mother. It bends down the leaves and keeps the wind away."

RUTH UNDERHILL,
QUOTED IN *DESERT PLANTS* 2 (AUTUMN 1980)

Homo sapiens are not the only species to grow through various ego states and stages of life. We are not the only species to be young, have adolescence, mature, and grow old and sometimes wise. Every species, whether it has roots and flowers, stands on two legs or four, needs elders to teach the young how to be that species. Elder trees teach young trees how to be tree, the archetype. Jacqueline Memory Paterson writes about European and Native American beliefs about the role of elder trees.

> The unique personality of the elder was anciently believed to come from the spirit of the "Elder Mother" who dwelt within the tree. The Elder Mother, called Elle or Hyldemoer in Scandinavian and Danish myth, worked strong earth magic and according to legend avenged all who harmed her host trees. No forester of old would touch elder, let alone cut it, before asking the Elder Mother's permission three times over and even then he was still in dread of her possible wrath. Likewise, in many country districts of Europe and Britain, wise people still show respect by touching their hats when passing elder trees, in continuance of ancient custom. Certain North American tribes also believe that elder is the Mother of the human race.[1]

Elder bears teach cubs how to be bear. In his book *The Presence of the Past*, Rupert Sheldrake writes: "When harvesting plants, I never take the elder plants, insuring that their wisdom and genetic strength can be passed on to the younger generations. According to the morphogenesis view, living organisms, such as badgers, willow trees, or earthworms, inherit not only genes but also habits of development and behaviour from past members of their own species and also from the long series of ancestral species from which their species has arisen."[2] We need sages, wise elders to take their place among us, to teach the children. We need elders who have owned their own sexuality unashamedly, unabashedly, humbly, unapologetically. And we need them to pass it on to the children through the teachings and by modeling healthy sexuality.

We tend often to take ourselves too seriously. This is especially true when talking to children about a topic we consider serious. Or scary. Or difficult. Or bad. Or naughty. Or seriously uncomfortable. One thing we all need to be aware of is that children are inherently intuitive and psychic. They feel vibrations, they sense our tentativeness, how we truly feel about something, and they know when we are lying. Their bullshit meters are very sensitive. Lying is damaging to them and to your relationship with them. When they sense you are lying, it brings your trustworthiness into question and it degrades their self-respect: Why would someone who loves me lie to me?

How do we talk to children about sex and sexuality? Start where we are, where they are. It's helpful if you can remember when you were their age, what was happening for you and your sexual curiosity. Be honest. Understand that children, at a very young age, are fascinated with their bodies, with our bodies, with sex. To raise sexually healthy children, capable of sexually intimate and healthy relationships, we need to be sexually healthy in ourselves and with our partners. Accepting that your children are sexual beings from the beginning is a very good start.

With that said, be cautious talking about sex with children until you have tried and enjoyed all kinds of sex—various positions, wet sex, oral sex, licking, touching, caressing, standing up sex, backward sex, sex under the sun and moon, sex on and in a river, battery-operated sex—at least a bazillion times. You ought to know what you are talking about. In other words, to the best of your ability, know what you are talking about.

When talking to children about sex, remember, it's about them. I recommend offering personal information only when asked for, or if you have an anecdote that seems to be supportive of the conversation and what was asked. Otherwise, stick to what's real. If you realize some of your fear about talking straight is that you don't have all the facts, now is the time to find them. Don't know where your cervix is and why you have one? Sadly, I had only a vague idea until mine got sick. On one visit with my gynecologist, she inserted a tiny tube with a camera on the end. I watched the monitor as I got an up-close-and-personal look at my cervix as it was healing. It was amazing and revealing to meet that part of me, to say hello "face-to-face," to know what it looked like, what I had been seeing as I prayed and talked with it over the six weeks of healing.

I don't know what the odds are that your child is going to ask you about masturbation, but in the event it does come up, are you comfortable talking about it? Most people aren't comfortable talking about masturbation though most everyone does it. Jocelyn Elders, surgeon general from

1994 to 1995, lost her job after fifteen months for suggesting that teaching masturbation wouldn't be out of place in our school system. Elders said: "I think that masturbation never got anybody pregnant, does not make anybody go crazy, and what we're about is preventing HIV in our bright young people. Nobody has to teach anybody how to masturbate, God taught us how. So I think that now, even in our society, they're saying that maybe this is something that we should stress more for couples and we know that they do already."[3]

Since they were old enough to understand language, I've been telling my granddaughters three primary things: how much I love them, that they can ask me anything, and that I will never lie to them. It's my job to encourage whatever thread of interest they want to follow for as long as they want to follow it. I support their natural curiosity and expose them to wild ecosystems. This includes collecting, and petting, snails, slugs, and worms. In those moments, I feel the trust and bond between the three of us grow deep roots. I take care not to impose my fears onto them. I give them room to explore with parameters, and I give them information on how to fight against what they don't want and for what they do want, to say what they need and want. I talk to them about what to do if they turn around in a crowd and can't see me or their mom: stay where you are. More people get lost by wandering off in a panic. Panic, from Pan, is the imaginal, and it stops rational thought in its tracks. James Hillman says, "The imaginal is never more vivid than when we are connected to it instinctually."[4] When in a panic, the imagination runs without rational thought or adult information.

I began having anatomy talks with my granddaughters when they were four and seven. They referred to both boy's and girl's genitals as "wieners." They giggled when I gave them the words labia, clitoris, and penis. The next day, the seven-year-old, pointing between her legs, asked me: "What was the el word for this part that girls have and boys don't?"

Don't fool yourself into thinking that you can wait until adolescence or puberty to have "the talk." Curiosity about the body and what feels good begins in the first year of life. We first learn that the breast and I are separate, that I can move my body this way and get from here to there, and that dirt is interesting to taste.

As soon as children discover they have a body with physical boundaries, they become fascinated with what it does and can do. Children begin exploring their body parts, including the genitals. It starts very young, younger than you may be comfortable knowing about. I learned this when my son was two years old. I heard him giggling to himself in his crib. I walked in to see him sitting up and playing with his penis. He was enjoying himself very much. He didn't see me, so I quietly backed out of the room and left him to enjoy himself. Toddlers, both boys and girls, find ways of pleasuring themselves before they are a year old.[5] They engage in genital play, fingering, or simple handling of their genitals.

Sensual touching begins in the moments immediately following birth when baby is placed on mom's breast. If she chooses to breast feed, the bond is reinforced. Fathers need to bond with infants immediately as well. Holding the infant in his arms next to his chest imprints his heartbeat and smell in the baby.

Babies need ample cuddling, skin-to-skin contact, and nurturing. This is their first experience of intimacy. Dressing them, diaper changing, and bathing them is their first experience of the sensuality of the body. Feeding time is nurturing and cuddling time. If your baby is a boy, you may notice an automatic response of erection during feeding, whether nursing or bottle feeding. It's a normal response. Take care to not discourage or interfere with it. Baby girls have clitoral erections, which, as we know, are less noticeable. It's not unusual for it to be accompanied by vaginal discharges so don't be alarmed if you notice extra fluid in the diaper.

At around four and five years old, children like to play doctor. They want to see and touch each other's bodies, though the idea of intercourse doesn't occur to them. It's normal behavior for that age. What's not normal or healthy is if older siblings or adults touch their bodies. Parents can and do until children learn how to bathe themselves. This is the age when kids begin learning how to navigate life, and how to resolve conflicts and put their things away. Marty Klein says, "That's when their sexuality starts developing, too." If you want to raise healthy, empowered children, let them explore their sexuality in a safe, comfortable environment; in their own home. If children are healthy, they "will become more sexual rather than less, and probably on a faster timetable than you're comfortable with."[6]

When I visit my granddaughters, we snuggle up together at bedtime with a storybook in my hands, I hug them, kiss them all over their faces, tell them how much I love them, how wonderful they are, and we giggle a lot. The conversation flows unhindered in the direction they want it to. They ask about breasts, pubic hair, and kissing boys. "Yuck," says the four-year-old.

We have fun with the teaching and learning. They are interested and curious, and I encourage those things in them. My job as their grandmother, our job as parents, is to show up and to tell the truth. Our job also is to make certain we are not talking with shame or shaming them for their natural curiosity. Hold the space for them as intelligent beings, capable of thinking and making decisions. The more honest information we give them, the better able they will be to make intelligent, informed decisions.

One time my granddaughters and I were having dinner out on our first night together. We looked at the menu, and I read the descriptions of meal choices and asked if anything sounded good to them. They decided what they would like to eat. When the waitress came to our table to take our order, I indicated for them to tell her. They both got shy and said, "You tell her. Mom always orders for us." Very quickly I assessed the situation, decided what response would best support them, support our relationship, and help them get the food they wanted without any drama. Thoughtfully, I took a deep breath, leaned forward, looked at them with grandmother eyes, and said: "Okay girls, here's the deal. When you're at home with your mom and your other grandma, you have certain ways of doing things that works for all of you. And when we're together we have ways of being together that work for us. Since we don't see each other very often, we need to figure it out more quickly. What I'm asking you to do is this: If you want something, anything, it's up to you to ask for it. So you get to tell the waitress what you want to order. It's really fun to do it. Will you both do that?" They looked at each other hesitantly, so I said, "It's all right, nothing bad will happen. I'm right here." As the sense of freedom and independence percolated, sly smiles crossed their faces. Having a restaurant meal just became even more interesting.

Talking with children about things that matter is to empower them with life skills, tools, and information. It's to build a foundation for them to be free, independent, autonomous, authentic, and shame free. Encourage them to feel and think at the same time. Children are like little detectives, inquisitively asking questions they want answers to. Without your help and an environment where they know they can ask you any-thing, they will absolutely find out for themselves from other sources, and there are many other sources.

Censoring gives the message that they are not capable of making their own decisions. Children need to be able to make mistakes, to discover where their own comfort zones are, what their limitations are. The stron-ger the foundation of trust, love, and intimacy you have with them, the healthier that process will be for all of you.

If you watch television, take note of how many obvious and subtle references there are to sex and sexuality in one hour. Sex is used as a sales pitch so much so that we equate a new car, certain beers, and clothing with being sexual or having sex. As adults, we screen out the meanings in them, but children are exposed to thousands of images and messages about sex long before their senses are dulled, and they are trained out of seeing and analyzing. Watch television with your children and be sensitive to opportunities to talk about what you see, not only in advertisements but in movies, documentaries, and television series. Point out the differ-ence between actors and real people.

They are like sponges taking in the values and beliefs from the media and of the adults in their lives. Seven-year-olds are well enough aware of adult standards and expectations to be sensitive to their own failures, fears, and mistakes. They are quite skilled at keeping secret their own interest in sex, though they may ask sideways with questions about preg-nancy and birth. Seven- to nine-year-olds continue to engage in same-gender sex games, girls primarily, while boys channel it into secret clubs and build clubhouses.

It's important to keep in mind that the onset of puberty is declining in age. Though studies are primarily aimed at girls, boys are not immune to the effects of pseudoestrogens and hormones in cows' milk, beef, and plastics, which have been found to initiate early puberty. Typically, girls reach puberty between the ages of 9 and 12 and boys between 10 and 14. In the last decade, there has been an increase in the number of 7-year-old girls developing breasts, acne, and pubic hair. Exposure to estrogen in food, plastics, and chemicals is common, and "[e]strogens do stimulate breast development," according to Stanley Korenman, an endocrinologist at the University of California, Los Angeles.[7] In the 1700s, the average onset of menses was between 17 and 18 years of age. It's been speculated that malnutrition in that time had something to do with the later onset. With the availability of more food and the increase of added hormones to meat and dairy products and chemicals in our water and lotions, the onset of puberty is happening at younger ages.

Children who are obese are prone to go through puberty at an earlier age. Mt. Sinai School of Medicine studied six- to eight-year-old girls in Cincinnati, San Francisco, and New York City. Urine samples were collected, and the presence of hormone-altering chemicals used in shampoo and lotions were found. Exposure to phthalates and fragrances were associated with early breast and pubic hair development.[8]

If you notice your child showing signs of early puberty understand that it may have psychological and emotional impacts for them. Imagine being the one girl in your second-grade class with breasts developing.

Children are the most creative about finding answers on their own and learn early to navigate the Internet. In an era of texting, Facebook, and Twitter, parents are outmaneuvered quickly if they aren't prepared and haven't set a solid foundation of open communication early on. If you don't know the answers, tell your child so and that you will find it for her or the two of you will search it out together. Having a healthy relationship with your own sexuality and intimacy—that is, owning your sexuality, what you know, what you don't know, and being honest with a sense of humor about it—goes a very long way to raising sexually healthy children. Hardly anything compares to it in strengthening the bond between you and your children. Having your own strong, clear foundations around sexuality and intimacy will be invaluable in maintaining close, intimate relationships with your children and as a family.

Parents do get nervous as they watch their children grow into sexual beings (as if they hadn't been sexual beings all along). We carry so much fear about touching and hugging and snuggling that, as our children get older, too often we pull back.

You'll have to find a balance that works to maintain a close relationship with your children, your need for privacy, and their need for sex education. What you decide to share should be based on what feels right to you, is supportive to their healthy development, and is not based on shame, guilt, or fear about sexuality.

Saying no demonstrates that in intimate relationships you can set limits and have a sense of modesty. You don't have to be angry when you say no; saying no can come from the love of the relationship, the child, or yourself and doesn't need to be hurtful or defensive or cause damage to the child or the relationship. Saying no models healthy limit setting, instills trust that you will answer when you feel good about it while encouraging the child to ask whatever he wants.

In all that my granddaughters and I do together, I encourage them to think and feel for themselves, and I repeatedly give them permission to say no. We cannot start early enough encouraging *them* to say no. They certainly understand the word's meaning. It's a valuable word two-year-olds learn and use very well and often.

Everyone needs to have permission to say no. If you haven't given it to yourself or the children in your lives, try it right now. Make it a meditation. My inability to say no was convoluted and confused with wanting to be the good girl. Not a very attractive or sexy habit at that. Reflexively, I gave up my needs and wants and happiness to please others. I habitually disempowered myself. Conversely, it is as important to be able to say yes consciously from free will and have some skill in thinking ahead to the consequences of a yes, or no.

Before we became puritanical about sex and sexuality, extended families in indigenous cultures shared the same sleeping space and sex just happened as a fact of life. There was no separation; everything was a part of life's natural rhythm. Everyone in the household knew how often sex happened, the sounds that were made, and children grew up seeing their parents' genitals. Because this way of life is foreign to us, just the thought of it can make us uncomfortable. Each of us has to examine our own feelings and find what works for us. Some families sleep together in a family bed when their children are small. Others have separate bedrooms. Some people are more comfortable with nudity than others. Whatever your personal comfort level, it helps to be calm and matter-of-fact about asserting your need for privacy. It is important to answer children's questions about sexuality as openly as possible with as little anxiety and fear as possible, for children pick that up very easily. There are ways to answer questions you find difficult with honesty and without the contamination of shame.

However you choose to respond to your children's inquiries and curiosities around sex and your sexual privacy, you might find it useful to first consider a few things:

- What will be the impact of your decisions on your child's sexual health and maturity?
- What will be the impact on you and your child's friendship and bond of trust?
- What is motivating your decision?
- Are you able to step outside cultural fears to make your own considered decisions?
- Your children will find answers to their questions, with or without your blessing and support; which would you prefer?

Understand the difference between privacy and secrecy; they are not even remotely the same thing though the two do get mixed up. Privacy is a conscious choice to be selective about what information you disclose about yourself. Secrecy, and I'm talking specifically about sexual secrets, keeps the past alive and toxic and it holds us as victims. Secrets isolate us, keep parts of us hidden from our partners and friends, prevent healing, cause doubt and low self-esteem, and can increase paranoid tendencies and fear of being found out. Our fears of conflict and of being rejected all get fed by secrets.

When we understand that increasing children's experience within the natural world increases the chances of them becoming healthy, sexual, sensual adults with healthier imaginations, more whole in themselves and with greater capacity for problem solving, only then can we truly see our role in facilitating that growth. As we grow more distant from nature, the physical and emotional distance between each other becomes greater. The natural environment is where children are sensitized; it is the world of sensations and beauty—where air and sun kiss skin, where bare feet touch the sensual Earth, where textures, tastes, smells, and colors are rich and vibrant and ever changing. It is the natural world where a child learns to inhabit her interbeing with the world into which she was born. In natural ecosystems, environments teeming with life, microbes, and the sexual reproduction of plants and animals, children learn the interplay of organisms, and the experience of their life among other life-forms is generated.

They need to feel bonded to and inseparable from the experience of living, which uncensored play in Nature fosters. Spending too much time in artificial environments, looking at life on the Internet or under microscopes, causes a sense of schizophrenia where a child's sense of place in the biotic community is never encouraged to grow. Without regular time in nature, a child's senses, sensibilities, and sensory acuity retreats.

Children learn lessons from the natural world that cannot be taught in classrooms or through lecturing or Internet searches: They are able to experience directly the changing seasons and how other life-forms respond to changes in the environment; how they prepare for winter, make nests, gather food, tend to their young—lessons that translate to human life. They learn that all animals have sex and can see it as a natural function of life and of being alive. More importantly, the education of their senses takes place formatively in the wild or Nature. It is through sensing, developing a keen awareness of subtle, sensory inputs, that they become discerning and learn to trust their bodies and their intuition. They learn what their fears are, how to assess danger, how each fear feels in their bodies and how to work it out in themselves. Nature is a great teacher of values; she is judgment free and unattached to outcomes.

Watch children at play in a natural environment. They are immersed in the now of the experience, their senses keenly tuned to the rhythmic movements and music of nature, their inner world and the outer world flow and intertwine unobstructed, one with the other. There is a silent, elegant communication that is taking place. They are "sitting" at the feet of Master and Mother of all that is in rapt attention; it is an attentiveness not found while sitting at desks in school buildings with fluorescent lights humming overhead. They sit on the bosom of the Great Mother, as she feeds and nourishes their bodies with myriad scents and colors of flowers, sounds of birdsong, the sacred dance of air, heat and cold, sun and moon. The elemental world of gnomes, sylphs, undines, and salamanders feeds their imaginations and fosters the knowing of other worlds and beings. This is the village it takes to raise a child. This is where their parents, our parents, and other parents and family are. We come through our human parents, but we are born to our family in the wild.

The ecological crisis we find ourselves in will not be remedied by more rules, more parental admonitions. The ecological crisis, as well as psychological dysfunctions, is mended by the balm of time in the natural world. When we are born, we need to be placed not only on the breast of our human parent, but we also need to be bonded with Earth.

ADOLESCENTS, SEX, AND INTIMACY

Adolescence comes from the Latin *adoescere,* meaning "to grow up." The term has been in common usage only since 1904 when Stanley Hall "discovered" this stage of growth, which he attributed to social changes in the early twentieth century. The National Child Labor Committee was formed in 1904 to abolish all child labor. Child labor laws keep children under sixteen out of the workforce, and universal education laws keep them in secondary schools longer, prolonging the period of dependence.

Adolescence is the time of life between puberty and being an adult. Because it is a time of becoming an adult, a grown-up, adolescents need adults who model healthy sexuality and maturity. Overcoming some of the culture's shames and fears are necessary to being an elder.

They need to see and experience the adults in their lives feeling and thinking, which then supports and encourages young adults to feel and think for themselves. Because being ill informed about sex can have serious consequences, particular attention needs to be paid to it.

Sex hormones are fully activated as children reach adolescence. During teenage years, adolescents begin to assert their independence, and rightfully so. They insist on being autonomous and try in earnest to separate their identity from their parents and siblings. People in this age group tend not to want to hear anything about sex from their parents unless they've had an intimate relationship before the terrible teen years. The teen years are the time when adolescents are learning to grow their own internal mother and father, and it's when they craft and adjust their own moral compass. They need permission to explore their bodies and experiment with dress, hair color, piercings, and tattoos if they wish. They need to find out for themselves what their limits are. Ideally, its best if this can all happen in an environment of love and caring and open communication. Teens are interested in sex; it's a biologically encoded reality that they become more focused on as hormones begin the cascade of bodily changes, altering the geography of their bodies.

There is an interesting phenomenon that happens between fathers and daughters and mothers and sons during adolescence. When our pre-teens reach adolescence, the changes that take place inside and externally can be quite dramatic. For girls, it's not just the visible physical changes—blossoming breasts and widening hips—but the hormonal changes that begin the onset of the menstrual cycle and make them fertile and ready to bear children. Pheromones—those chemicals released by the secreting individual that impact the behavior of the receiving individual—are released into the air bringing a whole new element into the family dynamics. There is young and newly awakened sexual energy in the house. The young woman experiments with her cleavage: How much can she show without being sent to her room to change into something else. Literally, she is being asked to change into something more acceptable so that everyone feels more comfortable while the sexual part of her is repressed and denied a life.

When this begins to happen and fathers and mothers have little or no information, relationship skills, or comfort with sexuality, they do the one thing they know, the one thing that damages the father/daughter or mother/son relationship—and sadly causes damage in young adults coming into sexual power—they shut down emotionally and create distance. The response that would be the most whole for everyone involved is for adults to grow up; work through their discomfort and lack of clarity about being sexual; understand and accept that their children are sexual beings; and start talking—break the silence and stigma around sexuality and sex.

Children and teens are human beings, read: sexual beings. They have fantasies, desires, needs, and questions. They need to feel good in their bodies, accepted and supported in the changes they are going through. We all know how challenging a time it can be; let's not make it any more painful and confusing.

Hans Hofmann notes that "[s]exuality is for the young a symbol of emancipation from family control and a foretaste of important, independent actions to come. Adolescent expectations about the creativity of sexuality are generally high and their criticisms of the failures of their elders are disarmingly perceptive."[9] What else must be emphasized is the intimate relationship between sexuality and self-understanding. Young adults need to unify what they know of themselves as human beings, how they feel and think about themselves and the reality of being a sexual being.

An understanding of the body and its role in expressing sexuality is so much more satisfying if there is self-acceptance, admiration of physical attributes and shame free. As Hofmann writes, "Sex can never be successfully abstracted from earthly enjoyment of the fleshly nature of man."[10]

Adolescents want and need to know about safe sex, how to use a condom, the pros and cons of various forms of birth control, where to get birth control, how to love and care for themselves and their evolving bodies, and how to nurture the relationships they will be exploring. One of the most loving things you can do is to give them information on what to do in the event of rape or sexual assault, such as where to get tested for sexually transmitted diseases.

They need to know and it's our job to give them accurate, up-to-date, honest, and truthful information. We cannot fairly expect them to take care of themselves, to act in their own best interests, to make informed choices, to advocate for themselves if we are withholding valuable information, information they must have. Research on teenage males published by the Urban Institute in 2000 suggests that although sex education has become almost universal, students are not receiving even general information early enough to fully protect themselves against unintended pregnancy and STDs.

If you are a parent depending on schools and teachers to provide your child with good and comprehensive sex education, you're fooling yourself and committing a grave disservice to your sons and daughters. Abstinence-only programs were originally instituted by the Clinton administration in 1996 as part of welfare reform; the Bush administration boosted these programs, which expired in June 2009. In March 2010, at the eleventh hour of the Health Reform Bill under the Obama administration, funding of abstinence-only programs was resurrected to the tune of $50 million dollars a year for five years. What's frightening is the definition of abstinence-only education, which states that it must teach that "a mutually faithful monogamous relationship in the context of marriage is the expected standard of human sexual activity" and that "sexual activity outside of the context of marriage is likely to have harmful effects." This should more accurately be called, abstinence-only propaganda.[11] "Expected standard"—by whom?

Current and extensive research pointing out that abstinence-only programs don't work. In fact, they fail miserably. For the first time in more than a decade, teen pregnancy rates rose 1 percent between 2005 and 2006 according to the Guttmacher Institute. It's nonpartisan and nonprofit, by the way. The rates rose again from 2006 to 2007. A congressionally mandated study conducted over nine years at a cost of almost $8 million concluded that these programs are not effective in stopping or even delaying teen sex and have no beneficial impact on young people's sexual behavior.[12]

> *Boys and girls in America have such a sad time together; sophistication demands that they submit to sex immediately without proper preliminary talk. Not courting talk—real straight talk about souls, for life is holy and every moment is precious.*
>
> JACK KEROUAC,
> ON THE ROAD

The earlier the foundation of self-esteem, self-worth, and a relationship of friendship that is created between you and your children, the easier the adolescent transition and all its inherent quandaries and milieu will be. They are human beings trying to find their way just as we did and still are. Regard them as thinking, intelligent beings, and they are likely to act as that. Regard them in ways that maintains their essential human dignity, whole and intact.

Learning the art of negotiation and making and keeping agreements are essential to healthy relating. You'll have a very difficult time trying to get your teenagers to keep agreements if they see you breaking yours all over the place. Only make agreements you're able and willing to keep. If you find that you are unable to keep an agreement you've made, renegotiate as soon as possible. When negotiating, it's important to acknowledge the agreement, the other person's investment in the agreement, and any inconvenience renegotiating may have caused and then offer alternatives.

If you and your teen can talk about whatever either of you needs to talk about, transition through these years will be much easier on all of you.

It's never too late to begin an intimate relationship with your teen if you don't have one already. It does get more difficult with surly teenagers who have a dozen years of repressed rage accumulated. In some instances, it will take tremendous self-effacement on your part to repair any damage that's been done to the relationship. Rage, which is primarily directed at you (it always goes for the closest target), is a natural and healthy response in teens who find themselves in a family and a culture that governs by lies, deceit, power struggles, and lack of accountability while they are being admonished to be something different.

I believe that parents and guardians need to be actively involved in what schools are teaching our children. Schools are businesses, and they don't always have the best interests of our children in mind. While many of us believe our children have a right to full disclosure when it comes to sex education, few of us have the emotional maturity to present the facts objectively. As long as parents, "intellectuals," academia, religious leaders, and politicians are confused themselves about the facts and nature of sex, confusion will be passed on. The prevalence of sexual activity and interest in sex among children and young adults will always be part of life. Meanwhile, as they are kept in the middle of groups competing for power over morality, nothing gets done and people continue to be repressed by widespread ignorance and fear around sexuality.

> *By the time many people are fourteen or fifteen, they have been divested of their loves, their ancient and intuitive tastes, one by one, until when they reach maturity there is no fun left, no zest, no gusto, no flavor. Others have criticized and they have criticized themselves, into embarrassment. When the circus pulls in at five of a dark, cold summer morn, and the calliope sounds, they do not rise and run, they turn in their sleep, and life passes by.*
>
> RAY BRADBURY,
> *ZEN IN THE ART OF WRITING*

A 2004 study by National Public Radio, the Kaiser Family Foundation (a private, nonpartisan, nonprofit organization focusing on major health-care issues), and Harvard's Kennedy School of Government found that only 7 percent of Americans say sex education should not be taught in schools. Among the remaining 93 percent, most parents seem to be generally content with whatever kind of sex education is taught by their local schools. However, there is disagreement about what kind of sex education should be taught. Fifteen percent of Americans believe abstinence from sexual intercourse should be the only thing taught with no information about how to obtain and use condoms or other forms of contraception. Forty-six percent believe that teaching "abstinence-plus" is the most appropriate approach. Abstinence-plus is an approach that considers that while some teens do not abstain from sexual intercourse, sex education should include information on condoms and contraceptives. Thirty-six percent believe that teaching abstinence is not the most important thing but that sex education should focus on teaching teens about responsible decision making regarding sex.[13]

Ultimately, the decision school administrators make regarding what sort of sex education program will be taught in their school district is far too often motivated by the greenback. Federal funding is the vehicle that drives the sex education our children are getting in school.

Sex education in schools was historically initiated by health advocates to teach children how to avoid pregnancy and sexually transmitted diseases, whereas abstinence-only education was entered into and pushed for by evangelical or born-again Christians (NPR/Kaiser/Kennedy School National Survey on Sex Education 2004) who believe it is morally wrong to engage in sexual relations before marriage. Seventy-eight percent of born-again or evangelical Christians believe that having sexual activity outside marriage is likely to have a detrimental affect on physical and psychological health.[14]

Sex education in Sweden's education system is compulsory and has been since 1956. Sweden believes in open communication as a primary foundation for healthy sexual and marital relations. And they don't pretend that people aren't having sex, teenagers included. (Is the United States even operating in the same century?) "Swedes generally view sexual intercourse as a natural and expected occurrence during teen years."[15]

The curriculum starts out at age 6 with information on sperm, eggs, and anatomy. From age 12 on the curriculum focus leans toward disease prevention, contraception, sex positions, and same-sex relations. The curriculum is intended to reach all students before age 15, the age of consent. There is a moral dimension involved as well; sex within loving relationships, gender and sexual equality are encouraged.[16]

Juxtaposed to the increase in teen pregnancy in the United States in the apron strings of abstinence-only programs, Sweden's teen pregnancy and sexually transmitted disease rates are among the lowest in the world. Sweden's teenage birthrate is 7 in 1,000 compared to 49 per 1,000 in the United States. Among fifteen- to nineteen-year-olds, the cases of gonorrhea in the United States are nearly six hundred times as great on a per capita basis. Pierre-Andre Michaud, chief of the Multidisciplinary Unit for Adolescent Health at the University of Lausanne Hospital in Switzerland and a leading researcher in European teen sexuality, dismisses the idea—widely held in the United States—that sex constitutes risky behavior for teens. In an editorial in May 2006, *Journal of Adolescent Health,* he wrote: "In many European countries—Switzerland in particular—sexual intercourse, at least from the age of 15 or 16 years, is considered acceptable and even part of normative adolescent behavior."[17] Switzerland has one of the world's lowest rates of abortion and teen pregnancy. Teens in Switzerland, Sweden and the Netherlands, have easy access to contraceptives, confidential health care and comprehensive sex education. In Sweden, teens have access to free medical care, free condoms and prescriptions for inexpensive oral contraceptives, and general advice at youth clinics—all without parental consent.

"Abstinence," says Michaud, "is not something the Swiss press on teens. We think it's unfair. It's useless. It's inefficient. We have been advocating the use of condoms . . . and I think that we tend to be successful."[18] And Joan-Carles Suris, head of the research group on adolescent medicine at the University of Lausanne, says it this way: "The main difference is that in the United States sexual activity is considered a risk. Here we consider it a pleasure."[19]

The message of responsible sex education is not restricted to the schoolroom. Throughout Sweden's cities there are youth clinics that provide continued education on and availability to low-cost contraception. Teens are given tools and information, even encouragement and permission to decide for themselves when they are ready for sex and then (horror of horrors) left to behave responsibly.[20]

Muslims who have immigrated to Sweden in the years since the Iraqi war are prohibiting their children from attending the sex education classes. Between 2003 and 2007, Sweden granted full refugee status to 24,799 Iraqis compared to 260 in Britain. With the increase in Muslim parents invoking a decades-old provision designed to give parents the option of taking their children out of Christian instruction, the Swedish government is set to abolish that provision. Sweden has a reputation for being sexually liberal,[21] and in 2008, the state-run pharmaceutical stores launched a line of sex toys aimed at women. The initiative was funded by tax dollars, and within a few days the products became the chain's bestsellers.[22]

Findings in a 2010 study done by the National Foundation for Educational Research in the UK (NFER) found a variety of approaches to sex education around the globe. Astonishingly, the United States isn't listed and if it were, it would be the most conservative and abusive approach on the planet. Norway begins sex education at age six and a few other countries like Finland and Japan delay it a few years, with most countries averaging sex and relationship education between ten and twelve years old. As students get older the curriculum becomes more sophisticated. In Finland, fifteen-year-olds receive an introductory sexual package including a condom.[23]

Interestingly, in the majority of countries parents do not have the right to withdraw their children from sex and relationship classes, though it is permitted in British Columbia and Singapore. Switzerland believes that sex education relies on the parents as well as institutions to "combat myths." In France, sex education is "one of the core social and civil competencies to be acquired in the course of mandatory education," in Victoria, sexuality education is seen as a "whole-school learning approach," while in Hungary schools have "an unavoidable duty to address the questions of sexual culture and behaviour."[24]

While schools extol critical thinking skills as part of the curriculum, it doesn't extend to sex education. Sex education that does exist in the United States primarily teaches abstinence only and sex values, it does not explore abstinence as an option, sexual activity as an option, values, relationships, intimacy, communication skills, the fluidity of human sexual responses, or sexual diversity and identity. Sex education is a top-down formula not community building, empowering, or pedagogical.

Change will come when we begin to genuinely care about giving genuine, heart-felt information for the benefit and welfare of our children. It will come when we care about empowering them through the dissemination of factual and objective information that encourages the transformation of information into knowledge and then wisdom. It will come about when we give up our positions that have roots in fear, ignorance, and power struggles.

Notes

INTRODUCTION. IT STOPS WITH ME

1. Hillman, *A Blue Fire,* 266.
2. Klein, *America's War on Sex,* 23 and 89.
3. Hanisch, "The Personal Is Political."
4. *Sex in the 90s,* MTV news special, 1996.
5. LaChapelle, *Sacred Land, Sacred Sex,* 254.
6. Escoffier, *Sexual Revolution,* 176.
7. Margulis and Sagan, *Dazzle Gradually,* 121.
8. Henry David Thoreau, *The Journal of Henry David Thoreau,* vol. 6, 740. The full sentence from Thoreau's journal reads, "This earth which is like a map spread out around me is but my inmost soul exposed."
9. White, *Kiss of the Yogini,* xiii.
10. Kakar, *Shamans, Mystics and Doctors,* 151.
11. Feuerstein, *Sacred Sexuality,* 210.

CHAPTER 1.
INTIMACY: FOOD THAT FEEDS
THE SOUL OF LOVE

1. Lerner, *The Dance of Intimacy,* 3.
2. Berne, *Games People Play,* 182.
3. Hofmann, *Sex Incorporated,* 7.

CHAPTER 2. AUTONOMOUS PERSONHOOD

1. Perlman, *The Power of Trees*, 2.
2. Buhner, *The Natural Testosterone Plan*, 22.
3. Matthews and Matthews, *The Encyclopaedia of Celtic Wisdom*, 299.
4. Ibid.
5. Frankl, *Man's Search for Meaning*, 121.
6. Ibid., 122.
7. Krishnamurti, *The Awakening of Intelligence*, 267.
8. Rand, *For the New Intellectual*, 124.
9. Bly, *A Little Book on the Human Shadow*, 18.
10. Estés, *Women Who Run with the Wolves*, 51.
11. Berne, *Sex in Human Loving*, 139.
12. Estés, *Women Who Run with the Wolves*, 342.

CHAPTER 3. GETTING TO KNOW YOU

1. Berne, *Intuition and Ego States*, 123.
2. Berne, *Games People Play*, 27.
3. Hollis, *The Middle Passage*, 103.
4. Bly, *A Little Book on the Human Shadow*, 24.
5. Frankl, *Man's Search for Meaning*, 147.
6. Hollis, *The Middle Passage*, 104.

CHAPTER 4. THE NUMINOUS

1. Eliade, *The Sacred and the Profane*, 14.
2. Ibid., 24.
3. Hamilton, *Mythology*, 57.
4. From www.gaianstudies.org.
5. Otto, *The Idea of the Holy*, xvi.

CHAPTER 5. HUMAN BEINGS: THE GROUND WHERE THE GODS RESIDE

1. Metzner, *Green Psychology*, 98.
2. Suzuki and Knudtson, *Wisdom of the Elders*, 49.

3. Weller, "Reclaiming Our Indigenous Soul."

4. Goldsmith, *The Way*, 124.

5. Suzuki, *The Sacred Balance*, 276.

6. Taylor, *The Prehistory of Sex*, 9.

7. Ibid., 142.

8. Ibid., 11.

9. Ibid., 187.

10. Sheldrake, *The Rebirth of Nature*, 59.

11. Ibid., 60.

12. Ryan and Jethá, *Sex at Dawn*, 13.

13. Phillips, "Am I a Spaceman?"

14. Wilhem Reich, lecture on somatic psychology at www.sonoma.edu/users/d /daniels/reich.

15. Moats, "MHS Homecoming Dance Canceled."

16. Klein, "CraigsList, Sex Trafficking, & the Next Moral Panic."

17. Sobel, "Beyond Ecophobia."

18. Davis, *The Father of Waters*, 87.

19. Ibid.

20. Ibid.

21. Mander, *In the Absence of the Sacred*, 187.

22. MacFarlane, *The Wild Places*, 30.

23. Ibid.

24. Ibid.

25. Abrams, *Becoming Animal*, 134.

26. Griffiths, *Wild*, 2.

27. Sheldrake, *The Rebirth of Nature*, 10.

28. Bell, "Haitians Challenge Monsanto's Influence."

29. Stock, "Manifest Haiti: Monsanto's Destiny."

30. Perlman, *The Power of Trees*, 12.

CHAPTER 6. FINDING THE WILD

1. Hillman, *The Soul's Code*, 13.

2. Wilson, *Biophilia*, 65–66.

3. Earnheart, Richard, "About the Artist," at www.richardearnheart.com /abouttheartist/htm.

4. For more information on the Müller-Lyer arrows see "94 Visual Phenomena & Optical Illusions by Michael Bach" at www.michaelbach.de/ot/. Click on the link for the Müller-Lyer Illusion.

5. Philip L Kilbride and H. W. Leibowitz, "The Ponzo Illusion among the Baganda of Uganda."

6. Nicolson, *Mountain Gloom and Mountain Glory,* 1.

7. Krishnamurti, *The Awakening of Intelligence,* 268.

8. Keleman, *The Human Ground,* 31.

9. Griffiths, *Wild,* 48.

10. Hillman, *A Blue Fire,* 9.

11. Leopold, *A Sand County Almanac,* 138.

12. Seed, "Think Like a Mountain."

13. Ferry, "Keepers of the World."

14. For more on Plato's worldview see the Indiana University webpage on Human Intelligence at www.indiana.edu/~intell/plato.shtml.

15. Feuerstein, *Sacred Sexuality,* 207.

16. Keeney, *The Bushman Way of Tracking God,* 215.

17. Ibid., 215.

18. Ibid., 249.

19. Keleman, *The Human Ground,* 35.

20. Keleman, *Your Body Speaks its Mind,* 58.

21. Mander, *In the Absence of the Sacred,* 85.

22. Ibid., 86.

23. Montagne, "Israel Kamakawiwo'ole: The Voice of Hawaii."

24. Abram, *Spell of the Sensuous,* 172.

25. Margulis and Sagan, *Dazzle Gradually,* 181.

CHAPTER 7. CHOOSING ANOTHER WAY

1. Malone and Malone, *The Art of Intimacy,* 260.

2. Johnson, *The Spiritual Practices of Rumi,* 140.

3. Hillman, *City and Soul,* 37.

4. Buhner, *The Secret Teachings of Plants,* 86.

5. Perlman, *The Power of Trees,* 24.

6. Blake, "The Marriage of Heaven and Earth," 38.

7. Metzner, *Green Psychology,* 108.

8. Dehiia, *Chola: Sacred Bronzes of Southern India.*

9. Dalrymple, "India: The Place of Sex," 33.

10. Riley, "Victorian Sex Rebels and Atheists."

CHAPTER 8. THE LANGUAGE OF LOVE

1. Hillman, *The Soul's Code,* 146.

2. From www.anthropine.eu/Anthropine/Media/praesentation/anthropine_english.

3. Wilhelm Reich, lecture on somatic psychology at www.sonoma.edu/users/d/daniels/reich.

CHAPTER 9. SACRED SEX

1. Schachter-Shalomi and Eve Ilsen, "Sacred Sex."

2. Johnson, *Rumi's Four Essential Practices,* 117.

3. Roach, *Bonk.*

4. Keeney, *The Bushman Way of Tracking God,* 80.

5. Otto, *The Idea of the Holy,* 42.

6. Halifax, *The Fruitful Darkness,* 18.

CHAPTER 10. THE DANCE OF TRUST

1. Hillman, *A Blue Fire,* 277.

2. Hofmann, *Sex Incorporated,* 13.

3. Hillman, *The Myth of Analysis*, 92.

4. Jack Morin, *The Erotic Mind,* 293.

5. Klein, *Your Sexual Secrets,* 48.

CHAPTER 11. HEALING SHAME

1. Brown, *I Thought It Was Just Me (but it isn't),* 30.

2. Nietzsche, from www.brainyquote.com/quotes/authors/f/friedrich_nietzsche_10.html.

3. Keleman, *The Human Ground,* 53.

CHAPTER 12.
FREEING OURSELVES FROM SEXUAL TYRANNY

1. Berne, *Sex in Human Loving,* 1.

2. Phoenix, *A Woman Whose Calling Is Men,* book 2, 27–28.

3. "Coins of Ancient Rome," www.dengedenge.com/2010/02/coins-of-ancient -rome.

4. Adams, "Pay for Play."

5. "The Sex Cult of Venus," http://heritage-key.com/rome/sex-cult-venus.

6. Diamant, *The Red Tent,* 158.

7. Mantegazza, *The Sexual Relations of Mankind,* 272–73.

8. Ibid., 270.

9. Seltzer, "Bishops Are Behind the 'Let Women Die' Act."

10. Baker, "The Deep Ecology of the Family."

11. Buhner, *Ensouling Language,* 271.

12. Miller, *Henry Miller on Writing,* 175.

13. "Obscene, Obscenity," The 'Lectric Law Library, www.lectlaw.com/def2 /o002.htm.

14. Heins, *Sex, Sin, and Blasphemy,* 17.

15. From http://ourpornourselves.org/about.

16. Ibid.

17. From www.pornharms.com.

18. From http:/news.ufl.edu/2004/11/29/sexual/revolution.

19. Cheesman, "6 Ways That Porn Runs the World."

20. Robinson and Wilson, "Porn-Induced Sexual Dysfunction Is a Growing Problem."

21. Shroeder, *Challenge to Sex Censors,* 31. Quoting an anonymous clergyman a century ago.

22. From http//abacus.bates.edu/admin/offices/scs/salt7.html.

23. From www.huffingtonpost.com/rep-jane-harman/finally-some-progress -in_b_125504.html.

24. From www.va.gov.

25. From www.orlandosentinel.com/news/local/orl-blogs,0,2664973.htmlpage.

26. Pendell, *Inspired Madness,* 69.

27. Cohn, "Did SEC Staffer Surf Porn?"

CHAPTER 13. HEALING THE HUMAN SOUL

1. Gandhi, *An Autobiography.*
2. Ibid, xvii.
3. From www.mosaicvoices.org.
4. Tompkins and Bird, *The Secret Life of Plants,* 107.
5. Taylor, *The Prehistory of Sex,* 60–61.
6. Bellows, "The Birth Control of Yesteryear."
7. Engel, *Wild Health,* 178.
8. Tompkins and Bird, *The Secret Life of Plants,* 121.
9. Ibid., 134.
10. Ibid., 137.
11. Ibid., 142.
12. Dobb, "New Life in a Death Trap."

EPILOGUE

1. Dale Pendell, interview with Emily Green, *Los Angeles Times,* 19 October 2003. From http://quantumtantra.com/pendell/html.
2. Bowden, *Blood Orchid,* 138, 140.
3. Fuller, *Critical Path,* xi
4. Fuller, from www.muzz.com/Buckminster_Fuller.aspx.
5. Krishnamurti, *Think on These Things,* 14.
6. Jong, *Sappho's Leap,* 88.
7. Reeves, *The Character of Leadership,* 119.
8. Berne, *Games People Play,* 184.

APPENDIX.
TALKING TO CHILDREN AND TEENS ABOUT SEX

1. Paterson, *Tree Wisdom,* 279.
2. Sheldrake, *The Presence of the Past,* 71.
3. From http://blogs.alternet.org/speakeasy/2010/10/20/dr-jocelyn-elders-marijuana-masturbation-and-medicine.
4. Hillman, *A Blue Fire,* 98.
5. Calderone and Ramey, *Talking with Your Child about Sex,* 5.

6. Klein, "'Catching' Your Kid Playing Doctor."

7. Carroll, "Growing Up Too Soon? Puberty Strikes 7-year-old Girls."

8. From www.niehs.hih.gov/research/supported/sep/2010/prenatal.

9. Hofmann, *Sex Incorporated,* 6.

10. Ibid., 11.

11. See www.advocatesforyouth.org/publications/429?task=view.

12. For information on sexual and reproductive health, policy analysis, and public education, see www.guttmacher.org.

13. From www.kff.org/newsmedia/upload/Sex-Education-in-America-Summary .pdf. See also www.npr.org/templates/story/story.php?storyId=1622610.

14. Ibid.

15. Reiss, *The End to Shame,* 62.

16. Grose, "Straight Facts about the Birds and Bees."

17. Agnvall, "Is Teen Sex Bad?"

18. Ibid.

19. Ibid.

20. Grose, "Straight Facts about the Birds and Bees."

21. Vaughan, "Swedish Muslims and Strawberry Condoms."

22. Stockholm Newsroom, "Swedes Convince Their State Shops to Sell Sex Toys."

23. Oscarsson, "Coming Home from School with Strawberry Condoms."

24. From www.nfer.ac.uk.

Bibliography and Recommended Reading

Abram, David. *Becoming Animal: An Earthly Cosmology*. New York: Pantheon Books, 2010.

———. *The Spell of the Sensuous: Perception and Language in a More-Than-Human World*. New York: Random House, 1996.

Adams, Cecil. "Pay for Play: Did the Romans Issue Sexually Depictive Tokens for Use in Foreign Brothels?" *The Straight Dope,* 18 January 2008. www .straightdope.com/columns/read/2355/pay-for-play.

Agnvall, Elizabeth. "Is Teen Sex Bad? Americans and Western Europeans Don't Agree on What's Normal and Acceptable But Many Health Experts Do." Special to *The Washington Post,* Tuesday, 16 May 2006.

Agustin, Laura Maria. *Sex at the Margins: Migration, Labour, Markets and the Rescue Industry*. London: Zed Books, 2007.

Anand, Margo. *The Art of Sexual Ecstasy: The Path of Sacred Sexuality for Western Lovers*. Los Angeles: Jeremy P. Tarcher/Putnam, 1989.

Baker, Jeannine Parvati. "The Deep Ecology of the Family." *Wise Woman Herbal Ezine,* January 2006. www.susunweed.com/herbal_ezine/January06/child-bearing.htm.

Barks, Coleman. *The Essential Rumi*. New York: HarperCollins, 1995.

Bartholomew, Alick. *Hidden Nature: The Startling Insights of Viktor Schauberger*. Kempton, Ill.: Adventures Unlimited Press, 2005.

Bateson, Gregory. *A Sacred Unity: Further Steps to an Ecology of Mind*. Edited by Rodney E. Donaldson. New York: Cornelia & Michael Bessie Books, 1991.

Bell, Beverly. "Haitians Challenge Monsanto's Influence." *Truthout,* 30 June 2011. www.truth-out.org/haitians-challenge-monsantos-influence/1309446649.

Bellows, Alan. "The Birth Control of Yesteryear." *Damn Interesting,* 21 May 2007. www.damninteresting.com/the-birth-control-of-yesteryear.

Berne, Eric. *Games People Play: The Basic Handbook of Transactional Analysis.* New York: Grove Press, 1964.

———. *Intuition and Ego States: The Origins of Transactional Analysis: A Series of Papers.* San Francisco: Harper & Row, 1977.

———. *Sex in Human Loving.* New York: Pocket Books, 1971.

Blake, William. *Blake: A Collection of Critical Essays.* Edited by Northrop Frye. Englewood Cliffs, N.J.: Prentice-Hall, 1966.

———. *The Complete Poetry & Prose of William Blake.* Edited by David V. Erdman. Commentary by Harold Bloom. New York: Anchor Books, 1988.

———. *Songs of Innocence and of Experience: Shewing the Two Contrary States of the Human Soul.* New York: The Orion Press, 1967.

Bly, Robert. *A Little Book on the Human Shadow.* San Francisco: Harper San Francisco, 1988.

———. *Morning Poems.* New York: Harper Perennial, 1998.

———. *Seven Sources of Shame.* East Montpelier, Vt.: Heaven and Earth, 1989.

———. *Loving a Woman in Two Worlds.* New York: Dial Press, 1985.

Bowden, Charles. *Blood Orchid: An Unnatural History of America.* New York: Farrar, Straus and Giroux, 1995.

———. *Blues for Cannibals: The Notes from Underground.* New York: North Point/Farrar, Straus and Giroux, 2002.

———. *Frog Mountain Blues.* Tucson: University of Arizona Press, 1994.

Bradbury, Ray. *Zen in the Art of Writing: Essays on Creativity.* Santa Barbara, Calif.: Joshua Odell Editions, Capra Press, 1989.

Brooks, Valerie. *Tantric Awakening: A Woman's Initiation into the Path of Ecstasy.* Rochester, Vt.: Destiny Books, 2001.

Brooks-Gordon, Belinda. *The Price of Sex: Prostitution, Policy and Society.* Cullompton, Devon, UK; Willan Publishing, 2006.

Brown, Brené. *I Thought It Was Just Me (but it isn't): Telling the Truth About Perfectionism, Inadequacy, and Power.* New York: Gotham Books, 2007.

Buhner, Stephen Harrod. *Ensouling Language: On the Art of Nonfiction and the Writer's Life.* Rochester, Vt.: Inner Traditions, 2010.

———. *The Lost Language of Plants: The Ecological Importance of Plant*

Medicines for Life on Earth. White River Junction, Vt.: Chelsea Green Publishing Company, 2002.

———. *The Natural Testosterone Plan: For Sexual Health and Healing*. Rochester, Vt.: Healing Arts Press, 2007.

———. *The Secret Teachings of Plants: The Intelligence of the Heart in the Direct Perception of Nature*. Rochester, Vt.: Bear & Company, 2004.

———. *The Taste of Wild Water*. Silver City, N.M.: Raven Press, 2009.

Caldecott, Moyra. *Myths of the Sacred Tree*. Rochester, Vt.: Destiny Books, 1993.

Calderone, Mary S., and James W. Ramey. *Talking with Your Child about Sex: Questions and Answers for Children from Birth to Puberty*. New York: Random House, 1982.

Callicott, J. Baird. *Earth's Insights: A Multicultural Survey of Ecological Ethics from the Mediterranean Basin to the Australian Outback*. Berkeley: University of California Press, 1994.

Campbell, Joseph. *Reflections on the Art of Living: A Joseph Campbell Companion*. New York: HarperCollins, 1991.

Carroll, Linda. "Growing Up Too Soon? Puberty Strikes 7-year-old Girls. MSNBC, 9 August 2010. www.msnbc.msn.com/id/38600414/ns/health-kids_and_parenting.

Cheesman, Ian. "6 Ways That Porn Runs the World." Cracked.com, 30 April 2009. www.cracked.com/article_17300_6-ways-that-porn-runs-the-world.html.

Chia, Mantak. *Healing Love Through the Tao: Cultivating Female Sexual Energy*. Rochester, Vt.: Destiny Books, 2005.

Coates, Peter. *Nature: Western Attitudes since Ancient Times*. Berkeley: University of California Press, 1998.

Cohn, Scott. "Did SEC Staffer Surf Porn While Investors Got Burned?" CNBC, 2 February 2011. www.cnbc.com/id/41391748.

Corrington, Robert S. *Wilhelm Reich; Psychoanalyst and Radical Naturalist*. New York: Farrar, Straus and Giroux, 2003.

Curcio, Joan L., Lois F. Berlin, and Patricia F. First. *Sexuality and the Schools: Handling the Critical Issues*. Thousand Oaks, Calif.: Corwin Press, 1996.

Dalrymple, William. "India: The Place of Sex." *The New York Review of Books*, 26 June 2008.

Daniélou, Alain. *The Phallus: Sacred Symbol of Male Creative Power*. Rochester, Vt.: Inner Traditions, 1995.

Davis, Norah Deakin, and Joseph Holmes. *The Father of Waters: A Mississippi River Chronicle.* San Francisco: Sierra Club Books, 1982.

Dehjia, Vidya, ed. *Chola: Sacred Bronzes of Southern India.* London: Royal Academy of Arts, 2007.

Devall, Bill, and George Sessions. *Deep Ecology: Living as if Nature Mattered.* Salt Lake City: Peregrine Smith Books, 1985.

Diamant, Anita. *The Red Tent.* New York: Picador, 1997.

Dobb, Edwin. "New Life in a Death Trap." *Discover Magazine,* December 2000. http://discovermagazine.com/2000/dec/featnewlife.

Douglas, Nik, and Penny Slinger. *Sexual Secrets: The Alchemy of Ecstasy.* Rochester, Vt.: Destiny Books, 1979.

Eisler, Riane. *Sacred Pleasure: Sex, Myth and the Politics of the Body; New Paths to Power and Love.* San Francisco: HarperCollins, 1996.

Eliade, Mircea. *The Sacred and the Profane.* New York: Harcourt Brace, 1987.

Ellis, Albert. *The Folklore of Sex.* Garden City, N.Y.: The Country Life Press, 1951.

Engel, Cindy. *Wild Health: Lessons in Natural Wellness from the Animal Kingdom.* New York: Houghton Mifflin Company, 2002.

Escoffier, Jeffrey, ed. *Sexual Revolution.* Foreword by Erica Jong. New York: Thunder's Mouth Press, 2003.

Estés, Clarissa Pinkola. *Women Who Run with the Wolves: Myths and Stories of the Wild Woman Archetype.* New York: Ballantine Books, 1992.

Ferrini, Paul. *Dancing with the Beloved: Opening Our Hearts to the Lessons of Love.* Greenfield, Mass.: Heartways Press, 2001.

———. *The Ecstatic Moment: A Practical Manual for Opening Your Heart and Staying in It.* Greenfield, Mass.: Heartways Press, 1996.

———. *The Wisdom of the Self: Authentic Experience and the Journey to Wholeness.* Greenfield, Mass.: Heartways Press, 1992.

Ferry, Stephen. "Keepers of the World." *National Geographic* 206, no. 4 (October 2004): 50.

Feuerstein, Georg. *Sacred Sexuality: The Erotic Spirit in the World's Great Religions.* Rochester, Vt.: Inner Traditions, 2003.

Flaceliere, Robert. *Love in Ancient Greece.* Translated by James Cleugh. New York: Crown Publishers, 1962.

Foreman, Dave. *Confessions of an Eco-Warrior.* New York: Harmony Books, 1991.

Foucault, Michel. *The History of Sexuality.* Vol. 1, *An Introduction.* New York: Random House, 1978.

Frankl, Viktor E. *Man's Search for Meaning.* New York: Washington Square Press, 1985.

Fromm, Erich. *Man for Himself: An Enquiry into the Psychology of Ethics.* New York: Holt, Rinehart and Winston, 1947.

———. *The Revolution of Hope: Toward a Humanized Technology.* New York: Harper & Row, 1968.

Fuller, R. Buckminster. *Operating Manual for Spaceship Earth.* New York: Simon and Schuster, University of Illinois Press, 1969.

———. *Critical Path,* 2nd ed. New York: St. Martin's Griffin, 1982.

Gandhi, Mohandas K. *Gandhi: An Autobiography: The Story of My Experiments with Truth.* Boston: Beacon Press, 1993.

Gil, Derek. *Quest: The Life of Elisabeth Kübler-Ross.* New York: Harper & Row, 1980.

Goldsmith, Edward. *The Way: An Ecological World-View.* Totnes, Devon, UK: Themis Books, 1996.

Greenwald, Jerry A. *Creative Intimacy: How to Break the Patterns That Poison Your Relationships.* New York: Simon and Schuster, 1975.

Griffiths, Jay. *Wild: An Elemental Journey.* New York: Jeremy P. Tarcher/Penguin, 2006.

Grose, Thomas K. "Straight Facts about the Birds and Bees." *U.S. News & World Report,* 18 March 2007. www.usnews.com/usnews/news/articles/070318/26sex.htm.

Halifax, Joan. *The Fruitful Darkness: Reconnecting with the Body of the Earth.* New York: HarperCollins, 1993.

Hamilton, Edith. *Mythology: Timeless Tales of Gods and Heroes.* Boston: Little, Brown and Company, 1942.

Hanisch, Carol. "The Personal Is Political." In *Feminist Revolution,* eds. Redstockings. New York: Random House, 1979. (Carol Hanisch's essay is dated March 1969, in this collection of feminist essays.)

Harris, Robbie H., and Michael Emberley. *It's Perfectly Normal: Changing Bodies, Growing up, Sex and Sexual Health.* Cambridge, Mass.: Candlewick Press.

Herzog, Dagmar. *Sex in Crisis: The New Sexual Revolution and the Future of American Politics.* New York: Basic Books, 2008.

Hillel, David. *Out of the Earth: Civilization and the Life of the Soil*. Berkeley: University of California Press, 1991.

Hillman, James. *A Blue Fire: Selected Writings by James Hillman*. Edited by Thomas Moore. New York: Harper & Row, 1989.

———. *City and Soul*, uniform ed., vol 2. Edited by Robert J. Leaver. 2006.

———. *Revisioning Psychology*. New York: HarperCollins, 1975.

———. *The Soul's Code*. New York: Warner Books, 1997.

———. *The Thought of the Heart and the Soul of the World*. Woodstock, Conn.: Spring Publications, 1995.

———. *The Myth of Analysis: Three Essays in Archetypal Psychology*. Evanston, Ill.: Northwestern University Press, 1998.

Hite, Shere. *The Hite Report: A Nationwide Study of Female Sexuality*. New York: Seven Stories Press, 1976.

———. *Women as Revolutionary Agents of Change: The Hite Reports and Beyond*. Madison: University of Wisconsin Press, 1993.

Hofmann, Hans F. *Sex Incorporated: A Positive View of the Sexual Revolution*. Boston: Beacon Press, 1967.

Hollis, James. *The Middle Passage: From Misery to Meaning in Midlife*. Toronto: Inner City Books, 1993.

James, William. *On Some of Life's Ideals*. New York: Henry Holt, 1900.

Johnson, Will. *The Spiritual Practices of Rumi: Radical Techniques for Beholding the Divine*. Rochester, Vt.: Inner Traditions, 2003.

———. *Rumi's Four Essential Practices: Ecstatic Body, Awakened Soul*. Rochester, Vt.: Inner Traditions, 2010,

Jong, Erica. *Sappho's Leap*. New York: W. W. Norton, 2003.

Jordon, June. *Some of Us Did Not Die: New and Selected Essays*. New York: Basic Books, 2002.

Kakar, Sudhir. *Shamans, Mystics and Doctors: A Psychological Inquiry into India and its Healing Traditions*. Chicago: University of Chicago Press, 1982.

Keeney, Bradford. *The Bushman Way of Tracking God*. New York: Aria Books, 2010.

Keleman, Stanley. *The Human Ground: Sexuality, Self and Survival*. Palo Alto, Calif.: Science and Behavior Books, 1975.

———. *Living Your Dying*. New York: Random House, 1974.

———. *Your Body Speaks Its Mind*. Berkeley, Calif.: Center Press, 1975.

Kellert, Stephen R., and Edward O. Wilson, eds. *The Biophilia Hypothesis*. Washington, D.C./ Covelo, Calif.: Island Press/Shearwater Books, 1993.

Kilbride, Philip L,, and H. W. Leibowitz. "The Ponzo Illusion among the Baganda of Uganda." *Annals of the New York Academy of Sciences* 285, Issues in Cross-Cultural Research (March 1977): 408–17.

Klein, Marty. *America's War on Sex: The Attack on Law, Lust and Liberty.* Westport, Conn.: Praeger Publishers, 2006.

———. *Ask Me Anything: A Sex Therapist Answers the Most Important Questions for the '90s.* Pacifica, Calif.: Pacifica Press, 1996.

———. "'Catching' Your Kid Playing Doctor." *Sexual Intelligence*, 30 August 2010. www.sexualintelligence.wordpress.com/2010/08/30 /"catching"-your-kid-playing-doctor.

———. "CraigsList, Sex Trafficking, & the Next Moral Panic." *Sexual Intelligence*, 6 September 2010. www.sexualintelligence.wordpress. com/2010/09/06.

———. *Your Sexual Secrets: When to Keep Them, When and How to Tell.* New York: E.P. Dutton, 1988.

Kövecses, Zoltán. "A Linguist's Quest for Love." *Journal of Social and Personal Relationships* 8, no.1 (February 1991): 77–97.

Krishnamurti, Jiddu. *The Awakening of Intelligence.* New York: Harper & Row, 1973.

———. *The First and Last Freedom.* New York: Harper & Row, 1954.

———. *Think on These Things.* Edited by J. D. Rajagopal. New York: Harper & Row, 1964.

LaChapelle, Dolores. *Earth Wisdom.* Silverton, Colo.: Finn Hill Arts, 1978.

———. *Sacred Land, Sacred Sex: Rapture of the Deep: Concerning Deep Ecology and Celebrating Life.* Silverton, Colo.: Finn Hill Arts, 1988.

Lai, Hsi. *The Sexual Teachings of the Jade Dragon: Taoist Methods for Male Sexual Revitalization.* Rochester, Vt.: Destiny Books, 2002.

———. *The Sexual Teachings of the White Tigress: Secrets of the Female Taoist Masters.* Rochester, Vt.: Destiny Books, 2001.

Larewnce, D. H. *Lady Chatterly's Lover.* New York: Bantam Classic Edition, 1983.

Lee, Victoria. *Ecstatic Lovemaking: An Intimate Guide to Soulful Sex.* Berkeley, Calif.: Conari Press, 1996.

Leopold, Aldo. *A Sand County Almanac.* New York: Ballantine Books, 1966.

Lerner, Harriet Goldhor. *The Dance of Intimacy.* New York: Harper and Row, 1989.

Levin, Pamela. *Becoming the Way We Are: Introduction to Personal Development in Recovery and in Life.* Deerfield Beach, Fla.: Health Communications, 1988.

Levine, Stephen, and Ondrea Levine. *Embracing the Beloved.* New York: Anchor Books, 1996.

Logsdon, Gene. *Living at Nature's Pace: Farming and the American Dream.* White River Junction, Vt.: Chelsea Green, 2000.

Lopez, Barry Holstun. *River Notes: The Dance of Herons.* New York: Avon Books, 1979.

Lorde, Audre. *Sister Outsider: Essays and Speeches.* Freedom, Calif.: The Crossing Press, 1984.

Louv, Richard. *Last Child in the Woods: Saving our Children from Nature-Deficit Disorder.* Chapel Hill, N.C.: Algonquin Books, 2008.

Lutz, Deborah. *Pleasure Bound: Victorian Sex Rebels and the New Eroticism.* New York: W. W. Norton, 2011.

MacFarlane, Robert. *The Wild Places.* London: Penguin Books, 2009.

Madaras, Lynda, and Area Madaras. *My Body, My Self for Boys.* New York: New Market Press.

———. *My Body, My Self for Girls.* New York: New Market Press, 2007.

Malone, Thomas Patrick, and Patrick Thomas Malone. *The Art of Intimacy.* New York: Prentice Hall Press, 1987,

Mander, Jerry. *In the Absence of the Sacred: The Failure of Technology and the Survival of the Indian Nations.* San Francisco: Sierra Club, 1991.

Mantegazza, Paolo. *The Sexual Relations of Mankind.* Translated by Samuel Putnam. New York: Eugenics Publishing Company, 1935.

Margulis, Lynn, and Dorion Sagan. *Dazzle Gradually: Reflections on the Nature of Nature.* Foreword by Roald Hoffmann. White River Junction, Vt.: Chelsea Green Publishing, 2007.

Matthews, Caitlin, and John Matthews. *The Encyclopaedia of Celtic Wisdom.* New York: Barnes and Noble Books, 1994.

Metzner, Ralph. *Green Psychology: Transforming Our Relationship to the Earth.* Rochester, Vt.: Park Street Press, 1999.

Miller, Henry. *The World of Sex.* New York: Grove Press, 1965.

Moats, Thatcher. "MHS Homecoming Dance Canceled, Due to 'Dirty Dancing,' Drug and Drinking Concerns." *The Barre-Montpelier Times Argus,* 8 October 2010. www.timesargus.com.

Montagne, Renee. "Israel Kamakawiwo'ole: The Voice of Hawaii." NPR, 26 December 2010. www.npr.org/2010/12/06/131812500/israel-kamakawiwo-ole-the-voice-of-hawaii?sl-emaf=.

Montagu, Ashley. *Growing Young.* New York: Berney & Garvey Publishers, 1981.

Moore, Thomas H., ed. *Henry Miller on Writing.* New York: New Directions Publishing, 1957.

Morin, Jack. *The Erotic Mind: Unlocking the Inner Sources of Sexual Passion and Fulfillment.* New York: Harper Collins, 1995.

Muir, Charles, and Caroline Muir. *Tantra: The Art of Conscious Loving.* San Francisco: Mercury House, 1989.

Nabhan, Gary Paul. *Cultures of Habit: On Nature, Culture and Story.* Washington, D.C.: Counterpoint, 1998.

Nicolson, Marjorie Hope. *Mountain Gloom and Mountain Glory: The Development of the Aesthetics of the Infinite.* Seattle: University of Washington Press, 1997.

Northrup, Christiane. *Women's Bodies, Women's Wisdom.* New York: Bantam Books, 1995.

Odier, Daniel. *Tantric Quest: An Encounter with Absolute Love.* Rochester, Vt.: Inner Traditions, 1997.

Oscarsson, Marcus. "Coming Home from School with Strawberry Condoms." *GlobalPost,* 30 May 2010. www.globalpost.com/dispatch/europe/090625/strawberry-condoms-14-year-olds-shock-muslims.

Otto, Herbert A., ed. *The New Sexuality.* Palo Alto, Calif.: Science and Behavior Books, 1971.

Otto, Rudolf. *The Idea of the Holy: An Inquiry into the Non-rational Factor in the Idea of the Divine and Its Relation to the Rational.* Translated by John W. Harvey. London: Oxford University Press, 1958.

Paterson, Jacqueline Memory. *Tree Wisdom: The Definitive Guidebook to the Myth, Folklore and Healing Power of Trees.* San Francisco: Thorsons, 1996.

Pendell, Dale. *Inspired Madness: The Gifts of Burning Man.* Berkeley, Calif.: Frog, Ltd., 2006.

———. interview at http://quantumtantra.com/pendell.html. Emily Green, *Los Angeles Times,* 10 October 2003.

Perlman, Michael. *The Power of Trees: The Reforesting of the Soul.* Woodstock, Conn.: Spring Publications, 1994.

Phillips, Adam. "Am I a Spaceman?" A review of *Adventures in the Orgasmatron: Wilhelm Reich and the Invention of Sex* by Christopher Turner. *London Review of Books* (August 2011).

Phoenix, Aphrodite. *The Woman Whose Calling Is Men.* 3 vols. Boca Raton, Fla.: Universal Publishers 2007.

Pisani, Elizabeth. *The Wisdom of Whores: Bureaucrats, Brothels and the Business of AIDS.* New York: W. W. Norton, 2008.

Plotkin, Bill. *Nature and the Human Soul: Cultivating Wholeness and Community in a Fragmented World.* Novato, Calif.: New World Library, 2008.

———. *Soulcraft: Crossing into the Mysteries of Nature and Psyche.* Novato, Calif.: New World Library, 2003.

Potter-Efron, Ronald, and Patricia Potter-Efron. *Letting Go of Shame.* San Francisco: Harper & Row, 1989.

Rand, Ayn. *For the New Intellectual.* New York: Random House, 1961.

Reeves, David W. *The Character of Leadership: The Roadmap and Compass That Guides you Through the Landmines of Management.* Bloomington, Ind.: iUniverse, 2010.

Reich, Wilhelm. *Ether, God and Devil: Cosmic Superimposition.* Translated by Therese Pol. New York: Welcome Rain Publishers, 2000.

Reiss, Ira L. *An End to Shame: Shaping Our Next Sexual Revolution.* With Harriet M. Reiss. Buffalo, N.Y.: Prometheus Books, 1990.

Riley, Cole. "Victorian Sex Rebels and Atheists: How Brave Artists Shook Up Prudish Mores." *SeXis Magazine,* February 16, 2011. www.alternet.org/story/149913/victorian_sex_rebels_and_atheists.

Roach, Mary. *Bonk: The Curious Coupling of Science and Sex.* New York: W. W. Norton, 2008.

Roark, Loralee, and Carol Normandy. *It's Not about Food.* New York: Perigee, 1998.

Robinson, Marnia, and Gary Wilson. "Porn-Induced Sexual Dysfunction Is a Growing Problem." *Psychology Today* (July 11, 2011).

Roszak, Theodore, Mary E. Gomes, and Allend D. Kanner. *Ecopsychology.* San Francisco: Sierra Club Books, 1995.

Rossellini, Isabella. *Green Porno.* New York: HarperCollins, 2009.

Roth, Geneen. *When Food Is Love.* New York: Plume, 1992.

Ryan, Christopher, and Cacilda Jethá. *Sex at Dawn: The Prehistoric Origins of Modern Sexuality.* New York: HarperCollins, 2010.

Satir, Virginia. *Peoplemaking*. Palo Alto, Calif.: Science and Behavior Books, 1972.

Schachter-Shalomi, Zalman, and Eve Ilsen. "Sacred Sex." *YES!* (October 20, 1997). www.yesmagazine.org/issues/sustainable-sex/sacred-sex.

Schenk, Roy U., and John Everingham, eds. *Men Healing Shame: An Anthology*. New York: Springer Publishing, 1995.

Seale, Alan. *Intuitive Living: A Sacred Path*. York Beach, Maine: Weiser Books, 1997.

Sears, James T., ed. *Sexuality and the Curriculum: The Politics and Practices of Sexuality Education*. New York: Teachers College Press, Columbia University, 1992.

Seed, John. "Think Like a Mountain." *Yoga Journal: The Magazine for Conscious Living* (March/April 1986): 76.

Seltzer, Sarah. "Bishops Are Behind the 'Let Women Die' Act and the Push Against Birth Control—Even as They're Under Fire for Sex Abuse Scandals." *AlterNet*, October 17, 2011. www.alternet.org/story/152765.

Sheldrake, Rupert. *The Presence of the Past*. Rochester, Vt.: Park Street Press, 1995.

———. *The Rebirth of Nature: The Greening of Science and God*. New York: Bantam Books, 1991.

Shroeder, Theodore. *A Challenge to Sex Censors*. Whitefish, Mont.: Kessinger Publishing, 2003.

Slovik, Scott. *Seeking Awareness in American Nature Writing: Henry Thoreau, Annie Dillard, Edward Abbey, Wendell Berry, Barry Lopez*. Salt Lake City: University of Utah, 1992.

Sobel, David. "Beyond Ecophobia." *Yes!*, November 2, 1998. www.yesmagazine. org/issues/education-for-life/803.

Steinsaltz, Adin. "Sex is a Meaningful Deed." *Parabola* 32, no. 2, Spiritual Teachings on Sex (Summer 2007).

Stock, Ryan. "Manifest Haiti: Monsanto's Destiny." Truthout, January 21, 2011. www.truth-out.org.

Stockholm Newsroom. "Swedes Convince Their State Shops to Sell Sex Toys." Reuters, March 7, 2008. www.reuters.com/article/2008/03/07/ us-sweden-sex-shops-idUSL0782566120080307.

Sundahl, Deborah. *Female Ejaculation & the G-Spot: Not Your Mother's Orgasm Book!* Forewords by Alice Ladas and Annie Sprinkle. Alameda, Calif.: Hunter House Publishers, 2003.

Suzuki, David. *The Sacred Balance: Rediscovering Our Place in Nature*. With Amanda McConnell. Vancouver, B.C. Canada: Greystone Books, 2007.

Suzuki, David, and Peter Knudtson. *Wisdom of the Elders: Honoring Sacred Native Visions of Nature*. New York: Bantam Books, 1992.

Taylor, G. Rattray. *Sex in History: The Story of Society's Changing Attitudes in Sex Throughout the Ages*. New York: Vanguard Press, 1970.

Taylor, Timothy. *The Prehistory of Sex: Four Million Years of Human Sexual Culture*. New York: Bantam, 1997.

Thoreau, Henry David. "Walking." *Works of Henry David Thoreau*. Edited by Lily Owens. New York: Avenel, 1981.

Tompkins, Peter, and Christopher Bird. *The Secret Life of Plants*. New York: Harper & Row, 1973.

Vaughan, Hal. "Swedish Muslims and Strawberry Condoms." The Hal Blog, 29 June 2009. http://halmasonberg.wordpress.com/tag/iraqis.

Weller, Francis. "Reclaiming Our Indigenous Soul." *Sacred Fire Magazine: The Heart of the Living World* 13 (2011): 32.

White, David Gordon. *Kiss of the Yogini: "Tantric Sex" in its South Asian Contexts*. Chicago: University of Chicago Press, 2006.

Wilson, Edward O. *Biophilia: The Human Bond with Other Species*. Cambridge, Mass.: Harvard University Press, 1984.

WEBSITES

Center for Sexual Pleasure and Health. http://thecsph.org

Damn Interesting. www.damninteresting.com

Examiner.com: National Sex & Relationships. www.examiner.com/sex-and-relationships-in-national?=1

The Foundation for Gaian Studies: www.gaianstudies.org

Gay History & Literature: Essays by Rictor Norton. http://rictornorton.co.uk

Guttmacher Institute. www.guttmacher.org

Heritage Key, a website about ancient history. http://heritage-key.com

Indiana University, series on human intelligence. www.indiana.edu/~intell/plato.shtml

Journal of Ultrasound in Medicine. www.jultrasoundmed.org

Kaiser Family Foundation. www.kff.org

The 'Lectric Law Library. www.lectlaw.com/def2/o002.htm

Live Strong. www.livestrong.com

Men Stuff: The National Men's Resource. www.menstuff.org

Miss Maggie Mayhem. http://missmaggiemayhem.com

National Foundation for Educational Research. www.nfer.ac.uk

National Institute of Environmental Health Sciences. *www.niehs.nih.gov*

94 Visual Phenomena & Optical Illusions by Michael Bach. www.michaelbach. de/ot/

Our Porn, Ourselves. www.ourpornourselves.org

Richard Earnheart, artist's website. www.richardearnheart.com/abouttheartist/ htm

Scientific American. www.scientificamerican.com/article.cfm?id=strange-but-true-males-can-lactate&pr

Sexual Intelligence. www.sexualintelligence.org

Sexuality & Modernity. www.isis.aust.com/stephan/writings/sexuality/vict.htm

Susie Bright's Journal. www.susiebright.com

The Straight Dope. www.straightdope.com

Truthout. www.truth-out.org

The University at Texas, Digital Writing & Research Lab. www.cwrl.utexas.edu

Wilhem Reich's somatic psychology lecture on Victor Daniels's website in the psychology department at Sonoma State University. www.sonoma.edu/ users/d/daniels/reich

Yes! magazine. www.yesmagazine.org

Index

BOOKS OF RELATED INTEREST

Plant Spirit Healing
A Guide to Working with Plant Consciousness
by Pam Montgomery

The Sexual Herbal
Prescriptions for Enhancing Love and Passion
by Brigitte Mars, A.H.G.

Wisdom of the Plant Devas
Herbal Medicine for a New Earth
by Thea Summer Deer

The Secret Teachings of Plants
The Intelligence of the Heart in the Direct Perception of Nature
by Stephen Harrod Buhner

The Sexual Practices of Quodoushka
Teachings from the Nagual Tradition
by Amara Charles

Moonrise
The Power of Women Leading from the Heart
Edited by Nina Simons with Anneke Campbell

Tantric Orgasm for Women
by Diana Richardson

Darwin's Unfinished Business
The Self-Organizing Intelligence of Nature
by Simon G. Powell

INNER TRADITIONS • BEAR & COMPANY
P.O. Box 388
Rochester, VT 05767
1-800-246-8648
www.InnerTraditions.com

Or contact your local bookseller